the brief, madcap life
of kay kendall

the brief, madcap life of

Kay Kendall

eve golden with kim kendall

THE UNIVERSITY PRESS OF KENTUCKY

Publication of this volume was made possible in part by a grant from the National Endowment for the Humanities.

Editorial and Sales Offices: The University Press of Kentucky
663 South Limestone Street, Lexington, Kentucky 40508-4008

02 03 04 05 06   5 4 3 2 1

Frontispiece: Kay Kendall. Photo courtesy of Kim Kendall.

Library of Congress Cataloging-in-Publication Data

Golden, Eve.
The brief, madcap life of Kay Kendall /
Eve Golden with Kim Kendall.
p. cm.
Includes bibliographical references and index.
ISBN 0-8131-2251-1 (alk. paper)
1. Kendall, Kay, 1927-1959 I. Kendall, Kim
Elizabeth, 1925- . II. Title.
PN2598.K623 G65 2002
791.43'028'092—dc21

This book is printed on acid-free recycled paper meeting
the requirements of the American National Standard
for Permanence in Paper for Printed Library Materials.

Manufactured in the United States of America.

"She was quite magic. Everywhere you went,
people used to stop and stare . . . she radiated."

—Roddy McDowell

"She was a wonderful, instinctive clown,
probably the most wonderful that we've ever had."

—Dirk Bogarde

"Oh, wifey, what's to become of me?"

—Kay Kendall

Contents

Contents   ix

Foreword

How This Book Came to Be

Maraday Wahlborg

The concept for this book was born in a far-off country in 1959, when Kay Kendall died so tragically. I was a teenager living in South Africa, and I idolized Kay. Her devil-may-care attitude, flamboyant personality, zest for life, beauty, and radiant smile were all captivating to a spotty-faced, gangling teenager. Her death stunned me and, far from forgetting about her, I decided that someday, somehow, her story would be told. My boxes of memorabilia grew through my life, changed countries with me and always remained part of me. Newspapers, magazines, and friends of Kay's received letters over the years requesting stories and photographs, and it proved to be an exciting study.

After settling in the U.S. in 1984, I had more time to think about Kay, and my hopes to see her story told remained steadfast. Modern communication made information available and simplified the project considerably. I knew that Kay had a sister somewhere and started trying to track down Kim—a daunting task, as I had no idea where she lived or what her married name was. A trip to London proved to be the turning point in my search. I received an article about the lighthouse in Withernsea that Kim had transformed into the Kay Kendall Memorial Museum. Not a minute was wasted! I immediately wrote to Kim in care of the museum.

My delight on receiving a phone call from Kim is indescribable. As it turned out, she had just started to record her own memories of Kay and was also determined to write a biography. Kim's cousin Fiona, a successful writer herself, had set the idea in motion, so my offer to do whatever research was needed came at the perfect moment. Kim commissioned me to set off around the world and do whatever it took to gather information on Kay. She was enormously generous and helpful in getting me appointments with people who would have been difficult to interview had I approached them as a stranger. Many of the people in show business who had known Kay were a little reluctant to trust an unknown researcher, but most of them duly granted me an interview.

I set off to meet and interview everyone who still remembered Kay Kendall. There were many moments of hilarity, many of frustration, and many of pure joy. The research involved a trip to Hollywood, several weeks in London, and a quick flight to Sweden to interview the gracious Princess Lilian, an old friend of Kay's. She told many stories that had us both in fits of laughter, as she lovingly fingered the heavy gold necklace that Kay had often worn and which now graced her own neck. People were extremely friendly and cooperative, and several interviews ran to four or five hours, sometimes with a gin and tonic to loosen them up and help them remember stories! Kay still lived on in London, and at times it was hard to believe how clearly and fondly she is remembered. Libraries, museums, restaurants, film studios, fellow actors, and personal friends were all approached with enthusiasm, usually with excellent results. Once people started talking, memories flooded back, often accompanied by tears and touching moments.

In Hollywood, Carol Matthau, a great friend of Kay's, talked for hours, sometimes stopping to wipe away a stray tear, sometimes whispering as she relived a part of her life very dear to her. Dinah Sheridan, a co-star in *Genevieve*, was wonderfully informative, and we spent a fascinating afternoon together. The late Sir Dirk Bogarde, Kay's very close friend and co-star, was initially resistant to the idea of talking to a stranger, but he soon relaxed and gave a colorful interview, remembering things in great detail and expressing himself with a flourish which befits a talented actor and writer such as he. Laurie Evans—Kay's agent—and his wife, Mary, spent a pleasant few hours chatting about her and filling me in on background to her film career. They spoke of the poignancy of Kay's marriage to Rex Harrison and were able to give me details of her final journey back to London, as they were among the few who saw her in the last days of her short life. Mary Evans still wears Kay's little gold ring on her pinkie. A trip to Kay's birthplace resulted in interviews with several of her relatives and a sentimental wander through the museum dedicated to her.

Other commitments kept Fiona from working on the project; but in 1999, Kim phoned and told me that Eve Golden wanted to write the biography. Eve duly received everything I had spent a lifetime collecting, and she and I have shared many funny moments as we've worked together on

Kay's quirky life. Eve conducted additional interviews and added reams of research material to which she had access as a seasoned biographer. The entire collection of memorabilia will be duly housed at the lighthouse in Withernsea, and Kay Kendall's beautiful smile and tales of her crazy life will live on forever.

Prologue

June 23, 1957, Universalist Church of the Divine Paternity, New York City

It was getting on toward midnight, but the Reverend Dr. Charles Francis Potter had agreed to keep his Upper West Side church open for this special, top-secret wedding. The bride and groom rushed in, accompanied by a small group: the bride's sister was matron of honor, the groom's lawyer was best man, the groom's dresser, and actress and friend Margaret Leighton lent moral support. Near the doorway of the small chapel, newsman Earl Wilson crept in with a camera. The press had known since the day before—when the couple had obtained a marriage license—that the ceremony was in the works. But only Wilson had sniffed out the time and the place.

That was surprising, as this could have been the most high-profile marriage of the summer. The groom was Rex Harrison, who, at the age of forty-nine, was at the peak of his success, starring on Broadway as Henry Higgins in *My Fair Lady*. The bride was thirty-year-old Kay Kendall, who had just capped a ten-year struggle up the show-business ladder by starring in her first Hollywood musical, *Les Girls*, with Gene Kelly. Even Harrison's enemies—and there were many—agreed that this was a love match, that the couple was simply mad for each other. Still, something seemed odd and off-kilter at this midnight ceremony.

The groom was attired in a gray suit, having just rushed over from the final curtain of his show at the Mark Hellinger Theater. The bride wore a simple beige dress of silk shantung, a silk scarf tied around her head, kerchief-style. She had been overcome with a case of the nervous giggles, which threatened to erupt into a full-blown attack of tears.

"Miss Kendall, if you can't control yourself, I really can't go on with it," snapped Dr. Potter impatiently.

Rex Harrison patted his bride's hand reassuringly and—her sister noticed—surreptitiously kicked her in the shins as well. Kay calmed down and the ceremony continued.

"Will you take the bride's right hand?" asked Potter, and Harrison grabbed Kay's left one.

Few people at the small ceremony knew just how bizarre this wedding—this whole marriage—really was. Only the groom, the best man and—perhaps—the bride. Rex Harrison's recent divorce from his second wife, actress Lilli Palmer, had been a scandal, precipitated by his very public affair with Kay. Hollywood had never quite forgiven him for the 1948 suicide of actress Carole Landis, which many felt he had caused. Now, this—only Harrison knew that this latest step would actually rehabilitate his reputation, turning him from the heartless cad "Sexy Rexy" into a saint. For Kay Kendall was dying of leukemia, and he had just signed on to be her nursemaid, to care for her in sickness and in health, till death should part them. The secret was also being kept from the bride herself—Rex Harrison had pledged that right up to the end Kay would never know that she was dying. Thus far, he had succeeded in keeping the secret.

As for Kay, she seemed to acknowledge this wedding as an end as much as a beginning. Since her teens, she had scrambled up through one show and movie after another, never letting her many hard knocks discourage her for long. After appearing in the biggest box-office flop in British film history, she had finally broken through to real stardom in 1953 with the low-budget comedy *Genevieve* and had since gone on strike from her studio for better parts. By 1957, she had become Britain's biggest, most glamorous comic star since Gertrude Lawrence; Kay was often compared to Carole Lombard and TV's Lucille Ball. "Kay has the happy facility of looking like the elegant Grace Kelly while cavorting à la Imogene Coca," according to *The Los Angeles Herald*. She had also hopped blithely from one romance to another since her teens: with directors, co-stars, agents, minor royalty, and millionaire playboys (some eligible bachelors, others very much married men). But now, at the very pinnacle of her success, she made it known that she was quite willing to give it all up. "I've had too many years of rushing around from hotel to hotel and town to town and waking up alone in the morning," she would soon tell Gilbert Millstein of *The New York Times*. "I've had too many hundreds of years of being by myself."

The vows were finally taken, and as the celebrity couple turned to go, Earl Wilson saw his chance: he began clicking away, his camera flashing in their faces. Kay burst into tears, and Harrison rushed her out while everyone muttered darkly about "the press—the terrible press!" News of the wedding hit the papers the next day:

"Professor 'iggins Weds His Fair Kay"

The newlyweds began what was to be a two-year public and private charade, more dramatic and sometimes more unbelievable than any of the movies they had starred in.

But then, Kay Kendall's life had always been theatrical, and it had never been dull.

Chapter One

"If anyone suggested anything, she was game for it."

May 21, 1927

It took him twenty-seven hours to cross the Atlantic after leaving Roosevelt Field in Long Island. By mid-afternoon, crowds were waiting at Le Bourget airfield northeast of Paris. By the time he was due over southern England, traffic was backed up for more than a mile outside his arrival place. It was nearly 9:00 P.M. when he flew over Cherbourg—by that time, some 150,000 people had gathered to greet him. French, American, British; reporters, well-wishers, cynics. The tiny, droning plane finally appeared as a dot on the horizon, and deafening cheers echoed as *The Spirit of St. Louis* swooped in for a landing at 10:24. It had taken Charles A. Lindbergh just over thirty-three and a half hours to become the first person to fly nonstop from America to France.

At the same moment in Withernsea, on the northeast coast of England, former actress Gladys Kendall had just given birth to her third and last baby, Justine Kay Kendall McCarthy. After having endured two difficult births, Gladys was less than thrilled with this third pregnancy and had tried every homemade remedy she could think of to end it: hot baths, jumping off chairs. But the determined baby was born anyway, weighing in at eleven pounds. All three babies were born in their mother's childhood home, Stanley House, next door to the town's landmark, the lighthouse. Gladys later recalled looking at her newborn daughter and wondering if she would ever ride in an airplane like the newly famous Lucky Lindy.

Kay Kendall was the offspring of two very colorful families: the Kendalls (her father's side) and the Drewerys (her mother's). The Drewerys were as well-known in their own circles as the Kendalls were in London. The family had lived in Withernsea—a small fishing village on the east coast of Yorkshire, about twenty miles from Hull—for as long as anyone could remember. There were Cooks in the family tree, and the Drewerys liked to claim that they were collateral descendants of the famed Captain James Cook.

Kay's maternal grandparents were Robert and Lavinia Drewery, both of whom lived to be ninety. Lavinia had been the maid at a local manor: Robert came courting the lady of the house and wound up marrying the maid instead. There was a rumor, though, that Lavinia was more than just a servant—her mother had been a sewing maid at Tranby Croft, the home of Arthur Wilson, where the Prince of Wales (later Edward VII) was a frequent guest. It was this home that figured in the notorious gambling trial of 1891, in which Edward was called to testify. Lavinia was the result of an unplanned pregnancy, and her mother was hurriedly married off to a local farmer—there was talk that Lavinia was actually one of Edward's many illegitimate children. "Don't you think we look like the royal family?" Kay would crow to her friends in later years.

A fisherman, merchant seaman, and Methodist lay preacher, Robert Drewery was coxswain of the Withernsea Lifeboat Crew. He helped dig the foundation for the 1893 lighthouse that still stands by Kay's birth-place. That lighthouse was much needed, as there were many wrecks per year on the Yorkshire coast. Gladys Kendall later remembered her girlhood being filled with sudden alarms and sea-borne traumas for the family. "The waves were mountains high," she wrote of one storm. "My father and my eldest brother Frank—only fourteen years old—were out in a lifeboat . . . With them were perhaps ten other men, all either fishermen or volunteers. How sickening to see the light of the boat disappear beyond a wave, and then the joy of seeing it come up again on the other side!"

Robert Drewery was a well-loved eccentric in town, fond of animals (and of practicing taxidermy on the ones he had shot). He kept a peregrine falcon and a wild fox as pets and was a good enough carpenter to build a new house for his family when it grew too large for its present quarters— Gladys Drewery (born in 1900) was one of ten children. The new house, Kay's birthplace, had four bedrooms, living room, front room, kitchen, and a beautiful garden backed by a wheat field. Gladys recalled that in her girlhood, "When the wheat had grown high and was ready for harvesting I would go and lie in it so I could weave my dreams and no one could find me."

Some of Gladys's dreams were of a stage career, though she readily admitted that she could neither sing nor dance. During the First World

War, the teenager left school to find work as a maid, like her mother and grandmother before her. "With four pretty teenaged daughters to look after, [father] and mother never had any peace of mind until we were all in our respective beds," she wrote. With the town full of soldiers, the Drewerys had their hands full making sure those respective beds were full of daughters and *only* daughters.

Gladys's show-business dreams came true when one of her sisters, Doris, married a road show manager, Sydney Parsons, who would later work as an assistant to film magnate J. Arthur Rank—a man who would have a great impact on Kay's life. Doris and her husband went on tour and took Gladys with them to help out backstage. Within a short time, Gladys was a chorus girl, touring the English seaside resorts and big cities. "It was one of the happiest times of my teenage years," she reminisced. "I never had the ambition to be a star. Often I would be chosen to do a bit part—and it was always a pleasure to know we would be in another town the next week." It was while touring in one of these shows that Gladys Drewery became acquainted with a brother-and-sister dance team on the same bill: Terry and Pat Kendall, whose mother was famed music-hall star Marie Kendall.

By far Kay's most famous relative was her paternal grandmother, Marie Kendall. Fifty-four years old at the time of Kay's birth, she was by no means retired, having recently completed a successful tour of Australia. Marie Kendall (born Marie Chester) made her first confirmed stage appearance, in male attire, at the age of twelve, at a music-hall benefit. She spent the late 1880s and early 1890s working her way up the ladder, touring as a male impersonator (then called "Girl Hero") throughout England as well as in Wales and Germany. Stardom finally came in 1893, when she put on skirts and introduced the song "One of the Girls." From then on her venues were the best music halls in London, and she also found good parts in pantomimes. From saucy Cockney songs ("He Says He's Going To Be a Regular Toff," "Did Your First Wife Ever Do That?," "Pearly Lizzie") to the sentimental hit "Just Like the Ivy, I'll Cling To You," Marie enjoyed a string of successes for the next twenty years. One of her grandsons, Cavan Kendall, remembered Marie as a real character into old age: she was "terribly funny." When he found out his grandmother had met famed artist Toulouse-Lautrec, Cavan begged her for stories about him. "Oh, dirty little man!" was her only comment.

By the mid-1920s, both music hall and Marie Kendall were slowing down a bit, though she was still a hard-working and popular performer. In 1895, she had married singer and songwriter Steven McCarthy, also born in 1873. Steven's father, John McCarthy, was a noted London character in his own right. The man who would become Kay's great-grandfather wore many hats: he was the life governor of several hospitals, a music-hall comic, singer, dancer and songwriter, and a member of the Water Rats theatrical union. He was also a landlord, a sideline that ties neatly into another family story: he may have been the same John McCarthy who was landlord to Mary Kelly, who on November 9, 1888, became the last-known victim of Jack the Ripper. (This McCarthy had to stand guard and wait for police at the death scene, 13 Miller's Court, after Kelly's body was found by his assistant.)

Marie Kendall and Steven McCarthy had four children: two boys (Terry and Shaun) and two girls (Moya and Pat). Terry, born in 1901, did not show any early signs of entering the family business. He ran away when the First World War broke out and became a ship's stoker. He jumped ship in the U.S. and worked on a paddleboat, then found work as a lumberjack in Canada. Finally arriving back in England in his twenties, he teamed up with his sister Pat—by the mid-1920s, the two were well on their way to becoming a successful dance act (all the more remarkable because Terry was self-taught, never having taken a dancing lesson in his life). In the 1920s and early 1930s, they rivaled other brother/sister dancers Fred and Adele Astaire and Buddy and Vilma Ebsen—their biggest success was in Noël Coward's 1925 revue *On with the Dance*, in which Terry played "Valentin the Boneless Wonder." Tall, dark, and more handsome than Astaire or Ebsen, Terry Kendall was a charmer and a marvelous broad comedian. His act was not always in the best of taste: one of Kay's favorite routines was when her father would remove pair after pair of trousers, finally revealing Union Jack drawers to the audience.

"I fell hook, line and sinker for Terry," said Gladys in the late 1970s, still smitten after all those years. In the spring of 1923, Terry Kendall and Gladys Drewery were married. "Terry dared not let his mother know we were married, as his mother and father were in the throes of a divorce," said Gladys. "In fact, he never did tell his mother until the day I brought our son to London to the apartment he and his mother were living in."

That son, Terry Junior, came along at the end of 1923; the first daughter, Patricia Kim Kendall McCarthy, in 1925; and—rounding out the family—Justine Kay Kendall McCarthy in 1927. Their London home was in a

basement flat on Elgin Avenue in Maida Vale. Gladys recalled a peram-
bulator built for three that allowed her to wheel newborn Kay, baby Kim,
and toddler Terry on shopping trips. The family took in boarders to help
with finances between shows, and Gladys became maid-of-all-work: cooking, cleaning, and taking care of her three children.

One of the boarders, Veronica Papworth, had once been private maid
to Marie of Rumania and had trunks full of aged hats and gowns—little
Kay was in heaven, trying them on and flouncing happily about as The
Queen of Rumania. "She told us how the Queen used to put ice on her
breasts to keep them firm," remembers Kim. "Also, how to mend our silk
stockings. We were quite impressed." Another boarder was chorus girl Cecily
Hill, who was appearing with Terry Kendall in the *Midnight Follies* at the
Dorchester. Hill (who was killed in a wartime air raid) introduced the
Kendall sisters to her boyfriend, the Maharajah of Jaipur: "A big, hand-
some man," recalls Kim. "He gave us each five pounds, and we were thrilled."

Being in a show-business family was not always easy on the young children. In 1926, Terry, Pat, and Gladys spent several months in the U.S., leaving babies Terry and Kim behind. Gladys later fondly recalled friendships
with Fanny Brice and Jack Benny and attending the viewing of Rudolph
Valentino in his casket: "One policeman said as we came out, 'It's a wonder
Rudy doesn't jump up and kiss all you pretty girls!'" In 1930, Terry and Pat
Kendall toured Australia and New Zealand, and Terry again took his wife
along. The girls were too young for the trip, so they were put into a boarding
school outside London; older brother Terry accompanied their parents. On
Kay's third birthday, only her grandmother Marie Kendall was able to attend
the celebration.

Kay was movie-mad as a child, saving her money for the shows and
sitting through them two and three times. She also attended the theater,
and Gladys recalled a London performance of *Peter Pan* to which she had
taken all three of her offspring. As Peter pleaded with Tinkerbell not to die,
the three Kendall children—rather than just applauding to show they did
believe in fairies—shrieked at the top of their lungs, "No! Please don't die!",
to the audience's vast amusement.

Kim and Kay spent two miserable terms at St. Leonard's boarding
school in Brighton, where the Dickensian headmistress Miss Hemsley
reigned. The students were forced to clean their plates at every meal—any
food left untouched would be re-served, cold, at the next meal. Kay was
never hungry and Kim was ravenous, so they worked out a system: Kay

would slip her food into a pouch and pass it to her sister, thus evading Miss Hemsley's wrath.

Holidays were spent in Withernsea with the Drewerys. Kay made her first public appearance there during the Bank Holiday Carnival in 1932, while on vacation. She and Kim were great fans of Terry Maxwell's Merry Mummer's Troupe, and that summer Maxwell needed three little drummer girls for their parade. Kay, Kim, and their cousin Jill Dootson were chosen (no doubt Gladys did some enthusiastic campaigning on their behalf). The three, in fluffy white tutus and big satin hats, pounding on drums, marched proudly in front on the Carnival Queen's float down Seaside Road.

Kay early showed signs of being a cut-up and incipient diva. Kim recalls walking down Elgin Avenue with her younger sister: A wealthy-looking couple passed them, and Kay loudly stage-whispered to Kim, "Isn't the mink lining of your coat terribly hot?" "We'd roar with laughter and dash off, thinking it was terribly funny," says Kim. Cousin James Drewery recalls Kay as being a comedienne from childhood. "She used to pull my leg something wicked. She was always joking and singing songs about me." By the age of five, she was able to bellow out, "Oh, Jim John, he's a funny old man, brushed his hair with a frying pan," in her best music-hall Cockney. She was particularly close to her grandfather, Robert Drewery, and maintained fond memories of him for the rest of her life.

Kay threw off all her London inhibitions during her Withernsea holidays, dashing stark-naked into the cold sea, playing hide-and-seek in the lighthouse with her sister, cousins, and neighborhood friends. Older brother Terry would take off on his own, putting as much distance between himself and his kid sisters as he could. The girls were avid bicyclists and would pedal furiously to Rimswell—two miles away—to visit friends.

As in most show-business families, the Kendalls' money came and went—sometimes each girl had her own nurse; sometimes there was no help at all in the home. "My dear father was always either working furiously or not working at all," says Kim. Jeffrey Hawks, of the popular musical instrument store Boosey and Hawks, befriended the Kendall girls, took them sailing on his yacht, and attempted to teach them to play accordions. They managed to master the song "Velia, Oh, Velia, the Witch of the Woods" but never progressed much beyond that. Though their father was the actor in the family, it was Gladys who pushed her children toward stage careers. They took ballet lessons at the Lydia Kyasht Dancing Academy on the Kilburn High Road, and at twelve years old Kim was already appearing in pantomimes. She and Kay also took tap-dancing lessons from their father, who regularly lost his temper and whacked the girls' legs with a switch.

Kay adored her father, who possessed equal parts of Irish fury and Irish humor. One day, when fooling about in their basement playroom, Kay managed to break his old walking cane off at the handle. Terrified, she shoved it back atop a wardrobe with the handle sticking out. The next time she misbehaved, Terry bellowed, "I'm going to kill you kids!" and ran downstairs for the cane. He dramatically grabbed it from the wardrobe and brandished the broken handle. Fortunately, he saw the humor in the situation and doubled up with laughter.

Then, in the mid-1930s, the Kendall family came apart at the seams. Terry's sister Pat retired from show business to marry naval officer John Cambridge, and Terry began auditioning new partners. A young blonde comedienne (and preacher's daughter) named Dora Spencer was approved by all—even Gladys—but soon their on-stage relationship became a backstage one as well. Terry discouraged his new partner's suitors, claiming he didn't want to have to break in yet another new dance partner. He changed her name to the more theatrical-sounding "Doric" and walked her home after shows. Eventually Gladys became suspicious.

"Doric is wonderful, but she's just a machine to me. She's my act," Terry would swear.

"When I would ask what they had been doing, it was either that they had been going the rounds of the agents looking for work—or they had gone to see a Ginger Rogers and Fred Astaire film—or they'd been to a tea dance, which was fashionable then," Gladys wrote. "One day when he came in I asked the usual question.

"What did you do today?"

"I sat in the hairdresser's with Doric all afternoon," he said.

"Naturally I bristled," Gladys recalled. "What in the world for?" she asked.

"I wanted to see if they did it properly," he answered.

That, said Gladys, was the last straw. Terry and Doric went off to Scotland for a tour, a divorce ensued, and soon he married his dancing partner. "I remember mother got something like three pounds a week—or was it a month?—with which to support three children," says Kim.

Terry and Doric Kendall continued as a successful comic dance act through the 1950s. They later had a son, Cavan Kendall, who had some success as a photographer and an actor on television *(The Railway Children, The Roving Reasons)* and movies *(Sexy Beast)*. Tragically for Terry, Doric would die a week after his daughter Kay.

Gladys was bitter over the divorce. She refused to let the girls see their beloved father until they were in their early teens and old enough to insist upon it. She never got over Terry: "My love lasted for more than fifty years," she recalled in old age. "I used to wonder why I got the nickname 'True-Blue Lou!'" In the 1960s, after Doric Kendall was dead and Gladys was living in America with her daughter Kim, Terry came to visit, and Gladys found that the flame of romance had not quite burned out, even after all those years of bitterness. But the two simply could not live together: "If she said 'white,' he said 'black,'" recalls Kim. Terry eventually remarried again. "To say I was devastated is putting it mildly," said Gladys. "To have it happen *twice* for a younger woman, it really hurts."

By grade school, Kay was showing a great talent for making friends, many of whom stayed close to her the rest of her life. Molly Simpson—who later became an actress under the name Patricia Coe—went to grade school with Kay and danced with her at Lydia Kyasht's ballet school, and the two quickly became partners in crime: "She was perfectly willing to get into any prank that—let's face it—I thought up," Simpson remembers. "If anyone suggested anything, she was game for it." The girls decided to take up cigarette smoking when Kay was about ten years old. They boldly bought some Player's at Baker Street Station and were caught by their parents before they could even light up. "It was so blatant," says Simpson ruefully, "I was no good at this sort of thing, actually." Another chum was Shirley Ann Hall (step-daughter of famed race-car driver E.R. Hall).

Religion was not a big part of the Kendalls' lives (though Gladys became a "born-again" Christian in later years). Kay was quiet and subdued in church, sometimes making rude jokes about religion and other times admonishing Kim in a horrified, hushed voice, "Please don't say anything like that!" Kay's own religious beliefs pretty much boiled down to a fear in the back of her mind that if it were all true she might really be in trouble someday.

Simpson remembers how hard her parents' divorce was on Kay, how attached she was to Terry. In 1938, troops began mobilizing, Neville Chamberlain was planning strategy in Munich, and people were growing jumpier every day about the possibility of war with Germany. Kay's first thought was for Terry—this was the only time Simpson remembers seeing her cry, sitting in the bathtub, sobbing with fear for her father. Terry snuck to school to see Kay, and she fell into his arms, heartbroken and terrified at the thought of his becoming a soldier. Happily for Kay, her father was too old to be drafted and wound up entertaining the troops with Doric.

Chapter Two

"Of course, there was nobody in London."

All through the late 1930s, the possibility of war was in everyone's mind. Like most families, the Kendalls listened to their radio and read their newspaper; and like many families, they were so busy with their own lives that they tried to push thoughts of war to the back of their thoughts. The theatrical family paid less attention to politics than most: King George VI's coronation just before Kay's tenth birthday and the Wallis Simpson crisis beforehand pretty much passed them by (though Kim remembers her mother wondering what the Prince of Wales saw in "that woman"). But by 1939, it became harder to deny that war was on the horizon: Germany took Czechoslovakia in March, and through the summer rumors flew that Poland would be next. Kim recalls the family huddled around the radio, like so many others, listening to Churchill's stirring and alarming wartime speeches.

In July 1939, Kay participated in a Lydia Kyasht "Evening of Ballet," along with her friends Shirley Ann Hall and Molly Simpson. Kay only had two featured numbers: as Dick Whittington in tights and high boots, and dancing "L'Elve." She was frustrated that she didn't get to be a flower fairy or a princess like her friends.

Kay and Kim spent the rest of the summer of 1939 with the Drewerys in Withernsea. On August 31, as Germany prepared to invade Poland, the British fleet mobilized and panicked parents began sending their children away from London into the country—into other countries, if they could manage to. Molly Simpson and Shirley Ann Hall were staying with Shirley's parents in Scotland, about twenty miles from Oban. Terry and Gladys agreed that it would be much safer to send the girls there; school could wait until the war situation worked itself out one way or the other.

The girls' temporary home was certainly no hardship: Trivnie Ardunie, the Halls' home, was a large rambling cottage on a mountainside leading down to the bay. Starvation wouldn't be a problem: the sisters caught plenty of salmon and lobsters, and Mr. Hall was able to bring home birds and rabbits to supplement the seafood.

Gladys stayed in the Elgin Avenue boardinghouse with Terry Junior; the two also visited friends' abandoned London homes to discourage burglars. Soon, Terry Junior joined the Merchant Service, and Gladys, on her own, returned to Withernsea for a visit with her family.

By the time the school year had started, it was evident that Kim and Kay would be in Scotland for some time—so they, along with Molly and Shirley, were sent off kicking and screaming to St. Margaret's convent school some two miles away for day lessons. "We will, I think, draw a veil over it," says Simpson with a shudder. Kay—with little religious background and a naturally rebellious sense of humor—barely survived. She was always so happy the day was over that she skipped, singing, the two miles back home while her three classmates trudged wearily behind—Simpson recalls once whacking Kay on the back of the head with her school bag and getting a "damn good hiding" from older sister Kim. The sisters were very close as young girls, and Kim was protective of her dotty young charge.

The four girls generally got along well, and they each had their own bedroom in the Halls' spacious home when they wanted to escape one another. Kay "kept us all sane," says Shirley Ann Hall. "She got away with everything." The four bartered their rations with each other: butter for margarine, sardines for beans, and sweets for favors. Kay was mad for sweets and never put on an ounce—Hall preferred sardines, so some satisfactory trading was accomplished. Kay had already developed an interest in perfume and makeup, but there was little to be had of that in 1939 Scotland. There was, however, a fairy-tale castle on the nearby bay, and the companionship of Annie the cook and Charlie the boatman, whose impenetrable Scots accents fascinated Kay and Kim.

Along with many other London evacuees in Scotland was Anna Duse, a dress and set designer who was also one of the girls' teachers from the Kyasht dancing school—so they were able to keep up their theatrical lessons as well as (actually, better than) their regular education. The girls participated in a charity concert in one of Oban's larger hotels. Kay swanned around happily dressed in a long black gown for her "Merry Widow Waltz" number. It was then that Simpson began to suspect that Kay had more potential than their other Kyasht schoolmates. "There was a little magic and I remember thinking, 'she will go far.'"

It wasn't long before Kay and Molly Simpson decided they'd had quite enough of country life and set out to walk all the way back to London, where the action was. They never bothered to pack food or clothing—"It shows how utterly stupid you can be when you are a child," says Simpson. Like most runaways, they changed their minds about two miles down the coast road but were too stubborn to turn around. (Kay, throughout her life, would remain too stubborn to turn around.) The Halls set out on rationed petrol in their small car and soon picked the girls up.

It was around that time that the Kendall sisters were confirmed, by the Bishop of Argyle. Mrs. Hall took all four girls to Oban for preparatory classes and finally for a group confirmation. The three older girls took this in stride.

"Do you have any questions?" the bishop asked.

Kay gazed curiously up at him and asked, "Why do all nuns smell of bread and butter?"

The cleric was stumped. He later told Mrs. Hall that he simply had no answer for that one.

Calling on her nascent dramatic skills, Kay had a habit of going "terribly solemn" while reciting her catechism.

"Don't overact, dear," Mrs. Hall would whisper.

Kay also managed to horrify the nuns at the local convent during a costume pageant: she dressed as Cupid in nude-appearing tights and leotards, and was sent straight back to the Halls' house to change.

Though she was only evacuated for a year, the period was long enough for Kay to discover the opposite sex, a discovery that she would take to with great enthusiasm. Shirley Ann Hall remembers that the girls took turns going to a nearby farm to get milk. One day, Kay uncharacteristically volunteered.

"Oh, I'll come and help you with the milk. I want to go to the farm. I'm *so* interested in dairy," Kay told Hall.

Shirley Ann suspected dirty work afoot, and she was right: a "quite dishy" young farmhand had caught Kay's eye. In the midst of milking, Hall found Kay and her beau getting to know one another on the other side of the cow.

"I shall never take you to the farm again," the scandalized eleven-year-old told Kay.

Gladys soon decided the danger of air attacks was overblown and sent for her daughters to return to London. Both were delighted. By the time the sisters arrived, their mother had left Maida Vale and taken a lovely flat at 10 Talbot House on St. Martin's Lane. It was right in the heart of London life: opposite the Coliseum, next door to the Duke of York's Theatre, down the street from the Hippodrome, and across the way was the eighteenth-century St. Martin-in-the-Fields church. A great many of Gladys's new neighbors were in the theater, which is perhaps how she managed to find the vacancy. "Of course, there was nobody in London and you had your choice of apartments," notes Kim. The lift operator, a dapper, fatherly World War I veteran named Monty, kept careful guard over the residents, making sure no one got past him without proving exactly why they were there.

Kay befriended Barbara Seabrook, a four-year-old who lived with her family in the same house. Kay would give the child piles of records and costume jewelry and became a fairy princess of elegance to her. "For somebody of that age to take an interest in a child is quite unusual," says Seabrook, "but she did. She was a very concerned, kind person." Seabrook recalls that all the residents had to sleep bundled up in their sleeping bags and pillows in the house's huge ground-floor entrance halls during nights when raids threatened. "I can't imagine how anybody thought we'd be safe through that," she says. Each time an air raid warning went off, the Kendall sisters had the same fight:

"Let's go wake mother up and get her," one would suggest.

"She'll kill us if we wake her up!" the other would answer.

Gladys was both hard of hearing and an insomniac, so the thought of interrupting her rare sleep usually led them to leave her in bed and to trust in luck.

Chapter Three

"That's Kay Kendall and she's supposed *to be in the chorus!"*

Kay developed early, and the neighborhood boys were not slow to notice. Tall and thin, she could put on full stage makeup and look like a woman in her twenties. Cousin Joy Drewery recalls the dance hall where teens would congregate with their beaus. "Kay would walk in and sort of lean up against the doorway or something like that and the boys would leave us and flock to Kay. She was so much more glamorous, her clothes were nicer. She just had an air about her that attracted everyone. . . . We would turn around in disgust and say, 'Oh, *she's* here again!'" Despite Kay's success with the boys, she was also developing a self-image problem. In her early teens, she was all legs, nose, and big goofy grin. Sister Kim, however, was a classic beauty, with a button nose and two years' head-start.

In late 1939, Kay got her first professional job, in the chorus of the out-of-town touring company of the George Black musical revue *Black Velvet*. (The more glamorous London production featured eighteen–year-old starlet Pat Kirkwood, Winston Churchill's son-in-law Vic Oliver, and a very young Julie Andrews.) George Black was the reigning king of the musical revue, sending productions on tour from the London Palladium all through the British Isles. ("A wonderful, great big, handsome man," Kim remembers, who called the towering showgirl "his six-foot-two of sex appeal.")

Kay's dancing talents were more enthusiastic than professional, but choreographer Wendy Toye was a friend of Terry Kendall's and gave his daughter a break.

"Who's that beautiful girl doing the solo?" an onlooker asked Toye during one performance.

"She's *not* doing a solo," snapped Toye. "That's Kay Kendall and she's *supposed* to be in the chorus!"

When Kay forgot her steps, says Shirley Ann Hall, "she'd make up something else and get away with it, because she got away with everything."

Terry visited his daughter during the run and was horrified to see his twelve-year-old baby at the railway station dolled up in a green gown and matching earrings, looking all for the world like a self-possessed and sexy young adult. She was also adult enough to expertly play her parents off one another. Her Aunt Moya was beloved by Terry and detested by Gladys. After a visit, Kay wrote to Terry about her delightful visit with "Auntie Moya, who is an angel," while Gladys got, "I've had to stay with 'Angel Moya'—what a bore!"

Kay was near to reaching her full height and realized that her future was not as a dancer. "From the time I was six I'd been studying ballet," she sighed dramatically. "I could dance well enough but soon outgrew myself and got too big for a ballerina. The tall ones look so awkward skipping about a stage. . . . I'm five-foot-nine. When I rose up on my toes I was ten-foot-six and my feet collapsed. Imagine how I'd look prancing about in a fluffy tutu!"

By early 1940, Kim had made her professional debut as a chorus girl at the Holborn Empire. Gladys earned extra money by baking pastries, which the sisters took around to the theater to sell to coworkers and patrons alike. She was quite a good cook, and Gladys's treats became a big hit; the girls told everyone that a new Italian bakery had opened. But quite soon both Gladys's rations and her patience ran out, and the sisters were confronted by disappointed customers.

"Oh, just tell them the Italian bakery closed!" Gladys snapped at them, putting an abrupt end to the added income.

Kay and Kim got jobs in the summer touring company of another George Black revue, *Black and Blue*, in Blackpool (Kim as a glamorous compere, Kay as a lowly chorine). Travel in the early days of the war was fraught with frustration; trains were off-schedule and packed with soldiers and relocating families. Adding to Kay's woes was her mother: Gladys lost no chance to remind her daughters that money was very short at home, so the sisters sent most of their meager salary to her. Bebe Lorenzi (who acted under the name Jean Walker) befriended Kay at the time—her connection to Kay's family went back much further (her mother had been in vaudeville with Marie, Terry, and Pat Kendall). Walker's father, jazz harpist Mario Lorenzi, was in *Black and Blue* and mentioned to his daughter that Kay had fainted from hunger more than once during the run. Still shooting up to her full adult height and thin as a beanpole, Kay needed all the food she could get. An American dance team, Billings and Chase, took her under their wing and made sure she joined them for dinner.

Already Kay had a reputation for putting on airs. She and a friend, Zena Marshall (a starlet who later married bandleader Paul Adams), met in a tiny, small-town pub when their touring companies crossed paths.

"My man, we would like something to eat," the starving, unknown chorine trilled to the barkeep.

The barkeep was not amused, though Marshall was astonished and delighted.

Kay spent the summer of 1941 in Blackpool with Kim in *Black and Blue*—and with a contingent of attractive Polish fliers and RAF men. She was still a virgin at this point, but this fact didn't keep Kay and Kim from having a moderately good time with the boys (they were too busy working, notes Kim, to have more than a moderately good time). Even as teenagers the sisters slept in the same bed while on tour and kissed each other goodnight. "A girl who was sleeping in the same room said we must be a couple of lesbians," Kim laughs. At the end of the tour, the show's stars were given huge bouquets of flowers, two of which Kay grabbed to take home to Gladys in London. The sisters, unable to find a cab to the train station, perched on the back of a milkwagon, precariously balancing luggage and the mounds of free flowers, which Kay refused to abandon.

Beryl Turner was one of the chorus girls who befriended the Kendall sisters during these years: "We worked together for over two years, going from one successful show to the other," she recalls today. Turner remembers the teenaged Kay as "very beautiful, a flawless complexion, lovely smile and teeth—perfection." But even at this age, with the early success coming her way, Kay was "never really satisfied with herself. She was always wishing her hair would grow long—it was beautiful hair, but unlike Kim's never grew. She admired Hedy Lamarr and always wished she had a nose like hers."

It was during the war that Kay began maturing: in the heart of London, in the depths of the Blitz, the teenager already looked more like a soigne café-society woman than the colt-like, rambunctious kid she still was. Her teen years were not easy ones when it came to getting along with her mother: Kay occasionally went to stay with one of her aunts after one too many battles with Gladys in the crowded, nerve-racked house.

Gladys had managed to bring her daughters back to London just in time for the Blitz, which began on September 7, 1940, with a daylight attack on the East End, killing 436 people and destroying entire blocks. On September 13, Buckingham Palace was bombed, and by the end of the month, nighttime raids made sleeping all but an impossibility. Gladys felt somewhat less silly for having brought the girls back to London when other towns—Coventry, Liverpool, Manchester—began receiving their share of bombings. By the last few days of 1940, England was ablaze. During the Blitz, Kay's birthplace in Withernsea was hit by an incendiary bomb, which crashed through the roof and right into the bedroom where Gladys had given birth. Happily, the fire was put out and the house eventually repaired. The last major raid of the Blitz occurred during a full moon, on the night of May 10, 1941: the Tower of London, the House of Commons, Westminster Abbey, and the British Museum all took hits, and 1,436 were killed in one night. By this time, Hitler had decided against an invasion of Britain, though the war was far from over. (By war's end, some sixty thousand civilians had been killed in air raids.) "There never seemed to be a night when the bombs weren't dropping," recalled Gladys. "In the daytime one could look up and see a dogfight going on between the Royal Air Force fighters and the enemy in a clear, blue, beautiful sunny sky while out walking or shopping."

Even the movies were no longer the great escape that they once were for Kay. Londoner Nancy Winter recalls movie-going as a child during the war: "If the siren went off there would be a notice flashed on the screen to inform everyone a raid was imminent, and then people could leave to take shelter if they wanted to." As big a movie fan as Kay, Winter adds, "I don't recall ever leaving, I wanted my sixpence worth!" Kay and Jean Walker felt the same way—Walker remembers being up in the cheap seats in theaters with Kay and staying put during air raid warnings.

For youngsters like Kay, who didn't remember the 1914–18 "war to end all wars," there was some excitement to be had even during the worst of the Blitz. She was working and living as a grown-up for the first time, in hectic, breathless London during wartime. Coming home nights after work was dangerous and terrifying in the blackout—even torches had to be pointed downward toward the sidewalks so not even a sliver of light would be visible to airplanes. Kay's growing enthusiasm for nightclubs and dance bands was not dampened by the disaster of March 8, 1941, when the Café de Paris took a direct hit: more than thirty patrons and employees were killed, including bandleader Ken "Snakehips" Johnson. But still Kay dolled herself up and sneaked into as many clubs as a glamorous, underaged girl could.

As Shirley Ann Hall remembers, "She was a very optimistic person—would never look on the black side and never think of the worst. . . . I mean, we were virtually children during the war and we would never say, 'Isn't it dreadful, the bombing? I'm so frightened.' We were always, 'You know, that's nothing!'" Roddy McDowell agreed that Kay was never fazed by imminent disaster, "because there's another adventure to be translated into a great good lark."

Shortly before his death in combat, fighter pilot Richard Hillary wrote that he "saw London as a city hysterically gay, a city doomed, with nerves so strained that a life of synthetic gaiety alone prevented them from snapping. . . . Though the sirens might scream and the bombs fall, restaurants and cocktail bars remained open and full every night of the week." Londoner Chloe Bowering recalled for the *Daily Mail,* "There was a huge increase in camaraderie among everybody. For the first time in our lives, we all had something in common. When you're confronted with danger like that, you don't dwell on it, or on the consequences of your actions." Kay was becoming a young lady in that era, when tomorrow might never come and today must be enjoyed to the fullest—that was a motto she would take with her throughout life, for better or for worse.

It was at this time that Kay made friends with Lilian Davies, a young singer and dancer from Wales. The girls roomed together, hit every London nightspot they could. Lilian would go on to have a life as exciting as Kay's: she married actor Ian Craig, then in 1943 began a lifelong love affair with the dashing Prince Bertil of Sweden. Bertil—like Edward VIII—could not marry her without losing his throne (actually, his potential regency to his nephew). But Lilian—unlike Wallis Simpson—gracefully stepped aside. The two finally wed in 1976, and Kay's pal became Princess Lilian of Sweden.

The girls first met at a cocktail party given by actor Buster Collier Jr., and before Lilian knew it, Kay had moved in with her, bag and baggage. "She was mad as a hatter, and we had so much fun," Princess Lilian recalls. "If she had money she'd go out and buy the most expensive pair of shoes or the most expensive blouse, and the next minute she'd be climbing up the walls with these lovely shoes on. She was absolutely nuts and didn't give a damn about anything." One friend recalled Kay going upstairs at a swanky party, disrobing, and coming back down wrapped only in other guests' fur coats.

Kay was perennially short on cash, whether or not she had a paycheck coming in. She would empty her purse if she knew a friend needed money and was seen giving ludicrous amounts to beggars on the street. If someone admired her brooch, Kay would unpin it and hand it over; and she once took a friend to Cartier's, had the salesman take out a tray of rings, and said, "There you are, darling, choose which one you want."

The two girls spent much of their money on shows, seeing everything that was playing in London. Saturday nights they went to the Caprice Hotel—showing off their best frocks—then off to the theater, sometimes the same show over and over if nothing new was playing. "She knew all the words, she knew all the lyrics, she knew everything," Lilian says. When she felt particularly down or broke, Kay would call up a fortune-teller she knew, telling Lilian, "We'll have to give her at least half a bottle of gin before she comes to see us!" Even at her most bankrupt, Kay managed to treat herself to odd little extravagances. Once she was passing a luggage store with Lilian when she dragged her friend in: "I left my crocodile bag there to be polished." "She was nuts," Lilian laughs. "She used to gargle with my perfumes and eau de toilettes before going out on dates—completely mad!"

Terry Junior's friend Walter "Tippo" Andrews remembers some of Kay's scattiness in this period. One night she managed to get some tickets to see a young Richard Attenborough in a show and invited Andrews along to the theater and dinner at Ley On's in Wardour Street, one of London's best Chinese restaurants. Kay strode up to the maître d'.

"We want the best table you have, and we've only got one pound to spend," Kay said, without a blush.

Andrews recalls with amazement that they "were shown to a very good table and had a jolly good dinner. My memory is unclear as to how we asked for the bill or for that matter how it was presented—Kay seemed to think it all entirely usual and natural."

Another time, Kay did manage to get hold of some serious money: she'd been to the dog races with a date, who had won big. In the taxi home, the gentleman bragged how he cared nothing for money and tossed a roll of it out the window.

"If you care nothing for money, *I* do!" Kay hollered. She dashed out of the taxi and went back to retrieve the roll.

"Kay, having used up her practicality for that week," says Andrews, went to Peter Jones and bought a hideous yellow silk taffeta settee, and to Fortnum and Mason's for huge bundles of fresh asparagus. She brought her haul home to her mother, who was suitably appalled. Gladys called Andrews and his wife, Sheila, over.

"Look what that silly girl has done!" she cried. "What can I do with it?"

Happily, it transpired that Sheila loved asparagus.

Kim and Kay both got work in *Gangway*, at the London Palladium, a musical comedy revue starring the married American film stars Bebe Daniels and Ben Lyon and lanky comic Tommy Trinder. Kim—variously decked out in no less than six specially designed Norman Hartnell gowns—announced the performers, and Kay (already as tall and leggy as her twenty–something fellow dancers) was in the chorus. Gladys somewhat ingenuously claimed, "Both girls were under age and I was sure I'd be put in prison for defaulting on the child labor law!" Kay certainly acted like the kid she still was: the mischievous Ben Lyon would chase her up the stairs with his walking stick, Kay shrieking wildly with laughter (she was regularly fined for showing up late or making too much noise backstage). She shared a dressing room and became good friends with starlet Peggy Dexter, who recalled that Kay had "two left feet, God bless her—she couldn't always remember the steps." Kay was also a hopeless slob who borrowed Peggy's makeup and consistently misplaced it. "I'd put out clean towels and line all her stuff up," said Dexter. "It would stay like that for five minutes."

Already, there were signs that Kay's health was not the best. Though she ate like a horse, Kay had, after her growth spurt, never put on enough weight. She was often white as a sheet, was always cold, and was diagnosed as anemic. "Kay was sent vials of what looked like blood from Paris," says Kim. "I don't know how she got them or who sent them to her, but I remember her taking them for her anemia. She always had dark shadows under her eyes." Peggy Dexter remembered weekends when Kay was so weak and lethargic all she could do was brush her hair and listen to gossip.

Kay's and Kim's work in *Gangway* came to an end when the Palladium was hit by a land mine, which was dropped from a plane but didn't explode. (Fortunately, it was one of the duds that slave laborers were able to create under the noses of their Nazi overseers.) The mine landed onstage, buoyed by a green parachute, which the cast and crew cut up and handed out as souvenirs. The theater had to be closed, the mine itself carefully removed, and repairs made.

"Let's go to Granny's!" decided Gladys, and soon the three Kendall women were on a train to Yorkshire, crowded among tired evacuees. Arriving in Withernsea in wartime was like going back to the nineteenth century. It was a lovely break from war and career worries for the girls, and a nice respite from her still-broken heart for Gladys. The three put on slacks, rode bicycles around the countryside (no cars, no petrol), and enjoyed one of their last carefree vacations as mother and daughters. The Drewerys begged the trio to stay out the war with them in Withernsea, but they were too full of ambition and adventure to stay away from London for long.

The London they returned to was coping with increasing rationing, begun in 1940. Kay and Kim rode their bikes everywhere, as inner-city transportation was disrupted. Even when busses were to be had, they were out of service by 9:00 at night (2:00 P.M. on Sundays). New clothes were not to be had, and Gladys was kept busy sewing the girls' dresses and theatrical costumes from old curtains and parachute silk. Silk stockings were a thing of the past, and many women came up with elaborate substitutes: one woman recalls a neighbor darkening her legs with gravy browning until the village dogs eagerly following her up and down the streets put an end to that idea. As for food, the Kendall girls had to content themselves with such dishes as powdered eggs, Spam, and prunes for dessert. Fish, while not rationed, was hard to come by. "The food was awful," Kim remembers. "Whale meat was served in restaurants—it looked like a roast but of course had a fishy taste." The grocer around the corner, though, would give the girls a full pound of chocolate for their ¾–pound coupons. They would gobble it down and "feel quite sick, but we'd do the same thing the following month." The tiny amounts of meat, milk, sugar, and tea allotted per person guaranteed that Kay and Kim had that lean and hungry fashion-model look throughout the war years. There was, of course, no central heating, so the sisters commandeered whatever taxis they could find and went on expeditions for buckets of coal.

Kay and Kim also put in time at the Stage Door Canteen, where they were very popular hostesses and dancing partners for the troops. It was there that Kay met actress Muriel Pavlow, with whom she later appeared in three films. "These two lovely tall girls—and I am five foot and a bit and never got beyond, so I was always terribly envious," Pavlow recalls.

Both sisters had odd regional accents—part Cockney, part Yorkshire—and they both knew their careers would not go far unless they spoke what later came to be known as BBC English. Gladys found them a singing and elocution teacher in London. Kay became as professional a singer as she was a dancer: just good enough to get away with it but not good enough to worry the pros. After months of repeating "How now, brown cow" and "Early in the morning before we are awake, we see the water lily on the water in the lake," Kay emerged with the perfectly modulated, non-regional voice that later became famous through her films.

With no jobs awaiting them, the Kendall sisters decided to make their own break. They formed a song-and-dance team and went into music halls, following in the footsteps of their grandmother Marie. The war opened stage employment for many an adventurous, hopeful actor; polished professionalism was no longer the most important attribute. "Huddled in shelters, sharing the common life of blackout and Blitz and for most of the time cut off from Europe, artists had returned to more native ways of feeling," wrote historian Harry Hopkins.

The untried and very nervous teenagers found a pianist and rehearsal room, managed to cobble together make-do costumes and dancing shoes under clothes rationing, and tried to find reliable train schedules when they got their first gig, in Dover. "I'm sure we looked beautiful," Kim says, "and although I'm sure we were *supposed* to be doing the same thing, we didn't." She recalls the quality of their act: they sang "Adios Muchachos" and told jokes:

"You know, my father was an electrician."

"Yeah, and you were his first shock!"

The girls and their mother found a nice theatrical boardinghouse, and everything seemed to be going well—until their second night, when an air raid siren sounded just after their show ended. Cast, audience, and passersby all rushed into Dover's natural caves, which the locals had transformed into underground dwellings for the duration: tables, cooking fires, candles. In the daytime, Kay strolled the nearly deserted boardwalk and flirted with the many available and agreeable soldiers and sailors. As for the audiences, "There weren't too many to see how bad we were," she later noted.

The Kendall sisters did not remain a two-act for long. "We were fired at the end of the first week," said Kay. "If I'd have been the manager I'd have fired me too, we were that awful."

Both girls went on the road with the Entertainment National Service Association, or ENSA (familiarly referred to as "Every Night Something Awful"). One of their stops was in Bury St. Edmonds, where they encountered a contingent of black American soldiers. The camp was run by white officers, and there was some ill feeling because the local girls were so charmed by these men, the first blacks most of them had met. The soldiers, in turn, were more than happy to mend fences and do farm work for the local girls, who "spoiled the life out of them," recalls Kim. The Kendall sisters were particularly taken by a handsome New Orleanian who was an expert on Charles Dickens, one of the town's former residents. He warned the sisters to be distant and ladylike to the black soldiers, but this advice went by the wayside when Kay encountered a huge rain puddle while crossing to the dressing room. One of the black soldiers picked her up, she delightedly put her arms around him and played up her maiden in distress act; Kim nervously noticed jealous looks from nearby white officers. "That was *not* what we were supposed to do!"

Kay had a harder time finding work on her own, according to her own (sometimes exaggerated) stories: "Nobody seemed to want me. Even the Government couldn't stand my act and sent me out of the country. They said it was to entertain the troops, but I knew better." (In fact, Kay never left the country during the war.)

Kay always managed to have a good time—and to dramatize herself and her life. With a perfectly straight face, she later told her friend Roddy McDowell about a supposed mishap she'd had while touring during the war. "She was asleep and woke up in the middle of the night and had to go to the bathroom and fumbled her way around," McDowell recalled the story going, "and fell out of the window and she didn't have any clothes on and she grabbed hold of the flagpole and she was hanging there screaming bloody murder and they turned searchlights on." Kay told these tales with such deadpan urgency that she invariably had her friends believing them.

Chapter Four

"We're going to take a chance with you . . ."

In 1944, Kay made her entrance into films. There was simply too much leisure time between stage shows, and the studios looked to be a promising source of income. Despite her unusual height, a beautiful young girl like Kay was bound to get well-paying work as an extra, at least. Both sisters got an appointment with producer and director Alexander Korda around this time—it didn't lead to any jobs, but "he gave us each five pounds," Kim recalls. "I haven't the vaguest idea why!"

Ealing Studios had a number of war-related successes (*The Big Blockade*, *The Foreman Went to War* and, most notably, *In Which We Serve*), but production head Michael Balcon decided to follow America's lead and begin concentrating on fluff-headed escapist movies. Kay provided background glamour in three of these Ealing extravaganzas, all released in the latter half of 1944. *Champagne Charlie* was a big-budget (loosely fact-based) musical about two Victorian music-hall singers, starring Tommy Trinder as George Leybourne and Stanley Holloway as Alfred Vance. Kay was lost amid the crowds of theater-audience extras: but Trinder, Holloway, and Betty Warren (as music-hall queen Bessie Bellwood) had a field day strutting their stuff, and the film proved to be enjoyable and atmospheric. (It was directed by Brazilian-born Alberto Cavalcanti, who later specialized in documentaries.)

Trinder also starred in *Fiddlers Three*, a very funny musical about two tars and a Wren (Trinder, Sonnie Hale, and Diana Decker) sent back to ancient Rome by a stroke of lightning; this film did well enough to be reissued in 1949. Kay and Kim can be briefly glimpsed as two tall and smiling "nubile young Circassians" for sale at a slave market, and later Kay appears at Nero's (very tame) orgy, where she clutches supposed soothsayer Trinder and purrs, "Tell me about my future!"

The popular comedy team of Bud Flanagan and Chesney Allen were the stars of the appropriately named *Dreaming*, which consisted mostly of the fantasies of Flanagan, who is hospitalized with a head injury. It was an enjoyable road movie not unlike the Bob Hope/Bing Crosby vehicles of the time. Kay appeared as a cigarette girl in a Stage Door Canteen sequence—she had only one line and rushed it so badly that it came out quite unintelligibly. Kay later remembered a hideous moment on the set of *Dreaming*, when director John Baxter shouted, "Put your leg up against the wall—it'll give the scene a bit more zip," and Kay obliged. "Nasty silence," she recalled with a shudder, "followed by a bellow from the director, 'Not you—YOU!' meaning, of course, the leading lady. I nearly died. There were at least eight million other extras there—and to be so singled out!"

Kay's biggest film of the war years was the ruinously expensive epic *Caesar and Cleopatra*, produced by J. Arthur Rank, who would later have a much more personal impact on Kay's life and career. Rank was a deeply religious Methodist who first got into the film business in 1935 to bring his moral views to the public. It wasn't long before he realized that British films were so badly organized and distributed that no one was seeing them, let alone being influenced by them. He worked his way into every aspect of the industry: production, distribution, promotion. By the mid-1940s he owned more than a thousand theaters and—through the Rank Organisation and General Film Distributors—he controlled more than half of all British film studios.

Rank knew little about the artistic side of producing, but he (like Louis B. Mayer in the U.S.) took a smotheringly paternal attitude toward the "children" in his employ. Actor Donald Sinden recalled that "One of the most hideous experiences each year was the Rank Organisation Christmas Dinner. . . . The Managing Director was at one end of a large table and the nearer you were to him, the more 'in' you were. If you were at the other end of the table you weren't going to last another year!" Contract actress Greta Gynt remembered going to Mr. Rank himself, unhappy about how little work she was being given: she was told, "Miss Gynt, do you think we'd have you under contract if we didn't want you to go into the right part for you?"

This side of J. Arthur Rank was still in the future for Kay: right now, she was just a faceless, nameless extra under his care. Based on the George Bernard Shaw play, *Caesar and Cleopatra* starred the emotionally fragile thirty–year-old Vivien Leigh as the Queen of Egypt and the short-tempered Claude Rains—fresh from several huge successes in America—as Caesar. The perfectionist stage director Gabriel Pascal, who had a long-term professional relationship with Shaw, was assigned to direct and produce. The whole production was a disaster waiting to happen, but no one could have predicted the extent of the trials to come, even for five-pound-a-day extras such as Kay (and Kim, who joined her on this film). Kay was not the only future star on the set: neophytes Jean Simmons (as a harp-playing slave girl) and Roger Moore also made brief appearances.

Filming started in June 1944, just after D-Day. Girls for extra work and sewing costumes were at a premium, as so many were either evacuated or working in factories. Kim recalls Pascal as a tyrant with a sadistic sense of humor: "All the virgins stand up," he ordered the extra girls, bellowing to the Kendall sisters, "Oh, sit down, you old bags." The shoot was enough to make anyone quit show business: that summer was so cold that the slave girls shivered in their chiffon costumes and tried to sneak wool underwear beneath. "Would the ladies on the palace steps please take off their underwear, which I know they are hiding underneath their gowns?" Pascal would shout through his megaphone.

"Every time we were on the palace steps with our palm leaves, supposedly fanning Cleopatra, there would be a whoosh! and an airplane would zoom across the screen and ruin the whole thing," says Kim. Claude Rains was grumpy about delays; Pascal ruled the players with furious tantrums. In September, Vivien Leigh suffered a miscarriage after a strenuous scene, further dampening spirits on the set. Even after the crew took off for location shots near Cairo, the bad luck continued: camels ate the papier-mâché shields, and sandstorms ground production to a halt. *Caesar and Cleopatra* wasn't released in England until late 1945 (and not in the U.S. until late 1946). George Bernard Shaw, critics, and audiences all considered it an overblown waste of five million dollars (possibly the most expensive film to date); seen today, the film is most notable for the stunning sets and cinematography. The Kendall sisters are lost in the crowd of palace-step extras in the final scene, wherein Caesar sets sail from Egypt back to Rome.

Kay advanced from unseen extra to bit player for her next film, the sugary Viennese musical *Waltz Time*, a British National production released in July 1945. The film concerned a young and pretty empress (Carole Raye) in love with a flirtatious captain of the Guards (London-born Peter Graves, not to be confused with the American actor of the same name). The whole thing was road-company Nelson Eddy/Jeannette MacDonald, the only interest coming from a cameo appearance by opera star Richard Tauber, filmed shortly before his death. Kay was in a handful of scenes, as the perkiest (and tallest, by a head) of the ladies in waiting to the court. She trills, "Your Highness, why can't we dance the waltz at court?" and is later caught teaching the other ladies the scandalous new step. She was billed dead-last in the closing credits, just above Tauber's cameo.

After this tiny career boost, Kay was given entre to J. Arthur Rank's famous "Charm School." He hired voice and acting coaches, teachers of deportment and charm, and tried to mold his own starlets much as major Hollywood studios had been doing since the 1920s. There was somewhat of an onus being known as a Charm School girl, as actress Honor Blackman recalled: "Everybody keeps putting me in the Charm School, but I was never there. People in the Charm School earned ten pounds a week, I earned one hundred pounds a week then." Rank was desperate to compete on the international market, and now with the war just over, the time seemed ripe. He began planning for the biggest-budgeted musical extravaganza ever filmed in England: it would be in color and would feature stage, music-hall, and radio stars, a bevy of Charm Schoolers, and the catchiest numbers that could be written or resurrected. The project, dubbed *London Town*, would, Rank hoped, be the opening volley to put the British film industry right up there alongside Hollywood. Kay had joined the Charm School at just the right moment.

The film's director was fifty-six-year-old Hollywood veteran Wesley Ruggles, younger brother of comic actor Charles Ruggles. Wesley had started as an actor, appearing with the Keystone Cops and Charlie Chaplin a decade before Kay's birth. He'd gone on to direct such sex symbols as Clara Bow (*The Plastic Age*), Carole Lombard (*No Man of Her Own* and *Bolero*), Mae West (*I'm No Angel*), and Claudette Colbert (*The Gilded Lily*). But his career had slowed down by the 1940s, and he was happy to get this offer from Rank. Handsome in a rumpled, middle-aged way, Ruggles had been the first of seven husbands of actress Arline Judge and had been married to French actress Marcelle Rogez since 1940.

Rank publicized a talent search to find the prettiest actresses in England to grace this film. Stars and starlets alike were screen-tested, Kay among them (her entre may have come through her acquaintance Buster Collier Jr., an associate producer of the film). She was dolled up in a dozen costumes, hairstyles, and makeups and shot and shot again—finally, Kay was cast as one of the "Dozen and One Girls" to be used as background color in musical numbers. But within a week or two, Ruggles had singled her out for a larger part—indeed, one of the female leads. "I think you've got something—we're going to take a chance with you," Kay later recalled being told by Ruggles. She was signed to a seven-year contract with Rank, and the newspapers carried a leggy photo of her, captioned "A Star is Born." She excitedly told her friend Jean Walker, "This is my break—this is the beginning!" Kay was understandably thrilled—but she was also smart enough to be terrified. With good reason, as it turned out.

Kay's abrupt discovery and promotion from "Dozen and One Girl" to star seems feasible enough on the face of it: looking at the other chorus girls, it's easy to see how she stood out. Her competition, while pleasant-looking enough, was hardly dazzling star material; there was nary a potential Audrey Hepburn or Vivien Leigh lurking amongst them. But Kay's ascent may have had another helping hand: she had lost her virginity to her director and was enjoying a passionate affair with him. She burbled happily to her sister about how in love she was and how she had no regrets: "Only do it for love, dear, nothing else—just for love." When reminded that her new passion had a wife, Kay retorted with a phrase she would be called on to use again in future years: "Well, that's just too bad. She found him first, but I'm here now!" The affair cooled down and the two parted without trauma as soon as filming ended and the cast and crew went their separate ways. But now that Kay had discovered the joys of sex, she became an enthusiastic—and not always very discriminating—participant.

Starring in *London Town* was forty-two-year-old revue and radio comic Sid Field. Often compared to Bob Hope, Field was a talented singer and dialect comic but was hardly a potential matinee idol. He played the role of small-time actor Jerry Sanford, who hits London to make his fortune. He's accompanied by his adoring daughter Peggy (played by thirteen–year-old Petula Clark, who'd gained great success as a radio singer and who had done a few film bits). Also in the film were glamorous Greta Gynt as a theatrical producer and Sonnie Hale as Field's competition. Music-hall great Tessie O'Shea was brought in to do a few numbers, as added insurance. Kay was billed seventh, in the largest role she'd yet had: she played Patsy, the leading lady of the show in which Jerry Sanford hopes to star (she was also given a romance with Field's character, in an effort to supply him with some reflected sex appeal).

London Town was shot in the fall of 1945 at Shepperton Studios, which had been used during the war to store airplanes for the RAF. Indeed, only two sound stages and a handful of dressing rooms were available for the film producers, and technical equipment was still in short supply. Ruggles was well-versed in comedy but not Technicolor musical extravaganzas; a lot of pressure was put on Kay to carry the film. Kay also had her first love scene onscreen with Field. "It was a very sad kiss," she recalled years later. "We all adored him and we knew he was already a very sick man, and we were all miserable. He was such a wonderful person."

To make things worse, Kay was putting on weight, for the first (and, as it turned out, only) time in her life. She still had her voracious teenage appetite, and now with the war over, it was a little easier to get her hands on food. The daily rushes showed her—while hardly chubby—becoming a bit more rounded. Kay put herself on a drastic diet and was, her sister recalls, "in agony." She couldn't sleep for hunger, which made early calls to the set all the harder to bear. Kim and their friend Beryl Turner visited her on the set, and Turner found Kay just as "sweet, warm and funny" as ever, but "confessing to be nervous about acting in her first film." Sid Field himself was in a state of terror: "When I saw that camera coming at me for the first time like a bloodthirsty dragon waiting to pick up my mistakes, my stomach screwed up," he later recalled. "I couldn't get a word out. My inside felt like a cavern of bats."

Kay was thrown in over her head—given the star treatment as far as costumes, hairstyles, and flattering lighting, she was also called upon to do much more in the way of Betty Grable-like singing and dancing than she was equipped for. A singer was brought in to dub Kay's voice (the fact that this woman sounded nothing like Kay didn't seem to faze anyone). Choreographer Freddie Carpenter put Kay through her paces and found that she was enthusiastic and hard-working but hardly capable of carrying a number on her own. She was showcased in two huge, Hollywood-style production numbers. In "My Heart Goes Crazy," she wore a series of long white gowns and traipsed around surrounded by a bevy of matronly looking chorines. "The 'ampstead Way" was an optimistic effort to duplicate the success of the wildly popular "Lambeth Walk" of the late 1930s. Kay and the cast also did music-hall turns, during which she looks visibly embarrassed, no doubt realizing she would be compared with her famously talented grandmother. Kay's voice-over didn't even attempt a Cockney accent while singing "A-dilly, a-dally," and when Tessie O'Shea burst onstage belting out "Any Old Iron," Kay was all but blown off the screen.

At the September 1946 opening of *London Town*, at the Odeon in Leicester Square, Kay was decked out in a sequined black gown—self-conscious about being so much taller than her co-star, Sid Field, she tossed her high heels away and appeared onstage with him wearing black socks. Rank hopefully (and foolishly) dubbed Kay "Britain's Lana Turner" and sent her out on a huge publicity tour. She sang (in her own voice) "The 'ampstead Way" on stage before the film unreeled. Pianist Derek Leask recalls accompanying Kay on one of these appearances, that October. "Audience reaction was lukewarm," he admits. "Kay arrived at the Astoria with a dancing partner to demonstrate 'The 'ampstead Way.' I did not rehearse with Kay prior to her appearance. We just went onstage and hoped for the best! It was a very unfavourable evening." Leask adds that "Kay was due to appear for the rest of the week, but the remaining five shows were cancelled."

She also made her radio debut in conjunction with the film's opening: on August 31, 1946, Kay appeared on the BBC show *In Town Tonight* to plug *London Town*. "Nobody had ever heard of me," Kay later said of this trying period. "I opened bazaars, signed autographs, went to premieres, and did everything a star was supposed to do. My photograph was on magazine covers and front pages of newspapers. And all before we'd even finished the picture." It was impossible for the nineteen-year-old not to get caught up in the excitement and optimism. Though still a teenager, Kay had been working professionally for seven years and had been preparing for this moment since she was a toddler.

Chapter Five

"You have no talent. Find some nice man and get married."

London Town has gone down in history as such a notorious flop that it is surprising to see that not all reviews were negative. *The London Times* called it "a triumph in its own class," adding that Sid Field had "ten times the talent" of Bob Hope. *Variety* felt it a "misfire" but praised Field and Tessie O'Shea—Kay was even mentioned by name as "a good-looking newcomer." Most critics, however, sided with *The Observer*, which called *London Town* "a sad error of judgment . . . a series of indifferent scenes." Viewed today, the film is not so much bad as too long by half. Field's stage routines do not age well, and—oddly—Ruggles never thought to dub audience laughter over them, making them seem to flop miserably in the show-within-a-show. Kay looks lovely and manages to get some personality and zip across in what was essentially a decorative role. She is beautifully gowned and made-up, her long auburn hair done in architecturally elaborate 1940s styles. Not even twenty years old, she looks at least thirty-five.

Audiences stayed away in droves, both in Britain and the U.S. (where the film was released as *My Heart Goes Crazy*). People wanted escapist entertainment, and there was as yet little competition from television, but there were too many brand-new imported Hollywood musicals to choose from: *Anchors Aweigh, Blue Skies, Tonight and Every Night, The Dolly Sisters*. As receipts fell and the film was ushered out of theaters ahead of time, everyone in the film industry realized that *London Town* looked to be the biggest financial disaster in recent memory. The hoped-for rebirth of the British musical had come to a grinding halt.

So did the careers of nearly everyone involved in the project. Wesley Ruggles skulked back to the U.S. and never directed another film. Bob Hope had no worries about Sid Field taking his place; Field's film career was essentially over (though he did score a stage success with *Harvey* shortly before his death in 1950). Only little Petula Clark was young enough to escape any blame and continued working steadily. Kay was hardly singled out for the film's failure, but all the brash, hopeful publicity about "Britain's Lana Turner" made her look—and feel—foolish. The late 1940s were the lowest point, the grimmest years, of Kay's life.

The seven-year Rank contract, which Kay had been so excited about a few months before, was now a chain around her neck. "I think I'm just going to do away with myself," she moaned to her cousin, Moya Collins. "They've got me under contract for seven years and they're not even using me." She needn't have worried: Rank did not exercise her option. Kay later raged about heartless producers who signed on and dropped vulnerable young performers, "picking up little girls in Pimlico or Ohio and making stars of them overnight. It's wicked to put such a burden on them. I started off far too miserably to ever catch up—the tatty publicity, the hired furs, the premieres and all the muck that goes with it."

The worst moment came when a Rank executive—Kay would never name him—called her into his office to release her. "You are a very ugly girl," she later recalled him saying. "You have no talent. You are too tall and you photograph horribly. Find some nice man and get married." It is questionable that any film executive—no matter how much money he'd lost— would say such a thing to a vulnerable and hard-working girl. But, no matter what his actual words, that is what Kay heard, and that is the message she all but branded on her heart. No matter what successes she achieved, both personally and professionally, she could never quite put behind her that executive summary: "No talent." "Ugly." "Photograph horribly."

Kay's personality in adulthood veered wildly from dazzling self-confidence to a bitter inferiority complex. Much—but not all—of this dated from her fall from grace in 1946. Kay's childhood consisted of adoration of her classically handsome father and a difficult relationship with her mother, who was pert but hardly a great beauty. She also had grown up as the kid sister of Kim, who was far more of a beauty than gangly, long-nosed Kay. This was never an issue between the sisters, but Kay came of age thinking of herself as something of an ugly duckling. No matter how much of a beauty she later became, she was never able to quite put these feelings behind her; instead, she was quick to make fun of herself to forestall anyone else's doing so.

Kay was still quite young—she turned twenty in May of 1947—but it seemed as though her life was over. Her professional life certainly seemed to be. But she didn't give up her career—Kay was an actress to the depths of her being. "If I weren't a real pro at heart, *London Town* would have finished me," she admitted years later. "But when you're born into show business, you just go on. I worked at my job. And I still do." Kay may have sounded philosophical and matter-of-fact in later years, but these were genuinely rock-bottom days for her. At one point she moved back in with her mother and sister, which alone was enough to depress her about her future. "I've had it," she moaned over and over. "I'm going to jump out of a window." A fed-up Kim finally opened a nearby window and snapped at her, "Help yourself!"

"I had ulcers with worry," Kay later recalled. "*London Town* was such a disaster that I left the country for two years and went around with touring repertory companies in Germany and Italy learning to act. And I picked up some pretty bad acting habits, too. I used to say all my lines to the people in the front row. Anyone further back than that didn't hear a thing." She later told Gilbert Millstein of *The New York Times* about those tours in Germany, Austria, and Italy, and that she had worked as an assistant stage manager in some touring rep companies. She even claimed, not very believably, to have turned down a film offer in the late 1940s, telling the producer, "Really, darling, I simply couldn't bear being discovered again." In fact, she had an agent, Bill Watts, sending photos out to studios and advising producers to "grab this babe. She's ripe for building into a Rosalind Russell type of comedienne." He received no response.

There are no scrapbooks, photos, or reviews from these years, so Kay's stage career cannot be traced from 1946 to 1950. Her family and friends do not recall attending any shows or getting any letters or calls about shows—indeed, knowing Kay's talent for exaggeration, she may well never have acted overseas at all. One of the few jobs that can be pinned down with any certainty during these dark years is Kay's television debut: on May 5, 1948, she appeared on the BBC variety show *Stars in Your Eyes*. She sang "Down By the Old Mill Stream," which must have provided one of the odder moments in early television.

While Kay struggled to recover her self-confidence and get her career back on track, England itself was still struggling to recover from the war. If people expected to promptly return to the calm and normalcy of the pre-war years, they were sadly disappointed. "After the war there were huge street parties all over the country and people danced around bonfires merrily hurling their ration books and ID cards into the flames," recalls Londoner Nancy Winter. "Unfortunately, the Socialists thought rationing was a good idea, fair rations for everyone. Bread was not rationed during the war, but it was *after* the war! People were given clothing coupons which didn't amount to much, so there was a lot of make-do-and-mend." Bombed-out building sites grew over with ragwort and willow-herb as reconstruction plans dragged out, remembers dancer Ronald Bruce. "The streets were still drab, unpainted and dim-lit," wrote Harry Hopkins. "In the West End, Oxford Street seemed to have become a succession of pin-table arcades and garish sideshows, offering such attractions as 'A REAL LIVE MERMAID IN A TANK OF GOLDFISH.'" German POWs and displaced Europeans still crowded towns and cities.

Then came the cold spell and fuel crisis of early 1947: in addition to lack of personal fuel rations, there were nationwide power cuts; trams and trains stopped; and in February, a record-breaking blizzard hit. Slowly, the bombed-out sites began filling up with modern "pre-fab" homes. Equipped with all the modern conveniences, they still gave parts of London a stark and cheap look. Vanishing, too, were the charming Victorian-era tea shops, to be replaced by Charles Forte's slick and garish but convenient milk bars. The last of the grand old Edwardian restaurants were vanishing: Frascati's, Quaglino's, the Caprice, the Carlton, the Holborn, all came to rubble. Food was still hard to come by—butchers shut their doors after supplies ran out; reconstituted eggs were nearly as hard to come by as real eggs. Pepper, vinegar, bananas—all nonexistent. Hopkins noted that "if there were piles of canned sardines on the shop shelves, it was merely because someone had neglected to provide the necessary openers."

All through the autumn of 1946, the tabloid press seemed torn between coverage of two handsome young men: the psychopathic murderer Neville Heath, and Princess Elizabeth's beau, Prince Philip of Greece and Denmark. Heath was executed; Philip was granted British citizenship and married his Princess, late in 1947—but as the decade wore on, hopeful starlet Kay Kendall still remained beneath the radar screens of public notice.

London filled with demobbed servicemen, and flats seemed impossible to come by at any price. Kay managed to share rooms with girls her age—first in Piccadilly, then in Mayfair. She traveled light, packing up and quickly moving if the rent came due before a paycheck came in. Anything was preferable to moving back in with her mother in St. Martin's Lane.

Her brother, Terry, had moved to Toronto and married, leaving Gladys all the more time to oversee her daughters' lives. Kay and her mother still had an on-again, off-again relationship. They would be getting on fine—then Gladys would visit Kay and notice that her daughter had inked moustaches onto her photos, and the two would be off and running again. "I haven't heard from Kay. This is her address," Gladys would tell Kay's friend Jean Walker. "Go 'round and see, is she eating all right?" Kay would airily apologize: "Is Glad pestering you again? Take no notice. I just haven't had time to write." Still, recalls Beryl Turner, the atmosphere was not always quite so electric at the Kendalls' house. "They were a lovely family," she says, "and we shared some terrific, fun times at their London flat. In spite of the seriousness of the war, they always managed to keep 'open house' for close friends, and to find fun and shared happiness."

Despite her self-consciousness about her looks, Kay applied for and got many modeling jobs in the late 1940s. Photos show her to be the height of New Look elegance in off-the-shoulder gowns, full, sweeping skirts, peasant blouses, and dirndls. It was around this time that Kay cut off her long Rita Hayworth-like mane of hair and opted for the shorter, curlier style that would exemplify the 1950s. It was a step she would later come to regret, as Kay's hair grew agonizingly slowly. In later years she longed for her flowing locks and tugged anxiously at her hair. But that awful "growing out" period took so long that filming always intervened and studio hairdressers just chopped it off short again.

One modeling assignment took her to the resort of Funchal in Madeira, which turned out to be anything but a vacation. Kay was seasick on the boat the whole way over and was still wobbly and nauseated during the shoot. Her return trip provided either a brush with death or another example of Kay's storytelling abilities: according to her, she booked a flight home to avoid another rocky boat. She either missed the plane or "was the last one off" before it crashed and exploded, killing everyone aboard. How the plane could have crashed after she'd left it beggars the imagination and leads one to believe this was just a typical example of Kay's growing talent for self-dramatization.

American theater invaded England in 1948 with the bright-as-paint musicals *Oklahoma!* and *Annie Get Your Gun*. Soon, U.S.-made dramas such as *A Streetcar Named Desire* and *Death of a Salesman* further crowded British playwrights off the boards. One of the more popular musicals in London in 1948 was *High Button Shoes,* and one of its more popular chorus members was nineteen-year-old Audrey Hepburn, making her London debut. Though most Hepburn biographies put Kay in the *High Button Shoes* cast, Hepburn's friend Nikolas Dana insists that "Kay was *not* in that show. There was a Kay in it—Kay Kimber, who played Mama—and that may have led to the confusion." Still, Audrey Hepburn did become friendly at about this time with the Kendall sisters, and Dana recalls seeing them around London together, "at some of the private clubs, like the Regency, where you needed a card to get in. Some of those clubs liked to have theater or movie people." Kay and Hepburn, both slim, adventurous beauties, quickly hit it off; Kay brought out Audrey's impish and mischievous side.

Hepburn, Kay, and Kim attended dance classes at King's Road in Chelsea every Saturday morning, along with such celebrities as Tyrone Power and Linda Christian (whom Power married in 1949), and Michael Wilding. "We'd all exercise together and sit kicking, fooling around," says Kim. "Afterwards we'd go across to the pub and we'd all drink lots of drinks." Hepburn was dating James Hanson, heir to the haulage and transportation corporation that bore his name. (It had been taken over by the government during the war and had just been resold to the Hanson family.) James and his sister Muriel were friends of Kim's; their brother Bill Hanson was just back from the war and was Captain of Britain's Equestrian Team in the 1948 Summer Olympics. The brothers naturally accompanied the group on their jaunts to nightclubs and restaurants in London, and Kay's romance with Bill Hanson became her first serious love affair. She was a dreadful social snob, and Bill Hanson's adoration of her did wonders for her self-image; she fed on it. But dating someone like him made her realize how little she'd accomplished and pointed out—to her, at least—her lack of social background. "Not bad for a Cockney chorus girl!" she'd crow to friends, knowing at the same time that exactly such behavior would put her beyond the pale of the social elite she both aspired to and made brutal fun of. Still, Hanson was great fun and the pair were friends as well as lovers.

Bill Hanson's friend Richard Cox Cowell says that Hanson convinced him to bring Kay to meet the Olympic Field Hockey Team. "The British Olympic Association always assigned hostesses—healthy, wholesome young English lasses, but none of them quite good looking," he recalls. Hanson drove Kay up to a practice in his new Rolls-Royce—Kay found herself surrounded by appreciative athletes, signing photos and warding off passes while her boyfriend and Cowell stood proudly by. As a result, "I got elected as Captain to the U.S. Olympic Team" by his grateful teammates, Cowell laughs.

Kay escaped from the *London Town* fallout and from England, too, with the help of her friend Valerie Nelson. Valerie whisked Kay off to California, where she lived in Beverly Hills with her husband Donald, who had been President Roosevelt's head of the War Production Board and who was currently president of the Society of Independent Motion Picture Producers association. It was Kay's first visit to the Hollywood community, and she was both dazzled and dazzling. Restaurateur "Prince" Mike Romanoff fell head over heels for her, loaning her money and making sure she had the best table and the best food in his establishment. She did not come equipped with trunks of clothing, so Kay relied on the kindness of strangers with deep closets. To one gala event, she wore one of Marlene Dietrich's old gowns, borrowed from a studio costume department. Unable to find anyone with shoes her size, Kay ingeniously wrapped ribbons around her feet and up her legs. Ingenious until she started to dance; the ribbons began to unwind and tripped up everyone in her path.

The most promising contact Kay made in Hollywood was with forty-four-year-old Famous Artists agent Charles Feldman, one of the first agents to sell directors and performers as a "package deal" to studios. He handled such clients as Greta Garbo, Marlene Dietrich, Lana Turner, and John Wayne; he could get nearly any producer on the phone in one try (though, admittedly, Louis B. Mayer hated him). In 1934 he had married starlet and photographer Jean Howard—after a stormy marriage, the two split up in 1946 and divorced two years later. Much to Hollywood's fascination, though, the couple continued to live side-by-side in their Hollywood home, giving elaborate parties. Feldman had helped launch the careers of youngsters such as Lauren Bacall, Kirk Douglas, and Lizbeth Scott, and Kay hoped he could do the same for her. An enjoyable romance resulted, but Feldman was unable to successfully sponsor the British beauty in Hollywood—and his residence with his ex-wife pretty much curtailed his extracurricular socializing. After two socially glittering but professionally unproductive months, Kay went with Bill Hanson to Richard Cox Cowell's New York apartment before returning home to take up her battered career.

Kay was not returning in triumph, as she'd hoped. Marriage to Bill Hanson was looking more and more unlikely, and she had failed to succeed in the family business as well. Kay skulked back into England determined to make something of herself but in such a cloud of depression and failure that she rarely spoke of this first U.S. trip. When she returned in 1957, most people assumed it was her first visit. But for now, Kay squared her shoulders and determined to take desperate efforts to get her life and career back on track.

Chapter Six

"I need someone to look after me, wifey."

Late in the 1940s, Kay took a step that would change her appearance and, she hoped, her career, for the better: she had her nose done. Rhinoplasty was nothing new—Fanny Brice had her nose bobbed back in the 1920s. And plastic surgery had made great leaps during the war. Kay was a believer in going right to the top, so she used her many social and government friends to approach the father of British plastic surgery, Sir Archibald McIndoe. McIndoe had established the Centre for Plastic and Jaw Surgery at the Queen Victoria Hospital in East Grinstead and did outstanding work rehabilitating burned and bomb-injured RAF pilots (he had been knighted in 1947 for his work). He founded the British Association of Plastic Surgeons and, when Kay met him, was a council member of the Royal College of Surgeons.

Archibald McIndoe did not make a habit of prettying-up starlets, so Kay's success with him is astonishing. But McIndoe was known for his psychological insights as well as for his surgical skill. Not only was Kay a promising actress held back by her previous association with *London Town*, but she was saddled with an inferiority complex easy for a doctor to discern. "Kay hated her nose," friends assert, and throughout her life Kay's own interviews are filled with jabs at her appearance: "People say I'm glamorous, but really, I'm not," she told reporter Jesse Zunser in 1957. "Why do you suppose producers make me get under those huge hats? To show my face? Don't believe it! Millions of women are more beautiful than I am—I mean, now, after all, let's face it!" Even years after her surgery, as Dinah Sheridan recalls, "she did *nothing* but grumble about her nose. She *loathed* it." She would tell friends, "I know what I look like—two profiles pasted together!"

The combination of Kay's crippling complex and her influential friends convinced McIndoe to bob her attractive, if somewhat long, nose. According to Kay, McIndoe could achieve one of two shapes: a ski-slope or a pug.

The one she chose was a more feminine version of Bob Hope's, or the Tin Man's from *The Wizard of Oz*—so pointed that it threatened to put out the eyes of her leading men. Somehow it worked and brought all her features together. It was slim, elegant, and aristocratic, which went well with Kay's light-as-air, Lady of the Manor personality. But it was also a tad silly-looking; just long and swoopy enough to give her a madcap appearance. Kay would wiggle her nose between her fingers and crow, "Look—no cartilage! It's all McIndoe!" It was similar to the look possessed by light comedienne Ina Claire, who once sighed, "Can you imagine anyone with a nose that tips up as mine does playing a noble, tragic character? I might get along fairly well being noble and sad until I suddenly turned my profile." Whether it was an accident or not, Kay's new nose typecast her as a comedienne. It turned out to be a fortuitous choice.

Kay never admitted to anyone that she'd hated her face enough to have a knife taken to it—she invented a horrific car crash to cover up. "She said she'd gone through the windscreen and had smashed up her face from the bridge of her nose to the chin," said her longtime friend Dirk Bogarde. "What rubbish!" says Kim Kendall. "We certainly would have known about any car crash." Indeed, toward the end of her life Kay herself completely forgot her own cover story and blithely told a reporter about her nose, "I got it from my mother, she has one just like it. It's awful, really—I have terrible sinus and this nose is so thin I can scarcely breathe through it." McIndoe later told surgeon Eric Gustavson that he himself hated the job he'd done on Kay's nose and had offered her a re-do, but that she refused, claiming that she loved it. McIndoe begged her not to tell anyone who her surgeon had been—a promise Kay obviously did not keep.

After the operation, Kay claimed to have no sense of smell or taste and would go through great theatrics over it. Once, while dining with Bogarde and his family, she ate a red pepper to prove she had no working taste buds. On another occasion she claimed to briefly have regained her sense of smell: "I can smell your cigar!" she cried happily to Bogarde's father. "She ran around the room and we gave her things to smell," Bogarde recalled. "There were roses, my mother's scent and various things—and it went within half an hour." "Oh, poor me," she'd laugh hopelessly, "I'm a ruin, a ruin. I need someone to look after me, wifey." As unlikely as this story is, Kim insists it has at least a basis in reality: "I used to have the same problem myself, no sense of smell," she affirms. "I think it might have something to do with lack of proper nutrition during the war—not enough zinc, or maybe the saccharine we had to use instead of sugar or something." Sadly, Kay's nose job did not improve her self-image.

As Kay's appearance had altered, so too British films had begun to change in the early 1950s (for one thing, the X-Certificate was introduced in 1951, giving rise to more adult films and subject matters). Then, there was the rise of the so-called "Ealing comedies," not all of them actually produced at Ealing Studios. In 1949 alone, *Kind Hearts and Coronets*, *Passport to Pimlico* and *Whiskey Galore* opened the door to a new breed of British comedy. Nineteen-fifty seemed to be the turning point, not only of the half-century, but as the year when Britain really began its new postwar life. Points rationing was ended in May; fish and steel were freed up. Bread, cream and petrol reappeared as facets of everyday life, some for the first time in a decade (it wasn't until 1954 that the last of wartime rationing, on meat, ended). On May 3, 1951, the Festival of Britain opened, along the Victoria Embankment. The last of the prewar fustiness seemed to be swept away in an hysteria of modern design: "Everything, the litter baskets, the signboards, the plant pots, the conical metal lampshades, seemed fresh and new," wrote one observer. Added another, "After that long grey winter, this galaxy of colour was like a glass of champagne. Everywhere I looked brought fresh impact—vivid reds, blues, greens, lemon yellows—bubbles pricking my nose."

The new decade also started very promisingly for Kay and ended a four-year streak of bad luck. For the first time since *London Town*, she stepped tentatively back in front of the movie camera. It was the tiniest of roles in a low-budget Ealing film, so if it flopped, there was not much to be lost. *Dance Hall* (1950) was an entertaining drama about four dance-mad factory girls and their beaus. The cast was packed with Rank Charm School hopefuls and various borrowed starlets: Petula Clark (now a grown-up eighteen and fully recovered from the disaster of *London Town*), fresh-faced brunettes Natasha Parry and Jane Hylton, curvy blonde Diana Dors (promoted as Britain's Marilyn Monroe, she instead became Britain's Jayne Mansfield). Kay—unbilled—appeared only fleetingly, just long enough to steal Natasha Parry's dance partner. The film was directed by Charles Crichton, whom screenwriter Diana Morgan called "bliss, lovely to work with—a lovely, funny man and very understanding." Not that he really had to understand Kay: she was onscreen for all of twenty seconds.

Dance Hall was the first time Kay really felt a part of Ealing Studios, remembered by Crichton as "a snug nursery where one was surrounded by talented playmates and supervised by a tolerant headmaster—Sir Michael

Balcon. Well, he was not all *that* tolerant." Actress Thora Hird agreed that Ealing was "the studio with the family feeling" but noted that not all family members were treated equally. "It had one restaurant with two doors in it," she said, "to separate the wheat from the chaff. If you were a star you went in one door." Even when it came to makeup, said Hird, "You could have eyelashes put on if you were a star, but if you weren't a star, you couldn't." At this point in her career, Kay still went eyelashless through the non-star door.

Kay's living conditions had always been somewhat thrown together. She moved from flat to flat, loudly telling people at parties, "everyone back to my place for coffee!" when in fact she had no place. Friends were used to her moving in on them at a moment's notice when she lost her apartment because of rent troubles or the previous owner's return. At one point she rented a flat from singer Judy Shirley, who had been a vocalist with Maurice Winnick's Orchestra in the 1930s and had branched out to a solo career. Shirley was now the girlfriend of liquor distributor Eustace Hoey. Hoey would periodically charge in to take back Shirley's minks, and she and Kay would frantically shove them into the clothesbin or the closet for safekeeping. "All her flats were scattered with cardboard boxes," recalls Kim. "Champagne, caviar, flowers in the corner—but no furniture."

Around 1950, Kay's affair with Bill Hanson began cooling off, and she took up with grocery-store tycoon James Sainsbury. Bill Hanson's brother, the current Lord Hanson, insists there were no hard feelings on either side. "James Sainsbury was a lovely man, a super guy, and I guess they just drifted apart," he says. "Bill had thought of marrying Kay, but I don't think it went beyond that." Kay's friend Princess Lilian recalls that there was a bit of social inequality involved, as well: Hanson would take Lilian aside and beg her, "Lilian, darling, tell her that she can't wear that . . . errr . . . that fur thing," and Lilian would snap back at him, "You should feel damned lucky that she's even going out with you!" Not long after the breakup, Bill Hanson did indeed marry (like Kay, he died quite young, in 1953).

Lilian introduced her to James Sainsbury. He and Lilian were good friends but not romantically involved, and the wealthy young man would take the poor actress out to dine frequently. One day Lilian chirped up brightly, "James, I think I know exactly the girl for you! Am I allowed to call her up and invite her to come and have dinner with us?" She got Kay on the phone and told her, "Katie, I've got a divine person here and he wants to meet you. All I ask you is, keep your trap shut!" The matchmaking paid off, and soon the couple was very much in love. Kay's St. Martin's Lane neighbor Barbara Seabrook remembers Sainsbury haunting the florist across the street and buying out the shop—"He was totally love-struck!"

James Sainsbury was forty-one when he and Kay met in 1950, and many thought they were the great love of each others' lives. "They were so much in love," says actress Dinah Sheridan. "She would talk of no one else but Jim Sainsbury—she was a very solitary, loyal and faithful girl." "I'm very much in love with her," Sainsbury told their mutual friend Lilian. Lilian suggested that he propose, but "he was a confirmed bachelor and didn't want to get married." Kay was still seeing Bill Hanson at the same time; juggling two men at once was not something she was quite organized enough to handle. She once made dates for both Hanson and Sainsbury to meet her for Sunday brunch at Les Ambassadeurs. She stood chatting happily with Bill Hanson and their friend Richard Cox Cowell, who recalls the scene when James Sainsbury walked in. "'Oh, *shit!*' bellowed Kay—as loud as you can get," says Cowell. "The whole room stopped." Lilian also remembers getting calls from one beau while Kay was out with the other: "She's just gone to post a letter, she won't be gone more than ten minutes," Lilian would improvise, then call Kay at Boyfriend One's house and tell her to call Boyfriend Two ("Ring him quickly, he wants to know where you are").

Kay's manic behavior and tumbling into ill-advised romances was not unusual for girls of her generation, says her friend Suzzie Dillon, who was married to musical star Jack Buchanan from 1949 till his death in 1957. "I think it was the postwar syndrome," she explains. "So many of my girlfriends had lived on the razor's edge during the war, on the brink of death. You didn't know if you were going to wake up the next morning—so you took what you got."

Kay took what she got career-wise, too, and there was very little available to her. If the job paid, she grabbed at it. She didn't even get billing in her next film, a rather lackluster musical called *Happy Go Lovely*. Shot at Elstree Studios late in 1950 and released early the next year, it starred perky American song-and-dance girl Vera-Ellen as a chorine put into the star's role because her producer mistakenly thinks she's dating a millionaire (David Niven). Kay played the put-upon secretary of the bullying theatrical producer (Cesar Romero). She had only two brief scenes and perhaps half-a-dozen lines; on her first entrance, she is knocked flat by Romero as they collide in a doorway. Tiny roles in two films was hardly the comeback Kay was hoping for.

Chapter Seven

"We made ourselves ill with laughter."

Films did not seem to be welcoming her back as 1951 began, but Kay had two lucky breaks in the still-infant television industry. On March 20, she was given a marvelous showcase role, as Martha Handsford in the BBC production *Sweethearts and Wives*, a comedy by Gilbert and Margareth Hackforth. On April 29 she played Mary, a farmer's daughter, in L. du Garde Peach's *The River*, a drama about a flood threatening a village (according to the *Radio Times,* it was a thinly veiled metaphor about the recent war). The BBC at the time had no casting director overseeing dramas, so Kay was given these choice roles by producers Kevin Sheldon (*Sweethearts and Wives*) and Dallas Dower (*The River*).

Another producer, Frank Launder, took note of Kay's TV work that spring. Launder, who had written the hit mystery *The Lady Vanishes*, tapped her for a supporting role in the film *Lady Godiva Rides Again,* filmed in the summer of 1951 and released in November. She was cast as Sylvie Clark, the older, cynical sister of a small-town innocent (Pauline Stroud) who becomes caught up in the whirl of a national beauty contest. Finally—for the first time—Kay had a good role in a good film. It was a small part, but Kay made the most of it. Indeed, hers is the first face seen in the film, gazing disgustedly out the window as the rain pours down. Rather than furs and sparkling gowns, she flounces about in plain cotton frocks, a tatty bathrobe and curling papers, rolling her eyes as her father (Stanley Holloway) makes rude noises in the background. Not only was Kay herself quite good, finally bursting forth as a wry comedienne, but the film as a whole was a delight (Diana Dors also had a nice turn, as a hardboiled beauty queen, as did Alistair Sims, playing a bankrupt film producer). Years later, Kay recalled Sylvie Clark as her favorite role: "I was a Cockney tart behind a sweet counter, and I adored it."

Kay's luck held out, and she was given another good-sized role— third-billed—in the charming comedy/drama *Curtain Up*, filmed by Rank late in 1951 and released early in 1952. Kay played Sandra Beverley, the leading lady of a small-town repertory company putting on a dreadful melodrama called *Tarnished Gold*. Kay was frustrated, though, that she had been given one of the more dramatic roles: Sandra is married to the philandering leading man (played by Liam Gaffney), who becomes jealous when she is offered a film contract. Additionally, she was pitted against two of the most accomplished scene-stealers in the business: Robert Morley (as the company's temperamental director) and Margaret Rutherford (as the befuddled playwright). With Morley and Rutherford shamelessly and delightfully double-taking, twitching, and blinking all over the place, the other cast members receded hopelessly into the background. *Curtain Up*, while an enjoyable diversion, did little for Kay's career.

Late in the year, Kay returned to the small screen, making a guest appearance in a July episode (*The Blonde Informer*) of a docudrama series, *I Made News*. And in December, she had a leading role, as Sue Kemp, on one of the BBC's earliest detective dramas. *The Inch Man*, starring Robert Ayres as the crime-solving Stephen Inch, lasted only through the 1951–52 season before dropping from the airwaves. But TV was still in its infancy, and Kay had her eyes set on a film career: she wouldn't act on TV again until 1957, and that would be in America.

Britain briefly ground to a halt when King George VI died on February 6, 1952. Though his illness had been long known, he had recently been seen shooting at Sandringham, and his daughter Elizabeth's trip to Kenya had reassured the public that his condition was stable. Plans for Elizabeth's coronation were put into effect—stalled again and again by the failing health of the late King's mother (who finally died at the end of March 1953).

There may have been a bracing change in the wind in England in 1952, but Kay's career remained mired in a series of unremarkable melodramas. Her glamour and fashion-model looks were showcased, but her gifts for comedy were completely buried. For Hammer Films, Kay was third-billed in a completely impenetrable crime quickie, *Wings of Danger*, co-starring American B actor Zachary Scott. There was no plot, as such: the film was based on a novel, *Dead on Course,* but something must have been lost in the translation. It seemed to involve a small airport, blackmail, gold smugglers, and code books. Kay played Alexia LaRoche, apparently a villainess: she looks glamorous and smouldery and simply says her lines with no idea what they mean or who her character is. Indeed, the whole film looks as if the cast had been given pages from completely different scripts just moments before the cameras were turned on. The only clue that Kay's character dies in a plane crash is when someone gestures toward the airfield and says, "Shame about the girl—she was a good looker."

Another Hammer film, also helmed by *Wings of Danger* director Terence Fisher, followed: *Mantrap* (released in the U.S. as *Man in Hiding*). Kay was billed ninth as Vera in this lurid crime drama starring Paul Henried as a detective who goes undercover to track an elusive killer. The only positive thing to come out of *Mantrap* was Kay's meeting Anthony Forwood, who had a supporting role in the film. Forwood was actress Glynis Johns's ex-husband and was now living with up-and-coming actor Dirk Bogarde. Forwood retired from acting in 1954 to become Bogarde's manager and companion (the two remained together until Forwood's death in 1988).

Kay clicked instantly with Bogarde and Forwood, and the threesome became lifelong friends. Bogarde had first spotted Kay back in the mid-1940s, when both were working at Ealing Studios. Like many, he was put off by her outlandish humor and grand duchess airs. "Oh, look, it's Mr. Bogarde," she would croon in what he called her "stand-uppy" voice as she breezed by him in the studio cafeteria. Bogarde had no interest in getting to know her any better. But Forwood insisted on bringing her to their home in Amersham (in Buckinghamshire), telling Bogarde, "She's very funny, she's brilliant and I think you'll like her."

Bogarde was not the only person to be frightened off by Kay's outre humor and sharp tongue. But when Kay calmed down, felt more comfortable, and put herself out to be friendly, she stopped performing and became the most attentive and supportive of friends. "She just enveloped you, and I don't mean like a praying mantis," recalled Roddy McDowell. "She was just completely attentive. She really looked at you, she really connected. She enjoyed people very much." Director Vincente Minnelli's wife, Lee, also found herself captured by Kay's charm: "When she talked to you, there was no one else in the room," says Minnelli. "She wasn't looking over your shoulder for someone else." This is the Kay whom Dirk Bogarde got to know and befriend.

Dirk Bogarde was on the rise in the early 1950s, more so than Kay. Born in 1921, he had his first real success as a killer in the play *Power Without Glory* (1947, also starring Kenneth More). Dark, brooding, and intense, Bogarde had since been signed to a long-term contract with Rank and had scored in *The Blue Lamp* and, most recently, the thriller *Hunted*.

Kay's first meeting with Bogarde and Forwood at home started out normally enough: with tea and a stroll around their grounds. Kay tossed herself onto a deck chair on the lawn, sipped a gin and tonic, and broke into what Bogarde recalled as her Dorothy Adorable voice: "What a sweet little housey-pousey you have! Do you do it all yourself? So clever . . . such a lot of work. . . . I've a teeny weeny little flat in horrid London, too awful, and no dear little garden like this." (Bogarde was swift to note that their "dear little garden" covered four acres.)

Kay continued to drop leaden hints about how close to the studios his housey-pousey was and how she hated the long drive so early in the morning and how she did *so* love the country. At the time, she was living in a tiny attic flat at the Connaught Hotel, a maid's room, for eighteen shillings a week. Before Bogarde or Forwood quite realized what had happened, Kay had talked herself into one of the guest bedrooms. The following weekend, she piled some suitcases, a white fox rug, and her anemia medications ("wretched blood capsules") into her room—Bogarde added that "There had never been a happier decision ever made." He and Forwood soon moved into a larger home, Beel House, nearby, and Kay was packed up along with the rest of the baggage. This new house included Bogarde's pride and joy, a glass-enclosed aviary, which he felt was very High Victorian and elegant. Kay took one look at it and dubbed it "the Outpatient's Department," which became its official nickname. A great one for nicknames, she also called Bogarde "Diggy" for his love of gardening. (Roddy McDowell, a good swimmer, was "Sammy the Seal.")

Kay had found a happy home with Bogarde and Forwood. Indeed, she was always comfortable around gay men. She didn't feel the need to flirt with them and could relax and treat them like pals. Bogarde remembered her lazing about weekends in jeans and a cashmere sweater, her hair a mess, no makeup on, mingling with other guests. She felt free to give vent to her emotions: after Bogarde bought a television, Kay would listen to concerts from Albert Hall, "knitting with her glasses on, crying and sobbing with grief at the music." Her tastes in pop music ran to Bing Crosby and Nat King Cole: "I just sit for hours listening to Nat King Cole," Kay said years later in a *Preview* magazine roundtable. "By just playing him long enough I can snap out of every mood." Fellow interviewee Kenneth More teased her, "great intellect, that girl! Such wit! Such conversational powers!" To which Kay bellowed, "Beast! I know I'm a low-brow, but I like romantic music. I could listen to it twenty-four hours a day."

Kay was not, of course, always on good behavior: Bogarde recalled a visit from actor Richard Todd, who rubbed her the wrong way. "Right, mates, goodnight, all!" she snapped in the middle of dinner and stormed off to her room. Bogarde tried to get her to come back down and be pleasant, but she loudly insisted, "He's a cunt and I don't want to see him!" Despite Kay's wild mood swings and Bogarde's earnest seriousness, the two got along like puppies: "We laughed, we got hysterical," he remembered shortly before his death in 1999. "I don't know what it was, it was such a long time ago and we were all so much younger, but we made ourselves ill with laughter."

Kay's romance with James Sainsbury continued to be a serious one; he could be as devilish a practical joker as Kay. The couple was spending a cold winter weekend with Bogarde and Forwood, when Sainsbury—annoyed at Kay's offhand treatment of him—vanished for hours. Worried about him, the group went on a search and saw his footprints disappearing into a nearby lake. "Oh, me poor little butcher boy, poor little butter-slapper!" Bogarde recalled Kay crying. But Sainsbury had backtracked over his own footprints and was hiding in the woods, immensely enjoying everyone's terror. "Kay was nice to him the rest of the weekend," Kim remembers.

Chapter Eight

"People think I'm the gayest thing on two legs, but I get awfully depressed at times."

While Kay's social life took off, her career was languishing. Still another stinker of a low-budget crime melodrama followed with *Street of Shadows* (filmed in 1952 and released in 1953). Kay had the pleasure of playing the second-billed love interest to Cesar Romero, to whom she'd been merely a nameless stooge in *Happy Go Lovely*. Romero was the manager of a "pintable saloon" and Kay the unhappy wife of a crooked police captain. She looks glamorous and sulky and barely changes facial expression throughout the film.

The next film Kay made in 1952 was her most enjoyable—for audiences, anyway—in some time: *It Started in Paradise* was the sort of glossy "woman's movie" that Susan Hayward and Lana Turner were making in the States. Produced by the Rank Organisation at a huge cost, it starred Jane Hylton (of *Dance Hall*) as an ambitious fashion designer who claws her way to the top of the couture world. Kay had a smallish role as the designer's star customer; she was breathtakingly beautiful in Technicolor and stylish gowns, though she looks far too old to be the "debutante of the season," as her character was described. Once again, though, Kay's talents were wasted while her aristocratic looks and voice were exploited: her "Lady Caroline" is bitchy and snobbish but wholly humorless. The only really juicy role in the film was a cheerfully vulgar nightclub singer played by Diana Decker—Kay would have killed for a part like that.

This was Kay's first of three films with Muriel Pavlow, who played the second female lead in *It Started in Paradise*. Both actresses hated the extreme-style, high-fashion costumes they were made to wear in the film: "I remember sitting, practically weeping in each other's arms, saying, 'Oh, the things they're making us wear! It's not right, it's not right,'" Pavlow says. Kay saw herself becoming typecast as a shady, glamorous sexpot: "I was their girl whenever anyone wanted anything like that," she later recalled, grimly. "I got simply fed up with terribly hard, bitchy, horsey sort of women. 'Please,' I begged them, 'shave my head if you have to, don't let me wear any makeup, but please stop smothering me in furs and smart tea-time talk!'"

Offscreen, however, Kay had no objections to furs and makeup, though her talk was hardly of the tea-time variety. There was a bumper crop of beautiful actresses, models, socialites, and royalty hitting London in those postwar years. In addition to the lovely Kendall sisters, there was Jean Simmons, Audrey Hepburn, and—of course—Princess Margaret. Kay, still a minor starlet, managed to make a huge splash in this circle. "She had half the men in London, you know," says her sometimes roommate Lilian. "The Marquis de Prima d'Riviera was mad about her, too. I had to cope with all her boyfriends—the phone never stopped and half the time I was making excuses by saying, 'she's with her mother,' or anything to get out of it." The Marquis was only able to withstand Kay's ribbing for so long, and she took every opportunity to tease him. At one well-publicized charity luncheon, Marina, Duchess of Kent, dropped a piece of jewelry under the table and dove down to retrieve it. The gentlemanly Marquis de Prima d'Riviera crawled under to help, which was reported on in the press the next day. Kay was immediately on the phone to him, bellowing in faux outrage: "*What* were you doing under that table with the Duchess of Kent?!"

Not only was Kay stunningly beautiful and always dressed in the latest gowns, she sparkled, drawing to her men and women alike by the force of her personality and her sometimes outlandish sense of humor. She also *liked* people and was having the time of her life, and this attracted even more moths to her flame. Night after night, Kay was seen dancing and dining at nightclubs and restaurants such as Ziggy's on Charles Street, Ciro's, the Savoy, the 400 Club, the Mill Roy, the Dorchester. *The* place to be seen was Les Ambassadeurs, a restaurant opened in the Rothschilds' house—it was here that Kay's friend Lilian first met Prince Bertil.

Kay was already known as a party girl, a reputation she shrugged off. "You work in the daytime as everyone else does," she told reporter Denis Myers early in 1953, "and then you can play at night. Oh, you have to ration your life while you're on a film, getting up at the crack of dawn to be at the studios, but on Saturdays and Sundays you can go gay." Two of the escorts Kay was "going gay" with were men-about-town in Princess Margaret's circle. In the early 1950s, she was still having a serious romance with James Sainsbury while at the same time carrying on with millionaire playboy Billy Wallace and David Montbatten, third Marquess of Milford Haven. Kay was thrilled to be seen with Milford Haven, who was a descendant of Queen Victoria and who'd been his cousin Prince Philip's best man at his 1947 wedding to Princess Elizabeth. Billy Wallace also proved to be an enchanting dancing partner and dinner companion—well over six feet tall, he was one of the few men in London who towered over Kay. Witty and wealthy, he lacked only looks (one of Princess Margaret's biographers referred to him as "the most chinless of the chinless wonders"). Wallace was the sole heir to a wealthy father and stepfather, and owned a huge family estate in Sussex. Both Kay and Margaret had entertained matrimonial thoughts about Wallace: indeed, Margaret was briefly engaged to him in 1948. But he proved not to be husband material for any woman until his only marriage, in 1965.

Kay laughed to a reporter about one beau, whom she refused to name. "He has a title, pots of money, a country mansion. But I can't stand him. No real personality like my other friends." What she really wanted, Kay sighed dramatically, was "one husband, ten children and three boxer puppies." And she knew very well that no Marquesses of Milford Haven were going to marry the scatty, goofy Yorkshire chorus girl. "It's the blood," she admitted sadly. "I would love it to have been blue just to please David and Billy." This didn't stop Kay from having romantic flings with titled admirers: around this time, her name was linked with two other handsome young royals, the Maharajah of Cooch Behar and Prince Carl Johan of Sweden (the youngest son of King Gustav VI and brother of her friend Lillian's lover, Bertil). The romance with Johan was a brief but fervid one. "We're planning to run away from it all and become beachcombers," Kay told her sister. "Of course, it was an absolute fantasy," notes Kim. "Neither of them wanted to cause a scandal in the royal family—besides, Johan's wife threatened to throw acid in Kay's face—at least, that was Kay's story. So they broke it off." But as usual, Kay remained close friends with her former hearthrob—when Johan showed up in New York, he was preceded by a telegram from Kay to Kim: "Johnny is coming to New York—love him for life." Still, she was already thinking seriously about marriage and was somewhat disconcerted that she was not the type men considered as bride material. She said jauntily that she couldn't see "Marie Kendall's granddaughter Katie happy in a stately home of England!" But only a moment later, she was telling the same reporter seriously that "People think I'm the gayest thing on two legs, but I get awfully depressed at times."

Only a year or two later, Kay airily brushed off these doomed romances: "Cooch Behar? Why, I don't even *know* him!" she hooted. As for Milford Haven and Billy Wallace, she insisted, "They are certainly good friends of mine, but there's never been the slightest romance of any kind." She added of Wallace, "Just because he's a friend of mine and I'd been dancing with him a couple of times, they'd dig out an ancient photo of me and say, 'Is there a romance in the house?' I hope they've dropped that once and for all."

One relationship that could not be brushed off in the early 1950s was with film producer Anthony Havelock-Allan. Born into the peerage, Havelock-Allan was forty-seven years old and a major player in the British film industry when he and Kay met. He'd worked his way up in the 1930s producing Quota Quickies, but had since been a power behind such hits as *Brief Encounter, In Which We Serve, This Happy Breed,* and *Great Expectations.* That last film starred his wife, actress Valerie Hobson. The couple had been married since 1939, but by the early 1950s the relationship was under some strain.

Although Kay was still heavily involved with James Sainsbury, she was also being courted by Havelock-Allan in the summer of 1952. "He was mad about her, sent her baskets of mimosas," Kim recalls. "And he had a lot of pull—her career really started taking off when she dated him." Cozying up to agents was a time-honored tradition in films, enough to spawn a joke about an actress so dumb she slept with the writers. But Kay's relationship with Havelock-Allen was more serious than that; she was never single-minded enough about her career to curl up on a casting couch. "Only do it for love," as she told her sister. And—despite Sainsbury lurking in the background—she and Havelock-Allen got quite serious. At least, *he* did.

He helped her get a role in a low-budget film, which Kay was only moderately grateful for: it was the least of four leads, and the project was being produced on a tiny budget with no real stars. From the first, no one expected much from *Genevieve.* Just before filming started, Kay and Anthony Havelock-Allen ended their romance. While Kay's relationship with Bill Hanson had ended on friendly, adult terms, she broke up with Havelock-Allen in a much more dramatic way—one not particularly to Kay's credit. He was still mad about her, sending her flowers and poems. The topic of marriage was tossed about, and Kay found herself, against her better judgment, making plans to become the next Mrs. Havelock-Allen. In the early 1950s, the only way to obtain a divorce was the old-fashioned "gentleman's way"—Havelock-Allen had to take himself off to a Brighton hotel with a paid corespondent. "Poor Tony," Kay told her sister. "She's the oddest-looking thing you've ever seen: she has blonde hair with a navy-blue parting!"

Havelock-Allen obtained his divorce from Valerie Hobson (who went on, in 1954, to marry scandal-plagued Conservative M.P. John Profumo). But by the time everything was properly arranged, Kay flew into a panic and changed her mind. Her sister called her on the carpet about it: Kay airily brushed off her former fiancé and career savior with the nasty (and inaccurate) comment, "Oh, he looks like an earwig." Havelock-Allen went on to have an affair with Grace Kelly, then a long, happy marriage. Even after the shoddy treatment he got from her, Havelock-Allen never spoke ill of Kay. "They all loved her," shrugs Kim. "Nobody seemed to take much offense."

Even with Havelock-Allen safely in the past, Kay still had the film role he had obtained for her. *Genevieve* was a small, light-hearted story about two young couples participating in the annual "Old Crock's Rally" from London to Brighton and back, driving antique cars (the real-life rallies had been held annually since 1928 by the Veteran Car Club). The film was budgeted for a very tight schedule of shooting, in September and October of 1952. Kay was billed third as Rosalind Peters, model-girlfriend of Ambrose Claverhouse (Kenneth More). Starring were John Gregson and Dinah Sheridan as Alan and Wendy McKim, a bright young barrister and his bride of three years. It was such a low-budget film that no one got paid much for it. The four leads earned two thousand pounds each and had to talk their way up to that. Larry Adler—who composed and played the film's enchantingly breezy harmonica score—was offered such a small amount that he elected to do it for a tiny percent of the film's profits instead. As it turned out, Adler was the only one to make any money out of *Genevieve*.

The director, thirty-seven-year-old Henry Cornelius, had worked with Max Reinhardt in pre-Hitler Berlin and later with René Clair and Alexander Korda. As associate producer for Michael Balcon he'd had a great success with *Passport to Pimlico* and was entrusted with the tiny budget and minuscule shooting time for *Genevieve*. Dinah Sheridan later said that Dirk Bogarde spotted the potential in the script and advised her to take the film if she were offered it. Cornelius had wanted Claire Bloom but had to settle for the lesser-known and less-expensive Sheridan. She recalled meeting him for the first time in a restaurant: "I see you're sitting with your back to the light because you know you're too old for this part," he bellowed. "That sort of thing went on all the way through," Sheridan sighs. "He was not a character I'd have enjoyed working for again."

Kay had similar misgivings about the director, who made his leanings for womanizing quite well-known early in the shooting. "We've got to be careful about this, you know," Kay whispered to Sheridan. "We'll have a whistle and if he's seen on the horizon, you go this way and I'll go that way and he can only catch one of us!" He caught Sheridan at least once, and she slapped him in front of the appreciative crew: "It was really quite a moment and Kay and I had hysterics afterward. He wasn't easy."

Interiors were filmed at Pinewood Studios, about an hour's drive from where Kay was living at the time, in Wilton Crescent (her bedroom contained an enormous bed, her white fur rug, and no other furniture at all). As October 1952 began, Kay started getting up at 5:30 A.M. in order to get to the studio to be in makeup by 6:30. This film was turning out to be the most difficult and physically exhausting project she'd ever worked on.

Chapter Nine

"*Come on, come on, getcher autographs here!*"

Despite the clever script, no one was expecting very much when *Genevieve* began shooting in the fall of 1952. None of the cast were stars; the director hardly had a promising attitude; and even the producer made it known that he was unhappy with the way the whole project was unfurling. Still, at least, the four leads quickly befriended one another. Thirty-eight-year-old Kenneth More was Kay's comic partner, playing the loudmouthed braggart to her increasingly annoyed fashion plate. More had been inching along in his acting career since his debut in *Scott of the Antarctic* (1948), and his films had been a smattering of hits and misses ever since. He was better-known than any of his *Genevieve* co-stars, but hardly a "name." Both of the male leads thought twice before taking their roles. Kenneth More knew the producers had wanted Guy Middleton for his part, and John Gregson was fully aware that Dirk Bogarde had been first choice for his. More was recently married and was concurrently playing a role onstage evenings: a daytime filming job would not leave him the time or energy a newlywed might want. Gregson had a more harrowing problem: he'd never driven in his life, had no license, and had to spend most of the film piloting a balky 1904 car. He started taking driving lessons as soon as he got the part, but steering the antique Darracq was worlds away from tooling down the road in a 1952 model. When filming began, Gregson was still unlicensed, and terrified behind the wheel.

It was a very cold autumn that year, and the cast and crew froze during the extensive outdoor filming. Cinematographer Christopher Challis managed to make the chilly, gray fall countryside look springlike and inviting (ironically, the actual London-to-Brighton rallies—held in November—often took place in the cold and rain). But Kay later remembered, "We were all fighting flu. In most of the exterior shots my teeth were chattering—even when I was smiling sweetie-sweetie into the lens." The cast got fatter- and fatter-looking throughout, bundling as many woollies underneath their costumes as they could squeeze on. Dinah Sheridan held a hot-water bottle under her lap robe, and a kindly propman furnished them all with brandy between takes. "I don't mind if you're cold," said director Cornelius, "but if you photograph blue, I do—come on, drink up!" At one point, Kay turned shivering to Sheridan and asked her, "Are we south of Scotland here?" When assured that they were, Kay breathed contentedly, "Oh, isn't that wonderful? Just to be south of *somewhere* makes me feel so warm!"

Despite the fact that the film took place on a London-to-Brighton rally, it was shot (other than a few establishing scenes in both towns) "behind every bush in Bucks," recalls Dinah Sheridan, "near Pinewood Studios. The propman had long wooden sticks with a sign that said, 'To Brighton.' For one scene they turned it this way and for the next scene they turned it that way. We never went anywhere near the Brighton road—the silly little lanes in *Genevieve* look nothing like the road to Brighton!"

Kay completely lost her self-control at least once, that Kenneth More recalled. Cornelius insisted on retake after retake of a scene showing Kay and More chugging up the road in a chilly drizzle (disguised by powerful arc lights). When Cornelius insisted on a sixth take, Kay leaped out of the car, grabbed a parasol from the back, "and began to beat Corny over the head with it. At first I thought she was just joking," More later wrote. "Then I realized she had gone hysterical with the cold and the misery of driving up and down in the rain. 'You miserable little bastard!' Kay cried as she belabored him. I knew exactly how she felt and sympathized with her."

Kay had more problems than Kenneth More realized: she had found out a week or two into filming that she was pregnant. There was never any question as to who was the father—James Sainsbury—or what was to be done. Even in 1952, a woman with connections and money could easily get a safe—if illegal—abortion. Kay, with her show-business and society friends, had no trouble finding an accommodating doctor. What is not known is if Sainsbury helped her financially with the procedure—or, indeed, if she ever told him she was pregnant. Whether or not he knew of this crisis, Kay's pregnancy and her abortion in late 1952 proved to be a pivotal point in their relationship. From the beginning of 1953, the two drifted apart. Sainsbury never married, and when he died in 1984, he left the bulk of his 18-million-pound estate to set up a leukemia research and treatment fund in Kay's name. "He never got over her," confirms Kay's friend Princess Lilian. "He decided too late—it was his own damn fault."

Dinah Sheridan discovered her co-star's dilemma while they were huddling in one of the extra's coaches, waiting for a scene to be set up. Kay was looking into her datebook and muttering, "Oh, God, oh God." Sheridan asked her what the matter was and Kay told her "Well, I'm just counting up—I've got to have 'flu.'" Kay took three days off and came back to work much sooner than she should have. Weak and anemic under the best of circumstances, she was in no shape to withstand jostling in antique cars and sitting about in the freezing cold. "She really was in a bad way," recalls Sheridan. "She shouldn't have been back at all."

Shortly after her abortion, Kay had to film her most important scene: in a Brighton restaurant, where—after too much champagne—she gets up and plays "Genevieve, Sweet Genevieve" on the trumpet. Kay studied with Kenny Baker, the jazz trumpeter with Ted Heath's Orchestra, learning the correct fingering and breathing methods. Baker dubbed Kay's solo, and for the rest of her life, she credited him with much of the scene's success (as big a story-teller as she was, Kay never once claimed to have played the trumpet herself). When Kay stepped up to play, she blatted out "nothing but the most appalling noises I have ever heard in my life," says Dinah Sheridan. But with Kay's clever miming and Baker's wonderful playing, the scene fit together seamlessly onscreen.

The night before the scene was filmed, the cast attended a party at Kenneth More's. John Gregson's wife was less than thrilled by the off-color stories being told, and lost her temper when More—true to the character he was playing in the film—told her to "come on, smile!" She slapped his face, leaving two ugly scratch marks down one cheek. Gregson wound up spending the night on More's sofa, and the two showed up to film the trumpet scene hung-over and scratched-up. Dinah Sheridan's fiance, John Davis—managing director of the Rank Organisation—chose that day to show up and watch the filming, to everyone's vast discomfort.

Another trauma came about a few days later, when Kay's character had to push More's antique Spyker out of an ankle-deep pond. Shrieking with cold, Kay lunged into the water and shoved mightily at the car, as More shouted, "No, not like that—get your shoulder into it!" Kay's moans of "I can't bear any more of this—I want to go home!" are painfully realistic. After one or two takes, she began to hemorrhage and indeed had to be sent home.

Kay began to collapse emotionally as well as physically at this point; happily, she had Dinah Sheridan to fall back on. Sheridan had been immediately drawn to her co-star, who struck her as "very beautiful and very delicate—you could almost see through one ear and out of the other. She was so light-headed and light-hearted." Kay's health was shaky, an abortion is never an easy experience to weather, and her relationship with Sainsbury had obviously reached a standoff. "I don't want to go home alone," she told Sheridan, who kindly asked if Kay wanted to come back to her place—"I hadn't got room for her, but I was testing to see how serious she was." Kay declined and asked Sheridan to come back to her flat, which she did, several times during filming. She put Kay to bed in white silk pyjamas (with James Sainsbury's initials on the pocket) and went into the kitchen to prepare some food. Settling Kay in for the night, she went home to her own family: "She seemed to be frightened, unstable," says Sheridan. "She didn't like her own company."

Kay and Sheridan talked sadly about the end of her relationship with Sainsbury. "Why don't you marry Jim?" Sheridan remembers asking. "You'd be so much happier, you'd be settled, you wouldn't be alone." Kay told her, "Oh, we've got to the door of the Registry Office two or three times, but he keeps saying, 'It's no good, you see. In my position I need a woman with a brain.'" It's rather unlikely James Sainsbury ever said such a thing, but that's what Kay convinced herself she had heard: just as she had heard that unnamed film executive call her "ugly" after *London Town*. And Kay did have a habit of saying just the wrong thing at the wrong time, just to be shocking: Whenever a Sainsbury's van would pass by, she would rub her hands together and gleefully crow, "Love those money-makers!" to Sainsbury's horror and embarrassment. She even turned to him once at a restaurant and asked in loud, ringing tones, "Why is it, James, you only make love to me on Wednesday once a week?" Very few men could put up with that on a long-term basis.

Late in filming, it briefly looked as though *Genevieve* would never be finished: the producer ran out of money. Rank's insurance company would have to fork over 20,000 pounds if the production defaulted, and this was not about to happen. *Genevieve* would have to be finished on an even thinner shoestring than it had been filmed on till this point. The company even tried to save money by having Kay and Dinah Sheridan double up in one tiny dressing room. Sheridan said it was fine with her, but Kay laughed, "Oh, that is sweet of you, but I don't want to dress with you—that's no fun! No, I'm going to bunk in with Kenneth More." And she did, too. Sheridan recalls them arriving each morning at 6:30 with a bottle of cham-

pagne and sharing the cramped quarters for the rest of filming. More recalled years later that he had received his first screen kiss from Kay on this
film: "It completely bowled me over," he told her. "It had the startling
effect of making me walk off the set on my hands and knees, hollering for
a tea break. You're dynamite, Kay, dynamite!" ("Thank you kindly, sir, compliment returned," she replied sweetly.)

The London police were pretty fed up with the production, as well:
The final scene had the four leads in their two cars racing toward
Westminster Bridge. They were causing so much traffic congestion with
the antique cars, camera cars and overturned fruit trucks required for the
last scene that they were finally threatened with jail and chased off the road
they needed—one with tramlines in which Kenneth More's car could get
stuck. Cornelius had to fill in with a take of the wheels getting caught on
the Old Kent Road, intercut it with waist-level shots of Kay and Kenneth
More, and splice it all together.

As soon as filming and post-production ended, the *Genevieve* cast
and crew put the little film behind them and pretty much forgot about it.
"From start to finish I had no confidence in myself or in the film," said
Kay. Rank, however, had regained the confidence in her he had once lost:
he signed Kay to a seven-year contract. She made sure it was a good contract, too, noting with satisfaction that "they sacked me once, so they didn't
re-engage me without a worthwhile contract." Kay threw a two-day party
and, remembered one guest, "kept us in fits from beginning to end."

The spring of 1953 was a festive time in England. The Queen's coronation was set for June 2, 1953. London—indeed, all of England—was
suffused with the gaiety of coronation fever: People hopefully and somewhat self-consciously spoke of themselves as "The New Elizabethans," and
London bedecked itself in pennants, arches, medallions and bunting. Visi-
tors from all over the world—officials and tourists alike—crowded into
London as *Genevieve* prepared for its opening. The Rank Organisation
took over a theater in Oxford Street from which to watch the coronation
procession, and everyone gathered at the Dorchester that night for a ball.
Kay turned down an invitation from a Hollywood producer and went on
her own.

One of the thrills of that season was Kay's presentation to the new
queen, at a Royal Command film performance. Muriel Pavlow, who was
also present, remembers the excitement of that evening, and that Rank—
to capitalize on the event—sent some of his contract players around the

country to make stage appearances before films. "There was a wonderful moment at some station," says Pavlow. "The train was held up and somebody recognized us and wanted autographs and we got the train window open." Kay, thoroughly enjoying her new spurt of stardom, waved a silk handkerchief over her head and bellowed happily, "Come on, come on, getcher autographs here!"

Not only were crowds packing the theaters to see *Genevieve*, but the newspapers fell all over themselves praising the film and its stars. Fred Majdalany of the *Daily Mail* called *Genevieve* "one of the three best English comedies since the war," and *The News of the World* wrote that it "sparkles with the authentic effervescence of youth . . . its people are the kind you like to have drop around the flat on a dreary Sunday evening." An anonymous critic praised *Genevieve* as "altogether more endearing than any light entertainment from a British studio for longer than I can remember." Several papers also noted the film's surprising sexual frisson. Richard Winnington of the *News Chronicle* found this turn of events refreshing, but the *Catholic Times* put its hands over its eyes at this "unsavory . . . smut." Their reviewer generally enjoyed the film and its stars, but tut-tutted at a scene wherein Kenneth More makes his intentions toward Kay known: "It left a bad taste in my mouth," the reviewer averred. The film's realism carried over to other areas than its sexuality: at one point in the day-long car race, Dinah Sheridan's character had to stop to find a toilet, a moment with which women in the audience certainly identified.

Kay herself came in for a lot of unreserved praise, as did all four stars. "Kay Kendall is a lovely girl and gives evidence of vivacity and high spirits unsuspected until now by me," wrote Leonard Mosley of the *Daily Express*. Cyril May of the *Sunday Times* felt that Kay "gives a good deal more dash to her portrayal of a highly pursuable popsy than is customary in our still rather inhibited studios." Another reviewer wrote that she "places a delicate tongue in beauty's cheek and turns in a cleverly judged comedy performance."

Kay's particular comic technique was already in place: she would sail into her scenes with a bemused half-smile and eyebrows cocked, as though she had just arrived at the wrong party but suspects this one might be fun, anyway. She worked hard at her craft and mightily resented critics' insinuations that her acting came naturally. "It really is desperately difficult being light and gay at nine o'clock on a Monday morning in a cold film studio," she told the *Daily Express*. "And when you've acted your heart out, people come up and say, 'it's simply *you*, darling!' I mean, *really*. I don't see the point of worrying oneself to a standstill and people turn around and say, 'darling, what gorgeous fun!' It isn't fun, believe me."

She also bridled at the ubiquitous tag "beautiful clown." "I wish people would stop calling me a clown," Kay groused shortly after *Genevieve*'s release. "Maybe a comedienne, although that does sound so pompous. . ." After the *London Town* debacle, Kay also objected when the press called her a star. "I am *not* a star, and I hate being called one," she snapped to one reporter. "There are only a very few stars here or in America. Vivien Leigh's a star, Dietrich is a star."

Genevieve remains, arguably, Kay's most enjoyable film. It was recently voted number 86 of the British Film Institute's Top 100 Films (the only one of Kay's films to make the list). It still shows up regularly on British television, though it is rarely if ever screened in the U.S. The film holds up quite well, and shows how lucky Henry Cornelius was to only be able to afford four such breezy and talented performers, to play such likeable and believable people.

Back in the bad old *London Town* days, Kay had been feted before the film's opening and politely ignored after. But *Genevieve* provided the opposite experience: as the spring of 1953 wore on and the film's success steamrolled on, the cast was pursued by reporters. One—Peter Vane—took her out for what he hoped would be great fun: a ride around the British countryside in a 1904 Renault. "*Such* fun," Kay smiled thinly. "It's just like a film I was in." Vane jounced Kay from Norbury to Thorton Heath to Crawley and finally up—slowly and torturously—Handcross Hill. Kay tried to be a good sport as the car broke down again and again, and fans—recognizing her in her antique car throne—stopped her for autographs. She had already been dragged along on two antique car rallies by The Veteran Car Club of Great Britain, and Vane was not able to get any fresh quotes for his piece. When they stopped for lunch, a visibly "wilting" Kay sighed, "If you don't mind, I'll have mine in an armchair."

Chapter Ten

"I have two hired killers looking for you at this very moment."

If Kay thought *Genevieve* would rocket her to stardom, that she'd become queen of the Rank Organisation, her next film brought her back down to earth with a thump. While *Genevieve* was still being edited and promoted, while Kay was bouncing about in antique cars with reporters, Rank dumped her into yet another low-budget, black-and-white melodrama. *The Square Ring* (released in July 1953) was a run-of-the-mill boxing story, with Kay as the wife of a fight manager, still carrying a torch for a washed-up boxer. Billed just above her was twenty-year-old Joan Collins, also being built up by Rank. Kay's was just the sort of role she'd been trying to escape since her return to films in 1950: glamorous, humorless, entirely free of personality.

Kay was not shy about making her displeasure known, about roles or anything else (she once stood on her chair in the Rank commissary and shouted, "Ladies and gentlemen, I want you all to join me in a gesture of protest at the salad being served today—I have found a baby alligator in mine."). She also had a very unusual clause written into her contract: no cheesecake photos. "Never show me legs, duck," she quipped to an unhappy cameraman. "No leg art, no swimsuit poses, no pin-up pictures." Rank had two choices for his burgeoning star: he could loan her out to other studios, or he could drop her into whatever projects he had available. To be fair, Rank *had* few good roles sitting about for a light, sophisticated comic. Scripts like *Genevieve* did not land on his desk every day.

Although her film career was taking off, Kay had never given up her theatrical roots. Between *The Square Ring*—filmed in early spring 1953—and *Meet Mr. Lucifer*—filmed that summer—she joined a touring company to sate her hunger for the stage and direct contact with a live audience. The show got little publicity; Rank had nothing to gain from a regional tour of a well-worn play. Kay played Cockney-turned-lady Eliza Doolittle in George Bernard Shaw's 1914 *Pygmalion*; she thoroughly enjoyed channeling her music-hall star grandmother for the early scenes and called on her own social ambitions for the "transformation." After a short run, Kay put the role behind her and forgot about it, until *Pygmalion* rose again to haunt her two years later.

Kay's next projec, was an odd number called *Meet Mr. Lucifer*, based on the play *Beggar My Neighbor*. Stanley Holloway played a small-time actor whose stage career is imperilled by the popularity of television. In a fantasy, Lucifer (also Holloway) shows him how TV can be used to destroy peoples' lives: an elderly man goes broke entertaining guests who want to watch his set; TV comes between a young couple; and a bachelor becomes obsessed by a Lonely Hearts singer. Kay played the dreamy-eyed vocalist; her victim was a young Gordon Jackson (later famed as Mr. Hudson on *Upstairs Downstairs*). *Meet Mr. Lucifer* was a timely film: British television really came of age in 1953, with TV cameras invading the coronation. Many families bought their first set just to participate in this national event. The medium took off like a rocket: between 1954 and 1959, British cinemas had to cut admission prices to compete with TV; still, more than eight hundred movie houses closed down. (American-style commercial television didn't arrive in Britain till late 1955, much to the horror of the intellectual elite). Most of Kay's films were plugged on TV, and throughout the 1950s she turned up on such promotional entertainment shows as *Current Release* and *In Town Tonight*. Though *Meet Mr. Lucifer* was too odd and disjointed to be a popular hit, it does give a sense to modern audiences of some of the real excitement TV must have caused in the early fifties.

Rank next put Kay into a witless, braying comedy called *Fast and Loose*, filmed in the autumn of 1953 and released the following February. After *Genevieve*—and even the oddities of *Meet Mr. Lucifer*—this role was such a letdown that Kay barely managed to walk through her performance with a slightly annoyed look on her face. The plot involved a lot of people gathering at a small-town inn and yelling at each other in what was supposed to be highly comical ways: a young husband and wife, the husband's ex-girlfriend (Kay), and the wife's parents (Stanley Holloway, in his fifth and last film with Kay, played the father). Everyone wildly overacted except for Kay, who looked distinctly bored throughout, as if she were mentally tallying the months left in her Rank contract. Still, the film's producer, Teddy Baird, voiced his belief in Kay, whom he felt had "that indefinable quality of the star. A quality that comes first from inspiration and then from slogging hard work."

Things got worse: Rank had no vehicles at all for Kay and loaned her out to an independent company late in 1953. Kay—who hated flying—was off to Cairo and Monte Carlo to film *Abdullah the Great* (which was released early in 1954). The romantic adventure was the brainchild of Gregory Ratoff, who produced, directed, and starred. The Russian-born Ratoff, then in his mid-fifties, had a long career in films and theater, both as actor and director (he's best-known today for his role as producer Max Fabian in *All About Eve*). *Abdullah the Great* was a questionable choice for a film title: in 1951, another Abdullah, the King of Transjordan and a friend of Britain's, had been assassinated, leading some moviegoers to expect a bio-pic. "It was great fun to make," Kay said to a newspaper reporter, adding optimistically, "I can tell you it'll be spectacular." Playing the role of a fashion model, however, grated on her: "That's not the sort of thing I really want to do. No more leg art. I want to act."

Abdullah the Great bears the dubious distinction of being, arguably, Kay's worst film—despite the very stiff competition. She played Ronnie, a model on assignment in a mythical Mideastern country, where she is loved by both the egotistical and oversexed king (Ratoff) and a revolutionary Army captain (Sydney Chaplin). What follows is two hours of kidnapping, attempted murder, revolution and lines like, "One word from you and I would have made you queen—and you laughed at me!" It was the worst kind of melodrama, not even bad enough to be funny.

But *Abdullah the Great* did have one side benefit (in addition to the lovely Jacques Fath gowns Kay got to wear). She embarked on a whirlwind romance with her darkly handsome twenty-eight-year-old co-star, Sydney Chaplin, the younger son of film legend Charles. Sydney had made his debut in his father's 1952 film *Limelight* and had since bounced back and forth from films to theater. "It's love," Kay sighed happily to reporter Donald Zec. "I just adore that man!" After filming completed, Sydney relocated to Paris and Hamburg to find work, and Kay spent her weekends following him from country to country, calling long-distance during the week. "That's one of the reasons I'm perpetually broke. I wish that Sydney was over here." Kay and Sydney (referred to by their friends as "Steak and Kidney") visited the Chaplins (Charles and his wife, Oona O'Neill) in Switzerland, and Kay became close to them and their daughter, Geraldine.

Kay's next film had to be an improvement, and it was: *Doctor in the*

House was a comic delight, to make and to watch. But, once again, her own role was less than she might have wished. Producer Betty Box had picked up the novel "Doctor in the House" for train reading, and "thought it would make a good film. . . . I was very lucky because I got a wonderful man called Nicholas Phipps who wrote the script." Muriel Pavlow, cast in a much better role than Kay's, remembers what a romp filming was: "We all loved the script. We had a ball—it was just the most enormous fun."

Doctor followed the adventures of four St. Swithins' medical students; the two leads were Kay's *Genevieve* co-star Kenneth More (in his usual hail-fellow-well-met characterization) and her pal Dirk Bogarde (as the wide-eyed, earnest Simon Sparrow). Kay had the smallest of the three female leads: Muriel Pavlow played Simon's eventual girlfriend and Suzanne Cloutier was More's fiancée (a young Shirley Eaton also had a marvelous bit as a landlady's slutty daughter). Kay played a chic woman whom Simon meets on the street and takes out to dinner—she had only two scenes but seemed relaxed and happy, making every moment count. Muriel Pavlow recalled Ralph Thomas as the most easygoing of directors. "For instance, I had to say a very long medical word when I was giving Dirk directions on how to reach a certain department; Ralph said to me, 'Don't worry, darling, you won't get it the first time but it's all right, we've plenty of time.'"

"It was a ragbag of all the old doctor jokes which everybody in hospitals knows," said Bogarde of the film. "Real student jokes, cleverly strung together." Bogarde was more a dramatic star than a comic, so he wisely played his role straight: "I had to be a real doctor; I would do things that were funny, but would never instigate anything funny." Thomas himself later admitted the wisdom of the cast playing everything seriously: "We didn't want to use actors who were professional funny men. We would cast the best actors we could get, actors we'd have cast if it was going to be a straight dramatic story about medicine . . . None of them ever did anything because they wanted to make it 'funny.' They played it within a very strict, tight limit of believability. . . . In our film, people liked and identified with the funny situations they had seen happen or which had happened to themselves as patients, doctors or nurses."

When it was released in March 1954, the film was a boon to audiences as well as to the cast and crew. Bogarde went on to appear in three sequels (as well as Shaw's *The Doctor's Dilemma*, which proved a vast disappointment for audiences expecting more of Simon Sparrow). Rank wanted to cast Kay in the 1955 *Doctor at Sea*, but by that time she had other fish to fry—French starlet Brigitte Bardot was hired in her place. With the huge success of *Doctor in the House*, Kay couldn't complain that she was being put into second-rate films. But she was being wasted in second-rate roles, and she complained loud and long about that. To fill in her free time, she even found herself appearing as a panelist on such TV quiz shows as *Guess My Story*, not a turn she was hoping her career would take.

By early 1954, the romance with Sydney Chaplin was beginning to wind down—Kay could be a very exhausting person to be with, and—as Chaplin's current wife, Margaret Beebe Chaplin, admits—"He had a very short attention span when it came to the ladies." He met another rising young starlet—Joan Collins—and was beginning to spark up a romance with her. Kay had met and bonded with Chaplin's friend Carol, who was then between marriages to author William Saroyan and actor Walter Matthau. Kay and Chaplin approached her at a restaurant, and the women were introduced: "She was adorable and said, 'Where are you staying?'" Carol Matthau recalls today. "I told them and she said, 'No, you'll go over and get your things. You're staying with us.'" The two women became lifelong friends, and Matthau was dubbed with Kay's favorite nickname for her elect, "wifey." She left her Savoy Hotel room and moved into the Kendall/Chaplin flat that very day. Kay was sharing a small apartment with Chaplin; it was pretty and comfortable but as tossed-together and cluttered as all of Kay's homes.

Soon Kay and Matthau had developed a close, schoolgirl relationship that left Chaplin feeling somewhat on the outside. He was to remain friends with both women, but this feeling of alienation marked the beginning of the end of his romance with Kay. Matthau recalls Kay playing a particularly nasty practical joke on Chaplin, as the three were dressing to go out. There was only enough hot water for one bath, so Kay insisted Matthau bathe first. "I'll take the second bath and we'll give Sydney the third." After the women had bathed, Kay impishly told Matthau "to tinkle in the tub." "I said, 'Good, I will,'" Matthau says. Kay followed suit, and the unsuspecting Chaplin then had his bath. "We did it just for no good reason at all, just to have fun," admits Matthau sheepishly.

"I don't know why I love [Sydney] so," Kay confided to her. "I mean, God, he's terrible in bed and he's fat and he's this and he's that. I'm madly in love with him!" Chaplin may have felt similar reservations about Kay, as he drew Matthau aside to confide in her that he was walking out on the relationship. "Sydney, you finally found a real girl," Matthau pleaded. "She is everything and more—I've never met anyone like her." Perhaps that was part of the problem: Kay was simply too much for any one sane man to handle. Chaplin packed up his suitcases and left.

Kay was never one to take these setbacks with calm equanimity. She and Matthau ordered up three bottles of wine and "enough Chinese food for six people." After the first bottle, Kay had an idea: the women called the local florist and had several large flower arrangements sent up. Chaplin was bound to call soon to see if Kay was alright, and Matthau was to tell him that she had keeled over dead from sorrow and shock. "Tell him you are in a terrible state and you need him to come right away and help with the body," Kay schemed. "What looks best when you're dead?" Matthau recalls Kay wondering to herself as she went through her closet. They decided on something flowing and lovely: "To be dead and sexy at the same time would be quite a feat," said Kay.

The evening came and went, as did another bottle of wine and the Chinese food. By the time Chaplin finally called, at 2:00 A.M., Kay and Matthau were fast asleep. Matthau somehow managed to remember their cover story and tried to convince Chaplin that Kay was lying there stone cold dead and that he had to come over and play undertaker. At that, "the corpse" came to and grabbed the phone, shrieking imprecations at Chaplin (who, by now, was probably convinced he was well out of this relationship). "I hope you are having a good time, because I am not," Matthau recalls Kay yelling into the phone. "I loved you with all my heart, and this is how you thank me. But that's alright, Sydney, have a good time. I have two hired killers looking for you at this very moment."

By the spring of 1954, Kay was insisting with a ladylike laugh to the press that "I am not and never was in love with Syd, although he's a sweet person. Oh, I know what's been reported about us, but it was nonsense." His friends agree that it took Chaplin a long time to get over his breakup with Kay—but by the time Kay was airily brushing off her romance with him, he was consoling himself with Joan Collins. Chaplin went on to another high-profile romance, with Judy Holliday, and Broadway success in *Bells Are Ringing, Funny Girl,* and *Subways Are for Sleeping.* And, eventually, he and Kay were able to put their woes behind them and remain friends. "He always said that she had a rare quality, because women liked her in spite of her beauty," says Margaret Beebe Chaplin. "She had something that didn't threaten other women, while being an incredible dame at the same time."

The next two years, 1954 and 1955, were to be the most traumatic of Kay's life and would decide her fate professionally as well. As 1954 began, she had just appeared in two hit films and was gaining the reputation of being one of Britain's up-and-coming stars. The 1946 failure of "Britain's Lana Turner" had largely been forgotten (though not by Kay herself), and she was now being referred to by reviewers as the new Carole Lombard.

Chapter Eleven

"You stupid, long-nosed English actor!"

Kay's next film would not have too big an impact on her career as an actress, but it would change her life. In the light comedy *The Constant Husband*, Rex Harrison plays a befuddled man who wakes up in a Welsh hotel suffering from amnesia—a doctor takes him back to London, where he slowly discovers he is a cad and a bounder, married to a successful photographer (Kay), a human cannonball (Nicole Maurey), and five other women. He goes on trial and, when all his wives offer to take him back and his own lawyer (Margaret Leighton) falls for him as well, he becomes a media heart-throb.

Kay began lunching at the Shepperton Studios cafeteria in the early spring of 1954, as pre-production on the film began: costume fittings, rehearsals, meetings with the cast and crew. It was there that she met for the first time her forty-six-year-old co-star. Actor Rex Harrison—tall, slim and handsome (in a rather equine manner)—had been a star since 1936, when he had his first big hits with the stage show *French Without Tears* and the film *Men Are Not Gods*. Born in Huyton in 1908, Harrison was schooled in nearby Liverpool and stormed London as a hopeful actor in 1927. The usual years of struggle ensued: repertory companies, small film roles, bit parts in West End shows. Since then, he had scored in such plays as *No Time for Comedy* and *Design for Living* and such films as *Major Barbara*, Noël Coward's *Blithe Spirit,* and as the romantically deceased sea captain in *The Ghost and Mrs. Muir.*

He became somewhat of a sex symbol—not along the lines of a Clark Gable or Errol Flynn but in a more intellectual and high-toned way. Harrison was one of the slim, dark young men who came of age in British film and theater in the late 1930s: Robert Donat, Stewart Granger, James Mason, David Niven, Michael Redgrave, Laurence Olivier. In the 1940s, these men exemplified the British leading man persona: handsome, upper-class, sexy, with a slightly cynical edge.

Harrison's private life had hardly held still while his career flourished. He married for the first time in 1934; he and his wife, Collette Thomas, had a son, Noel, the following year. By 1940, this first marriage was beginning to fray around the edges, and Harrison took up with the stunningly beautiful Polish-born actress Lilli Palmer. Making her stage debut in Berlin, Palmer had entered British films by 1935 and was quickly a minor, but rising, star. Like Rex Harrison, Palmer varied her successful film career with stage appearances. By the war years, Palmer was one of the busiest actresses in London.

Through the early 1940s, Lilli Palmer lived openly as Rex Harrison's mistress while his long-suffering wife did war work; this scandalous situation would come back to haunt Palmer a decade later. Finally, Collette charged Harrison and Palmer with cohabitation and a divorce ensued. The couple married in 1943, and Harrison's second son, Carey, was born in 1944. The attractive and talented Harrisons went on to co-star onscreen in *The Rake's Progress*, *The Long Dark Hall*, and *The Four-Poster*. By 1948 Harrison was in Hollywood starring in Preston Sturges's delightful dark comedy *Unfaithfully Yours*. An unhappy title, as it turned out.

While in Hollywood, "Sexy Rexy," as the press had dubbed him, began a torrid affair with twenty-nine-year-old blonde bombshell Carole Landis, star of such films as *One Million B.C.* and *Orchestra Wives*. Landis had also become somewhat of a heroine by touring the war zones and telling of her exploits in the book and film *Four Jills in a Jeep*. Landis—who was still married to her fourth husband—somehow got the notion that Rex Harrison was going to leave his wife and marry her. When she was disabused of this idea, she killed herself with an overdose of barbiturates. Harrison found her body, lying on her bedroom floor, on the afternoon of July 5, 1948 (the two had dined together the night before).

Lilli Palmer nobly stood by her husband's side through the inquiries and press assaults, but Harrison's name was ruined in Hollywood; he had killed one of their own. Rumors were spreading that Landis had not been dead yet when Harrison had discovered her, and that he—rather than calling a doctor—had wasted precious time calling his studio PR people for advice. Columnist Hedda Hopper in particular made it her duty to keep after Rex Harrison and hound him from the country. His 20th Century-Fox contract was canceled, and Harrison was "exiled" east to Broadway, where he appeared in *Anne of a Thousand Days* and *Bell, Book and Candle* (with Palmer), and—in London—in he played a role in *The Cocktail Party*.

He didn't return to Hollywood until 1952 and wasn't to have another hit film there until 1964—by which time he would have long since "redeemed himself" in everyone's eyes (except those of Hedda Hopper, who was not one to forget).

While the Landis scandal slowly simmered and eventually began to fade, Rex Harrison and Lilli Palmer built the loveliest of movie-star retreats far away from Hollywood. In 1949, they managed to get a building permit in Portofino, a small resort town on the Italian Riviera. They only wangled it because the Germans had torn down the mansion of the Countess Besozzi to construct a gun emplacement overlooking the Bay of Paraggi and Portofino harbor. It was the perfect setting for an occupying army and just as perfect for a home. The gun turrets were blown up (Palmer lit the fuse) and the Harrisons built a large, rambling getaway surrounded by a vineyard. The house (eventually named the Villa San Genesio, after the patron saint of actors) was sprawling, sunny, and accommodating. It was soon a gathering spot for the international show-biz set; as the 1950s wore on, Portofino itself became a popular jet-set resort, and the Harrisons found themselves the center of a glamorous group who neither knew nor cared about Carole Landis. Noël Coward, the Duke and Duchess of Windsor, Greta Garbo; the elite of the publishing, theatrical, and film worlds stopped in for visits of varying lengths.

The Rex Harrison Kay met in the spring of 1954 was still—shakily—married to Lilli Palmer. He had just flopped in the epic film *King Richard and the Crusaders* and was happy to return to light twentieth-century comedy. He was also very happy to meet his new co-star. "She was very easy, full of fun, beautifully inconsequential, flirtatious, impertinent, and rakish," Harrison recalled some two decades later in his memoirs. He also romanticized Kay in a way which would have had her hooting in derision: "I felt instinctively that here was a unique sad-gay sprite, adrift, yet clearly totally at home even in that drab cafeteria." Sad, Chaplinesque little sprite she may very well have been—but anyone who said so to Kay's face would never have heard the end of it.

Harrison immediately fell head over heels for her, as was apparent to everyone but Kay herself. She and Harrison dined out with Gladys Kendall one night, after which Kay's mother told her, "You know, darling, this man is absolutely madly in love with you!" Kay looked blankly at Gladys and replied, "Oh, really, mother! He's twenty years older than I am, and he's got a concave chest and he's going bald." Either Gladys had put a flea in

Kay's ear, or Harrison's famous charm began to work its magic, for soon his feelings were reciprocated: Kay fell for Harrison, and she fell hard. The next time the trio dined out, Gladys mentioned that Harrison looked a bit tired, and Kay all but bit her mother's head off: "Tired? Have you ever seen a man in such marvelous condition? Look at that bearing!"

Kay's friends, most of them, were leery of this new beau. Not only was he two decades her senior and married, but he had a reputation as a womanizer and an insufferable snob. One of Kay's former lovers, Anthony Havelock-Allan, also had a rather low opinion of Harrison. He told reporter Wendy Leigh in 2000 that in his early days, Harrison was "not at all difficult . . . because he was eager to get on. But the more successful he became, the more difficult he became and the less other actors liked acting with him. . . . I think he made a decision and said to himself, 'I am not going to waste my time being nice to anybody. No one has been very nice to me, and if I make it, I am only going to be nice to myself.'"

The Constant Husband was filmed in three months, in the spring and early summer of 1954—if he spent any longer in his birth country, the tight-fisted Harrison would be liable for British taxes. One of the other delights on the set for Kay was the costume designer, Anna Duse—the same woman who had been her childhood ballet teacher and fellow war evacuee in Scotland. The film did rather well on its release in April 1955: Bosley Crowther in *The New York Times* called it a "flighty and photogenic farce" with "cute plot twists and some occasionally quite witty words." Seen today, the film is pleasant and diverting, and it is easy to see the sparks between Kay and Harrison. The best of the film is their scenes together, and friends later laughed at some of the foreshadowing of their relationship. It could have been taken from real life when Harrison's character asks Kay's, "What kind of a person am I?" and she replies, "You're careless and untidy, very selfish, you snap at me in the morning and you spend ages in the bathroom—in fact, you're awfully sweet and I love you very much." According to one of Harrison's biographers, Kay was more than slightly playful on the set, grabbing her co-star's crotch out of camera range during one scene and eliciting a "moment of completely off-guard surprise on his face."

Kay's role was a relatively small one for a lead (she appeared only at the beginning and the end of the film), and as soon as she had a few days off, she would spend time with American actor Steve Cochran, with whom she was carrying on a heated affair. The darkly handsome, rough-edged

Cochran (who was to die mysteriously on a small yacht in 1965) was never a top-flight star. But he was sexy, funny, and had a wonderfully raffish sense of humor. Harrison's first biographer and longtime friend Roy Moseley recalls visiting Cochran at his Hamilton Mews flat and finding the actor in a dressing gown. Down the stairs came Kay, also in a dressing gown. "What do you think of my latest conquest?" she asked a startled Moseley. "Cochran played around, and she loved it," he says. "She was no prude, she loved his kind of jokes and sexual innuendo." Rex Harrison was not accustomed to sharing his women, and his interest grew. "This was very frustrating," Harrison later recalled. "It was frightening that somebody I knew only superficially should have such a violent effect on me."

But soon Kay began to favor Harrison over Cochran and spent more and more time with him, flitting about London. Although Harrison had been in London himself off and on since 1927—the year of Kay's birth— she knew nooks and crannies he'd never heard of. "She was a true Cockney, and she loved her city," said Harrison. "She made it seem like a village, and most particularly her village." Harrison's son Noel was playing guitar in a nightclub called Esmeralda's Barn, and the couple spent time there. They hit coffee shops, bookstores, and all the restaurants Kay couldn't afford to eat in only a few years earlier. Noel fell for Kay as his father had: "Kay was exuberant, generous, and good with my father," he says. "She would slap him down when he got uppity, calling him 'You stupid, long-nosed English actor.' They were real equals. She brought out the lighthearted side of him."

One thing Kay had trouble doing was inviting Rex Harrison up to her flat; she was still moving from apartment to apartment on a monthly— sometimes weekly—basis. Harrison simply did not know people who lived like this, and it threw him off balance. Kay would desert a flat either to avoid paying the rent or because she just didn't care for it anymore; she would move into a place even drearier or more expensive, and barely unpack before moving again. It was very hard for a hopeful suitor to track her down. Harrison was baffled by this bizarre creature, quite unlike his sensible current wife: "[Kay] always went to extremes, it seemed: totally broke, frozen stiff in the cold, always wearing clothes quite unsuited to the weather."

Unlike most women Harrison knew, Kay would also not accept any guff from him; she could dish it out as well as she could take it. "She was perfectly capable of saying, 'Oh, come off it, you stuffy bugger'—which he was," laughs her sister. Even in this early—still very much secret—stage of their relationship, the two engaged in "great battles, fisticuffs, runnings away, reconciliations, and an incessant hectic activity. . . . She was always funny, even when doing the most impossibly stupid things, which indeed she never stopped doing . . . it was as if some demon was driving her to live recklessly, almost dottily."

Meanwhile, Mrs. Rex Harrison—Lilli Palmer—was in Germany, making the film *Feuerwerk*. Word of the Kendall/Harrison goings-on had not yet reached the press, but the gossip grapevine had already alerted Palmer that perhaps all was not well in her marriage. Harrison had had many other affairs, and Palmer trusted that Kay Kendall would prove to be another passing fancy. So, at this point, did Rex Harrison. "Lilli was very tolerant of my father's many infidelities," Noel Harrison told writer Wendy Leigh in 2000. "When I was in my teens he told me how wonderful it was going off to the Cannes Film Festival, where, within minutes of him checking in, girls would be knocking on his bedroom door. I'm sure Lilli didn't like it, but she put up with it, because she loved him."

Kay had other ideas—she had set her cap for Rex Harrison, and her old cry of "she may have got him first, but I'm here now!" was heard echoing again throughout London. Harrison's work on *The Constant Husband* ended, and he took off to Munich to join his wife. When her film wrapped, they drove to their Portofino home to spend what they hoped would be a relaxing summer with friends: guests and drop-ins that season included Laurence Olivier and Vivien Leigh (themselves in the midst of one of their many marital traumas), actor Jean-Pierre Aumont, the Duke and Duchess of Windsor, and the Earl of Warwick.

Within a week, however, Harrison was back in London, ostensibly to pick up his son Carey from boarding school. He and Kay flew to each other and spent as much time as they could together without alarming Carey or tipping off the press and their friends. Harrison returned to Portofino, and Kay tried to occupy herself. In August, she and Carol Matthau visited Matthau's sister, Elinor, the Baroness de la Boullerie, in Geneva. The sisters and Kay would sit out on the terrace having drinks at sunset, while Kay alternately fumed about Sydney Chaplin and mused about Rex Harrison. Eventually, she had to take action: Carol Matthau and Kay took a train to Geneva, along with Matthau's children, eight-year-old Lucy and ten-year-old Aram. There, they visited with Sydney's father and step-mother, Charles and Oona O'Neill Chaplin (long after the breakup with Sydney, Kay continued her closeness with his family).

As she saw the Chaplin episode coming to an end, Kay began obsessing over Rex Harrison. She conned Matthau and her children into an August trip to Santa Margherita, a bustling tourist town near Portofino. "I will never forget that train ride," says Matthau. "I know he's there," Kay insisted. "I know he's there and will be glad to see me. In fact, he invited me there." The two women took a cab from the airport to the Hotel Eden, which Kay had booked beforehand. Matthau overtipped the taxi driver and the financially scatterbrained Kay shrieked, "You really don't understand lire, darling—hand it all over to me!" The women prepared for dinner while Kay went on and on about Harrison, his house, and dreadful things he had apparently told Kay about Lilli Palmer. "He told me he never even wanted to marry her," Kay insisted. "One day they were walking and she said, 'Oh, I have an idea,' and he said, 'What?' and she said, 'Let's get married.' They did, but he had never been happy and he had never been faithful to her." Enough recitations of these tales, and Kay had convinced herself that she was doing everyone a favor by breaking up that awful marriage.

Chapter Twelve

"It's about the worst case I know."

Back at Portofino, the Harrisons were hosting Hugh "Binkie" Beaumont, one of Britain's leading theatrical producers and managing director of the firm H.M. Tennant, Ltd. Socially ebullient, Beaumont was a close friend of the Harrisons' as well as of Laurence Olivier and Vivien Leigh. At Portofino, Beaumont was going over the script of *Bell, Book and Candle*, which the Harrisons were to revive onstage in London late in 1954. As they went over the play—about a beautiful witch who entrances her neighbor, a publisher—friends flitted in and out of the house and the summer seemed to be wearing on amiably.

Kay, meanwhile, was spinning her plans over in Santa Margherita; somehow, she discovered that the Harrisons had dinner reservations on a certain night with the Duke and Duchess of Windsor. Kay had Harrison paged and the two enjoyed some hurried moments before he had to return to the restaurant. "She had arranged it all, but she was damned if she was going to admit it to me then," wrote Harrison. It actually seems more likely that she had called the Portofino house, and Harrison had told her himself where and when they would be dining.

Kay later told Dirk Bogarde an even more melodramatic—and unlikely—version of the events in Portofino that night. "I'm going to see that fucking wife of his and get rid of her!" she growled enthusiastically to Bogarde. She later told him that she had showed up in the middle of a dinner party at the Harrison home, "banged on the window, peered through and waved her hands at Rex and said, 'Here I am!' and he was absolutely shattered and had to come out in the middle of a dinner party."

The story got better and better with each re-telling, but real-life events were astonishing enough without the embroidery. Kay managed to wangle an invitation for dinner at the Portofino house for herself and Carol Matthau. "He wants to marry me," Kay told her while they dressed for dinner, adding that she "was not even sure she wanted to get married." Still burned from Sydney Chaplin, Kay was like a dog chasing a car—even if she caught Rex Harrison, she wasn't sure what she was actually going to do with him. Lilli Palmer was the perfect hostess, and Kay ran about exploring the house—especially the master bedroom, where she saw to her distress that Harrison and Palmer shared one large bed. Palmer drew Carol Matthau aside and began quizzing her about Kay: How long had they known each other? What sort of person was she? How did they meet? If Palmer wasn't yet sure what was going on, she had some very strong forebodings.

That night, Rex Harrison had a momentary bout of insanity and invited Kay and Matthau to a yachting party the next day: the Earl of Warwick had invited the Harrisons and Binkie Beaumont on an all-day cruise, and wouldn't it be great fun? To everyone's dismay, Kay accepted. But she and Harrison couldn't wait that long—at ten o'clock the next morning, Matthau greeted Kay, who was returning from a mysterious outing, limping, and covered in prickles and brambles. "We did it in the woods!" a delighted Kay told her shocked friend. Brushed off and presentable again, Kay went off to the Earl's yacht, where the expected social disaster ensued. Lilli Palmer knew her husband had been flirting with his recent co-star, but until that day—the three of them, trapped on that yacht—she'd had no idea just how serious things had become. "All at once, there it was," Palmer wrote in her 1975 memoirs. "In the open, as clear as daylight. The impact hit me full force." Harrison agreed in his own book that the yachting trip might not have been the brightest of his ideas: "Kay and I were too obviously in love to be anything but embarrassing to anyone else, and Lilli had every reason to be both upset and cross." What Harrison remembered, but Palmer conveniently forgot, was that a decade earlier Palmer herself had been living openly with Harrison while he was still married to his first wife.

According to Carol Matthau, the confrontation was straightforward and as melodramatic as anything in Kay's Rank films. "Why are you doing this to my husband and to my marriage and me? Why?" Palmer demanded of an uncharacteristically appalled and embarrassed Kay. Whether through guilt or fear (they were out to sea, after all), Kay backtracked and tried to calm Palmer down, assuring her that there was nothing between her and Harrison. But Harrison had decided to make a clean breast of it, to the entertainment of everyone on the yacht. He confronted his wife and his lover and said, "Kay, don't tell that to Lilli. We *have* been together and we're in love. . . . Stop lying to her." Kay began to cry; Palmer became hysterical and demanded to be put ashore in a dinghy. As Harrison concluded in his memoirs, with vast understatement, "The evening ended icily."

A day or two later, another crisis developed: Matthau's daughter, Lucy, had a sudden, severe attack of appendicitis and had to be rushed to a clinic—Matthau had no insurance and not much money on her. Happily, Lucy pulled through and William Saroyan came across with the cash. So when Kay came rushing to the hospital yelling, "Wifey! Wifey! I've got the money!" she was met with less tearful gratitude than she'd hoped. Kay had persuaded the notoriously cheap Harrison to pay the bills and snapped to Matthau, "You are a fucking fool—you should have taken money from everyone. . . . You're going to be poor, darling, I don't know what would happen to you if it wasn't for me." Kay sensibly pocketed the cash: "Well, I can't give it back to Rex, he'll think I'm insane."

The rest of the summer was shot, as far as Rex Harrison and Lilli Palmer were concerned: Kay had recaptured Rex. A few days after the disastrous yatching trip, the illicit couple hopped into Harrison's old Jaguar and took off—no notes, no apologies—to the Apennines, a mountain range running through Italy, where they roughed it in a farmhouse. Then off to Genoa, where they played at being anonymous tourists: they ambled slowly and aimlessly around, dining in cafes and following interesting characters for blocks. They spotted an elderly couple enjoying a tremendous verbal battle and felt they had seen themselves in thirty–odd years.

Meanwhile, Lilli Palmer packed up what was left of her pride and went back to London, where she took rooms at the Connaught Hotel in Mayfair and studied for her and Harrison's upcoming *Bell, Book and Candle* run, set to open on October 5. Her husband and co-star was, by this time, outside Paris with Kay, at Jean-Pierre Aumont's country home. In September, Harrison skulked guiltily back to London and joined his wife at the Connaught, where, Binkie Beaumont was relieved to see, they both behaved professionally and went ahead with rehearsals. Their play opened to great reviews and full houses—only a few discreet hints had surfaced in the press about Kay and Harrison's romance, so few audience members (except for show-business insiders) were amusing themselves with the backstage drama.

And there *was* a lot of backstage drama (the show was referred to by insiders, of course, as *Bell, Book and Kendall*). Kay once went to see a matinee performance of the show, and half the audience turned around to stare

Above left, Kay's paternal grandmother, Marie Kendall (photo: Andy Aliffe). *Above right,* Baby Kay, c. 1929 (photo: Kim Kendall). *Below,* A rare family reunion, c. 1950. *From left*: Terry, Kim, Gladys, and Kay Kendall (photo: Kim Kendall).

Left, Kay, on her third birthday, practices her movie-star smile (with siblings Terry Jr. and Kim) (photo: Kim Kendall). *Right,* Kay (left) and Kim at the beach, Christmas 1934 (photo: Kim Kendall).

Left, Kay, about age ten, caught up in the excitement of a dancing-school recital (photo: Kim Kendall). *Right,* The dance team of Terry and Pat Kendall, Kay's father and aunt, c. 1930 (photo: Kim Kendall).

Above left, Kay's parents, Terry and Gladys Kendall, in the early 1930s (photo: Kim Kendall). *Above, top right,* Gladys Kendall with her parents, Robert and Lavinia Drewery (photo: Kim Kendall). *Above, bottom right,* Kay, second from left, with her brother Terry, mother, and sister Kim, 1930 (photo: Kim Kendall). *Below,* Kay (left) and Kim with their famous grandmother, Marie Kendall (photo: Kim Kendall).

Above left, Beanpole-thin Kay grows into her teens (photo: Kim Kendall). *Above right,* Madly keen to entertain the troops: Kim, 19, and Kay, 17, join the war effort (photo: Kim Kendall). *Below,* Kim and Kay, fifth and sixth from left, enjoy themselves in Blackpool with the RAF and some Polish Night Fliers, 1944. Sadly, Mum, second from left, was there to chaperon (photo: Kim Kendall).

Above, The hopeful young chorus girl, c.1942 (photo: Kim Kendall). *Below left,* Photos like this one (from *Waltz Time,* 1945) convinced Kay to have her nose bobbed (photo: Corbis-Bettmann). *Below right,* Sid Field, left, and Petula Clark, stars of *London Town* (1946), with director Wesley Ruggles—who gave Kay some very personal coaching (photo: Photofest).

Above left, Glamour still from *London Town,* 1946 (photo: Maraday Wahlborg). *Above right,* A Star is Stillborn: Kay dances up a storm in poster art for the retitled American release of *London Town* (photo: The Everett Collection). *Below,* At the races with Bill Hanson, late 1940s (photo: Maraday Wahlborg).

 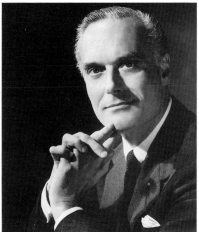

Above left, As the overdressed "debutante of the season" in *It Started in Paradise,* 1952 (photo: Maraday Wahlborg). *Above right,* Grocery-store heir James Sainsbury, with whom Kay had a romance in the early 1950s (photo: Sainsbury plc). *Below,* The hopeful starlet ponders her future, c. 1950 (photo: Corbis-Bettmann).

Left top, With expert scene-stealers Margaret Rutherford and Robert Morley in *Curtain Up*, 1952 (photo: Maraday Wahlborg). *Left bottom*, With Zachary Scott in the dreary 1952 melodrama *Wings of Danger* (photo: Maraday Walhborg). *Right*, A Star Is Born: Kay's first entrance in *Genevieve*, 1953 (with co-star John Gregson) (photo: Maraday Wahlborg). *Below*, Kay bursts forth in a Brighton club in *Genevieve* (photo: Maraday Wahlborg).

Left top, The genial *Genevieve* four-some: John Gregson, Dinah Sheridan, Kenneth More, and Kay (photo: Corbis-Bettmann). *Left bottom,* With Gregory Ratoff in *Abdullah the Great,* 1955 (photo: Photofest). *Right,* Sydney Chaplin, Kay's romantic interest on- and offscreen during *Abdullah the Great,* filmed early in 1954 (photo: Photofest). *Below,* Kenneth More, Kay, and her good friend Dirk Bogarde in *Doctor in the House,* 1954 (photo: Culver Pictures).

Glamour still, early 1950s (photo: Wisconsin Center for Film and Theater Research).

Right, Rex Harrison and Lilli Palmer toward the end of their marriage, during the scandal- and trauma-plagued run of *Bell, Book and Candle* (photo: Photofest). *Below,* Carole Landis. Many in Hollywood blamed Rex Harrison for her 1948 suicide (photo: The Metaluna Collection).

Left top, Spring 1954: Kay and Rex Harrison meet while filming *The Constant Husband* (photo: The Everett Collection). *Left bottom*, Sheltering with Robert Taylor in *The Adventures of Quentin Durward*, 1955 (photo: Culver Pictures). *Above*, Kay and Rex Harrison in *The Constant Husband* (photo: Photofest).

Above left, Kay between scenes of *The Adventures of Quentin Durward* (photo: Maraday Wahlborg). *Above right,* On the set of *Simon and Laura,* 1955 (photo: Jerry Ohlinger's). *Below,* With Peter Finch, left, and Ian Carmichael in *Simon and Laura* (photo: Culver Pictures).

Above left, The height of mid-1950s glamour (photo: Photofest). *Above right,* On the Hollywood soundstage of *Les Girls* (1957) with Gladys Cooper's borrowed Corgi, June (photo: Jerry Ohlinger's). *Right,* Visibly uncomfortable with *Les Girls* cheesecake (photo: Culver Pictures).

Left, Surrounded by *Les Girls* co-stars Mitzi Gaynor, Gene Kelly, and Taina Elg (photo: Maraday Wahlborg). *Right,* The Harrisons return from their Bermuda honeymoon, July 1957 (photo: Corbis-Bettmann).

Top, The Harrisons backstage at the Mark Hellinger Theater two days after their wedding (photo: The Everett Collection). *Bottom,* Kay made her U.S. television debut on *The Polly Bergen Show* in November 1957. *Left to right:* Kay, Howard Morris, and Bergen (photo: Corbis-Bettmann).

Above, The Harrisons in *The Reluctant Debutante,* 1958 (photo: Photofest). *Below,* Kay, Harrison, and director Vincente Minnelli in rehearsal for *The Reluctant Debutante,* Paris, March 1958 (photo: Photofest).

Kay in her London backyard in the spring of 1958 (photo: Maraday Wahlborg).

Three bored girls-about-town in London with their friend Noël Coward, early 1959. *From left to right,* Vivien Leigh, Kay, Coward, and Lauren Bacall (photo: Eric Conklin/Donald Smith).

Kay and Harrison (without his usual toupee) on an Italian Riviera vacation, September 1958 (photo: Corbis-Bettmann).

Signs of illness (and sun damage) are obvious in this unretouched portrait from Kay's late 1958 stage vehicle, *The Bright One* (photo: Photofest).

Left, With a painting of her co-star Yul Brynner, in her last film, *Once More With Feeling!,* released in 1960 (photo: Jerry Ohlinger's). *Below,* A fading Kay (on the set with Yul Brynner) struggles through the filming of *Once More With Feeling!* summer 1959 (photo: The Everett Collection).

"I'm not coming here to die!" snapped Kay as she re-entered the London Clinic—but, obviously, she was (photo: Atlantic Syndication Partners).

Kay's grave in St. John's churchyard, London (photo: David Conway).

(photo: Photofest)

at her rather than the stage. Athene Seyler, who was co-starring in the play, told Roy Moseley that "It was bad taste on everybody's part that she should come. . . . Everybody knew that she was in the theatre. It made me very uncomfortable." Palmer went to her old friend Noël Coward for brotherly advice, but he was only able to sigh, "It's about the worst case I know. I've witnessed fairly bad pickles. . . . My advice has always been to get out of town and stay out—until a decision is made one way or the other. But with you and Rex, playing those hot love scenes every night. . . . Honestly, I don't know what to say to you."

As Palmer moaned in her memoirs, "How was I going to get through the run of the play? I hated myself for crying and carrying on, behaving hysterically in a way I had always despised in other women. . . . There we were, chained together by a contract we couldn't get out of." Kay tried to stay out of the way, but Harrison made things worse by calmly suggesting to his wife, "Maybe you ought to have a lover. Maybe that would help you." Palmer later explained, "He meant it kindly, not cynically." She failed to add in her memoirs that she herself was already eyeing Harrison's successor, Argentinean actor Carlos Thompson.

The intrusion of Kay into her marriage "was horrible for my mother, and it clearly was theft," says Carey Harrison. "It was a big rupture in my mother's life, one she might never have really gotten over." But even after the split, says Carey, Lilli Palmer couldn't totally blame her husband, who, he notes, "wasn't an unduly predatory male—but he *was* susceptible. If my mother's anger was more toward Kay than Rex, it's because he *let* himself be stolen. My mother always said they'd survived the war, the Carole Landis scandal; they'd come through the fire, and she thought they were home-free."

Several months into the run of *Bell, Book and Candle*, the Harrisons moved out of their rooms at the Connaught Hotel and rented a flat in Jack Buchanan's house at 44 Mount Street. Buchanan's young wife, Suzzie—today Mrs. C. Douglas Dillon—befriended the couple. Rex Harrison, she recalls, idolized Jack Buchanan: "Indeed, when he was starting, he based his mannerisms on Jack's. They were very much alike in body language and sense of timing onstage. They were not alike in character or temperament, thank God, because Rex could be extremely difficult and my chap had a lovely nature." Suzzie Dillon also enjoyed Lilli Palmer's company, finding her "attractive and intelligent." The Buchanans heard rumors in the theater community that Harrison had set Kay up in a flat at the Connaught, a block down the street. Despite her friendship with Lilli Palmer, Suzzie Dillon also found herself drawn to Kay: "She was great fun, natural and very attractive. No wonder the spoilt Rex found her irresistible. To be with Kay was a joy, the room lit up when she entered." Dillon admits that Kay regularly referred to Palmer as "that frightful German Hausfrau" but that "she would laugh as she said it. I never heard her to be cruel or overly critical."

Diana Dors and her husband invited Kay and Harrison to lunch at the Riverside Inn in Cookham. The ride over was sparking with tension, Dors later recalled: Kay was needling Harrison about Lilli Palmer and what his ultimate intentions were; Harrison kept muttering darkly, "Oh, for God's sake, Mousey, let's not start that bloody nonsense again." Dors even claimed Harrison actually struck Kay—though none of Kay's other friends recall such incidents. After lunch, the foursome took off in Dors's cruiser for a ride on the Thames: Kay, after glaring at Harrison for some time, dramatically leaped over the side, and Harrison (with no good grace) jumped after her to "save" her. The two finished the day in bathrobes, while Dors draped their clothes out to dry.

Kay seemed to try and shake herself loose from her obsession with Harrison, but she had no luck whatsoever. She annoyed Dirk Bogarde with her lovesickness: "Kate went mooning around about him for quite a while, a-dither for some days and nights, and I said to her, 'Look, you are getting over-interested in this man.'" Kay defensively snapped back at Bogarde, "Oh, for Christ sake, he's a *dreadful* old man. He's older than my father and he's got the most *disgusting* breath of any man I've ever met!" Then she would ask Bogarde if she couldn't bring him down for the following weekend.

"It was dreadful for Lilli," recalled Bogarde. "She adored Rex. She never got over Rex. She hated Kate—but Kate was a very naughty girl." The melodramatic romantic triangle even intruded on the bucolic Bogarde/Forwood home. "Lilli used to telephone every so often with a very, very bad accent," said Bogarde, "a foreign accent—but a bad one. I knew it was Lilli, but she changed it all the time. She asked if she could speak to Mr. Radishon and all that rubbish." Palmer partially blamed Bogarde for joining in on the deception. Years later, when the two were co-starring in the film *Sebastian*, Palmer picked up a letter opener on the set and quietly said to Bogarde, "Isn't it funny, darling, a few years ago I would have pushed this straight into your back. You stole my husband."

Kay also stole Palmer's son and stepson—or at least earned their devoted affection. Carey Harrison, who was a preteen when Kay entered the scene, says today that "There were no hard feelings on my part, which I suppose is rather disloyal of me. I adored Katie, she was a wonderful presence in my life." Kay was smart enough not to try and be a mother to Carey: "I already *had* a mother. But Kay was delightful, she was fun and affectionate and a joy to be around. She was so witty that we were all a little in love with her." Noel Harrison was in his twenties and never saw Kay as a homewrecker: "I grew up with my mother, Collette, so Lilli was the marriage breaker in my experience," he says, "though I didn't think of *her* like that, either." Noel found Kay to be "a divinely, deliciously naughty girl. Totally irreverent, regal as a queen." Lilli Palmer, Noel feels, "was a good and incredibly loyal wife, good housekeeper, good manager, good mother, kind stepmother. It wasn't exactly a 'stuffy' household," he adds, "but it gave the impression that anything more than tiny doses of naughtiness should be curbed. It was a wonderful change to see [my father] with someone loose who could mock him, tease him, be giddy with him and delight him with her naughtiness."

Rex Harrison and Lilli Palmer stayed with *Bell, Book and Candle* through early summer 1954, their marriage (and, some felt, their performances) deteriorating steadily through the run. The pointed backstage "Bell, Book and Kendall" jokes did nothing for Palmer's mood. She finally left to make a film in Germany and was replaced by Joan Greenwood. Then Harrison left in July, his role taken by Robert Flemyng, who had been recommended for it by his acquaintance Kay.

Finally, late in the year, Binkie Beaumont suggested Kay herself go on tour with the show, opposite Flemyng. Friends of the Harrisons felt that Beaumont had done this solely to keep Kay out of the couple's hair. Between film assignments, Kay bravely played the role recently abandoned by her arch-rival, trying not to imagine what it might have been like had Harrison and not Flemyng been acting opposite her. Flemyng eventually became close friends with Kay, but this tour started out badly, he told Harrison biographer Alexander Walker. "I told Binkie, 'I don't want Kay Kendall, she can't act,'" he recounted. He was so offhand and rude to her that both Beaumont and Harrison wrote, telling him to ease up, and Kay collapsed in tears. "The play was a success," said Flemyng, "because everyone said, 'Oh, there's the girl who was in *Genevieve*,' and came to see it."

Chapter Thirteen

"I am not thinking of matrimony either with Mr. Harrison or anybody else."

As it became more apparent to her friends that this relationship with Rex Harrison was not simply a passing fancy, they became concerned. Many of them looked fondly back on Sydney Chaplin, Bill Hanson, and James Sainsbury as much more suited to Kay than this pompous ladies' man. "Oh, Rex was *never* the love of her life," snaps Kim Kendall. "She was so crazy about Bill Hanson she couldn't see straight!" Other friends feel that Chaplin better fit that description. Decades older than Kay, Harrison was well past his prime as "Sexy Rexy." But for once, she had latched onto a man who could keep her on her toes mentally and emotionally as well as physically. "She was terribly funny with Rex," says Laurie Evans, who was later Kay's agent. "She was a match for Rex, which nobody else was, intellectually and on a sense-of-humor basis. Lilli was not gifted with a sense of humor."

All her life, Kay had lived in a dreamy Noël Coward comedy of her own making. A drama queen from childhood, she had been looking for a leading man as self-obsessed and witty as she; and now she had found someone to play Elyot to her Amanda in a twenty-four-hour-a-day production of *Private Lives*; a Nick Charles to her Nora, a Petruchio to her Katharine. Actress Nancy Olson told one of Harrison's biographers that the couple's public fights had "great humour and tremendous style. It was like a contest to see who could be the most outrageously nasty, but with an undercurrent of such amusement with it all and tremendous fun. It was not lethal venom—but theatrical venom. They played the part well and they enjoyed their own performance tremendously."

Carol Matthau recalls a romantic restaurant dinner during which "Kay suddenly showed the stress [of their ongoing triangle] by throwing her drink in Rex's face. He barely moved, but he threw his drink in her face. . . . I came to learn this was normal behavior for these two." Kay's friend Princess Lilian remembers that "We were always laughing and giggling because she was so rude and insulting to Rex—he was *so* pompous." She particularly enjoyed taking him down a peg or two in public, at one party yelling at him, "Sexy Rexy! Who said *you* were sexy?!" Those who had felt the sharp edge of Harrison's temper through the years were delighted, and Kay gained many admirers for this alone.

It was during this time that Kay first got to know her half-brother, Cavan Kendall, the son of Terry and his second wife, Doric. Cavan was twelve years old in 1954 and in boarding school. Kay tried her best to befriend the pre-teen; she would hire a hotel room for the weekend and take him to the beach or to restaurants. He remembered Kay sitting up in bed, surrounded by framed photos of Rex Harrison, along with one or two of Dirk Bogarde. His school chums, who thought his half-sister "quite dishy," were green with jealousy. She brought him a St. Christopher's medal from Cartier's in Paris and, in a totally different approach, introduced him to champagne cocktails. For breakfast. "I didn't know what it was at the time, and it certainly tasted good, so I knocked it back," he recalled. "I think I giggled for the next four hours."

Kay also had the pleasure of introducing Harrison to her beloved father—as well as her stepmother, the bête noire of Gladys Kendall's existence. The glamorous couple would show up with a bottle of Chianti, and the Kendalls would lay out a spread of shepherd's pie. Cavan noted how much Kay and Harrison loved getting away from it all, "sitting on the settee watching TV and having dinner on their lap on their own." Kay hoped that being in such a settled family atmosphere would give Harrison ideas—but he still showed no signs of wanting to make their relationship official.

In the fall of 1954, the theater gave Kay perhaps the best role she would ever play: the delicately bitter, sarcastic ghost Elvira in a touring company of Noël Coward's 1941 play *Blithe Spirit*. The role (which had been created in London and New York by Kay Hammond and Leonora Corbett, respectively) could have been written for Kay and had a lot of Coward's lifetime friend and frequent co-star Gertrude Lawrence in it as well (coincidentally, Rex Harrison had played Elvira's put-upon husband Charles in the 1945 film version). Elvira—who comes back from the spirit world to haunt Charles and his second wife—flits through the play teasing spiritualist Madame Arcati, flirting with her husband, and tormenting his new wife, Ruth. "I remember how fascinating she was, and how maddening," Charles recalls of his dead wife, " . . . I remember her gay charm when she had achieved her own way and her extreme acidity when she didn't."

Elvira's taunting of the earthly married pair certainly brought to mind Kay's current relationship with Rex Harrison and Lilli Palmer, and her sniping ("You invite mockery, Charles. It's something to do with your personality, I think. A certain seedy grandeur!") would be a hallmark of Kay's baiting of Harrison for the rest of her life. There was even a certain dark clairvoyance to the dialogue, as Elvira sadly remarks, "Why shouldn't I have fun? I died young, didn't I?" Airy, scatty, and very blithe indeed, Elvira was the kind of role that J. Arthur Rank was totally unable to offer Kay, and she threw herself into it with great enthusiasm.

Noël Coward took to Kay immediately, despite being a friend of Rex Harrison's and Lilli Palmer's. He saw a lot of Gertrude Lawrence in her and was unable to take sides in the romantic triangle: "Rex Harrison has fallen in love with Kay Kendall and is breaking Lilli's heart," he noted in his diary on September 12, 1954, but he stayed on good terms with all three of the principals. By then, the company was in rehearsal, with Coward himself directing: Dennis Price played Charles, and Irene Handl the potentially scene-stealing Madame Arcati. By October 7 they were in Dublin. "Kay Kendall is a good girl, I think, in spite of having an affair with Rex and upsetting Lilli," Coward tut-tutted in his ever-present diary. "Her wig was no good so she dyed her hair grey, which showed enthusiasm and horsesense. She gives a performance of great charm; all she needs is experience and a bit more technical assurance." Kay must have been reassured that the play was not being stolen from her: Coward also wrote that "Irene Handl, who could be brilliant as Madame Arcati, is still floundering and mistiming."

Roy Moseley saw Kay in *Blithe Spirit* when it played the Golder's Green theater outside London. "She was not as good as I expected," he says. "Somehow she was not at home in it, and the whole production was lackluster." Coward had given over the direction to actress Joyce Carey, "which was a disaster," Moseley feels. "Coward wanted Kay in the role, but she and Margot Grahame, who played Ruth, did not get along at all, and Kay was very down because of what was going on with Rex."

The play's producers, Lance Hamilton and Charles Russell, raved to the press about Kay's unique talents. "She's so vital, so spontaneous," said Hamilton. "Her reactions are so accurate. She has no barriers." Russell added that calling Kay "scatty" and "common" was actually a compliment. "'Common' doesn't mean in Britain what it means in America. It's what

Gertie Lawrence was and what Kay is. She has a wonderful, down-to-earth sophistication and she can get away with it, something she couldn't do if she were really a dreary, vulgar girl." When the show arrived in Leeds, Kay tried to make amends with her mother, asking her to bring her Aunt Nan to a show. She picked them up in her car, took them to lunch at her hotel, and had them shown to front-row seats. Past arguments temporarily forgotten, Gladys bragged happily to fellow audience members about being the Star's Mother.

Returning to London in December 1954, Kay was still glowing from her excursion with Coward's inspired dialogue and in no mood for the dull fare Rank continued to hand her. "She's been offered plenty of scripts and has turned them all down," said Rank's managing director (and Dinah Sheridan's new husband) John Davis. She rejected *Doctor at Sea* as well as two films (*Value for Money* and *As Long As They're Happy*) in which she was replaced by Diana Dors. "She's a clever actress," Kay said of Dors, "but can you imagine *me* playing a Diana part? I'm not even a beauty, for that matter," she concluded, managing to once more let her insecurities show.

On December 21, Rank put Kay on suspension; her surprisingly meager salary of one hundred and fifty pounds a week (from her 1952 contract) was withheld and the fight taken to the press. Kay's current agent, George Routledge, told reporters that "She is not a temperamental star. It is not that the parts are not big enough. She just wants to be sure they are right for her and will advance her career." Kay herself tried to keep things on a professional level: "Nobody can blame Rank for not paying me when I wouldn't work," she told a reporter. "But the parts they offered weren't— well, *me*. . . . I felt they were getting me nowhere." Kay's strike lasted through the New Year holiday and until the end of January 1955, when Rank agreed to loan her out to MGM for their big-budget production of *The Adventures of Quentin Durward*, loosely based on Sir Walter Scott's heroic 1823 novel. It was filmed in France in the summer of 1955 (to be released in January of the following year) and co-starred—to Kay's delight—Hollywood heart-throb Robert Taylor. What Rank neglected to mention was that Kay's role had already been turned down by Grace Kelly.

Quentin Durward was part of Rank's attempt to make high-profile pictures that would do well internationally. They hooked up with MGM, which had a huge, ten-soundstage production studio at Borehamwood. The 1950s were boom years for historical epics of swashbuckling swordsmen and fair ladies: such Saturday matinee fare as *Rogues of Sherwood For-*

est, Prince of Pirates, The Story of Robin Hood, The Prisoner of Zenda, Scaramouche, The Crimson Pirate, The Black Shield of Falworth and many others were cluttering the screen, with varying degrees of success.

Robert Taylor had begun to make a career of these period adventures: he had recently starred in *Ivanhoe* and *Knights of the Round Table*. At the age of forty-four, Taylor's best days as a movie idol were behind him. He'd come to fame at MGM in the late 1930s, supporting such stars as Jean Harlow, Greta Garbo, and Joan Crawford; he was married (from 1939 to 1952) to occasional co-star Barbara Stanwyck. Taylor had shot to stardom in *A Yank at Oxford, Waterloo Bridge,* and *Billy the Kid*—but by the mid-1950s, his generation of stars was being cut loose, just as the American studio system itself was falling prey to television and the breakup of the studios' monopolies over distribution and exhibition. Actually, it was Kay Kendall who was on her way up in 1955—Taylor, though still a name to be reckoned with, was a star on the decline.

Kay was thrilled with the high budget, the location filming—the Loire Valley (Chenoceau Castle) and near Chartres (Maintenon Castle)—and her co-stars Taylor (as Quentin Durward) and Robert Morley (as King Louis XI). The film was directed by Richard Thorpe and overseen by producer Pandro Berman, one of MGM's longtime big-shots. Thorpe might not have been the happiest of choices to direct the film. He had been at the helm of scores of Westerns since the 1920s and had recently directed some similar period adventures: Robert Taylor's *Ivanhoe* and *Knights of the Round Table*, as well as *The Prisoner of Zenda*. But none of the films from Thorpe's five-decade career have gone on to become classics.

Cast as Isabelle de Croye, Kay portrayed a fifteenth-century French noblewoman sold into marriage to a wealthy old Scotsman, who sends his dashing nephew (Taylor) to collect her. The expected happens: they fall in love, she is kidnaped by an evil "renegade count," and all hell breaks loose. Rescue comes in the portly shape of Louis XI (Morley turned in an agreeably hammy performance). At the fadeout, Isabelle and her romantic Quentin ride happily off into the French countryside.

Kay played the publicity game and burbled happily to the press about the film: "This is my first costume picture, and I wasn't at all sure about my fitness for the undertaking," she told *Los Angeles Times* reporter Edwin Schallert, brushing off her early bit parts in four other costume films. "Nothing I had done in the past on the screen enabled me to obtain the part I play. . . . I am finding the change from my other roles most interesting.

Nevertheless," Kay wisely realized, "I am convinced that I am a modern at heart, and that pictures of the modern type will be my logical choice in the future, with an occasional historical film." Kay also took time to deny in a haughty manner the rumors of her affair with Rex Harrison. "This is all just gossip," she snapped to Schallert in her best Grand Lady of the Manor voice. "I am surprised that rumors like that should be circulating . . . and I will certainly appreciate your making it clear to people that there is nothing to those reports." She had co-starred with Mr. Harrison in a recent film, of course, but "I hardly think that justifies any talk of romance. Certainly I am not thinking of matrimony either with Mr. Harrison or anybody else at the present time."

For all the money and star power, *Quentin Durward* turned out to be nearly as dismal as Kay's previous venture into romantic adventure, *Abdullah the Great*. This time, she had medieval costumes and lines to deal with as well—always the most light and modern of actresses, she was plainly uncomfortable and knew how silly she looked and sounded. "Oh, cavalier, your silence is so sad—even the roses are weeping," she intones, sounding for all the world like the lead in a middle-school production. There were lots of sword fights, loud declaiming, chases on horseback, and no discernable sexual electricity between Kay and Robert Taylor. Even the big set-piece—a sword fight with Taylor and the villain swinging wildly from bell ropes in a burning church belfry—comes off as unintentionally hilarious.

Later, Kay laughed ruefully about the role: "They shaved my eyebrows and put an orange wig on me—I looked like Danny Kaye having a fit in drag!" MGM, however, was impressed enough with Kay to offer Rank a good sum of money to buy out her contract—Rank refused, to Kay's disgust, and looked about for further homegrown projects for her. When a reporter found Kay at home and asked about losing out on this MGM deal, she shouted furiously at him, "You go and ask Mr. Rank—I've spent three years telling them I'm not happy. *You* have a go."

Much more up her alley, she thought, was the light domestic comedy *Simon and Laura*, from the play of the same name. Filmed in the late summer of 1955, *Simon and Laura* was a parody of the star-couple domestic sitcoms so popular in the mid-1950s (most notably *I Love Lucy* and *The George Burns and Gracie Allen Show* in the U.S., and *Life with the Lyons* in Britain). Kay and Peter Finch played Simon and Laura Foster, a battling stage duo on the verge of divorce, who are corralled into doing a daily domestic comedy. Ian Carmichael co-starred as TV producer David Prentice, and Muriel Pavlow played his romantic interest, scriptwriter Janet Honeyman.

The film was directed by fifty-year-old Muriel Box, then one of the more important women in the British film industry. She was married to writer and producer Sydney Box (whose sister, Betty, was an important producer in her own right). Muriel Box had worked her way up as a playwright and producer and had begun to direct films in 1952. *Simon and Laura* was her fifth feature assignment, and she had definite ideas as to whom she wanted to cast. Coral Browne had played Laura Foster onstage but wasn't a big enough name to draw film fans. Box knew she wanted Kay and Peter Finch in the lead roles—and she also wanted Ian Carmichael, who had played in the stage version but who was not yet a big box-office name. "Normally the casting is left to the director but Rank had no hesitation in saying if they disagreed with you," Muriel Box later recalled. "With Ian Carmichael, I really dug in my heels because I knew he would be excellent in the part." Box was right—he all but stole the film.

Peter Finch came to the verge of a nervous collapse while filming, carrying on as if it were his first outing before the cameras: "I feel all these camera angles cramping my style," he would moan. "I become totally strained and awkward." Finch, at the age of thirty-nine, still had no toehold on stardom. He'd been in films since the 1930s, but his first real success had come as a radio actor in Australia. By 1955, Finch was alternating between classical stage roles and such middling film dramas as *Elephant Walk* and *Father Brown*. *Simon and Laura* was only his second comedy—he'd just completed his first, *Josephine and Men*, with Glynis Johns. *Simon and Laura* was also Finch's first film under his new long-term Rank contract—the studio was planning on building him into a major star, and the pressure was not sitting well on the actor. The fact that he was forced to wear a silly-looking false moustache and have his reddish hair blackened, with white streaks, certainly didn't help his temper. He developed quite a crush on Kay, though, later sighing about her romance with Rex Harrison, "a steadier and more stable man and, let's face it, a much better comedian than I am."

Peter Finch's nerves were contagious, and Kay was soon in a state herself, flubbing lines and rushing off to her dressing room in floods of tears. Muriel Box recalled that "Nothing I said could reassure her, and on the first morning of shooting, she was in an absolute panic. I went to the dressing room on the second morning to calm her down but she had convinced herself that I had come to say she was not strong enough for the part. She refused to believe me when I said I had cast her because I thought she was ideal for it, and was certain to make a big hit."

During that first jittery week of production, Kay and Finch asked to be shown the few rushes that had been shot. They, along with Box and editor Jean Barker, sat silently watching the scenes already in the can. The two stars rose silently, corralled executive producer Earl St. John and producer Teddy Baird, and demanded that Muriel Box be replaced: they did not care for the way the film was being shot or the way they were being directed. Box was called into St. John's office and found her stars glumly staring at the floor. When the difficult situation was explained to her, Box exclaimed, "I can't understand why—they both play ideally together and I'm delighted with the little I've seen so far!"

A series of highly uncomfortable meetings was held, during which Finch made his unhappiness with high, mannered comedy known. Box patiently tried to explain the importance of split-second timing and camera angles with this type of film, "which had to be visualized by the director in terms of shots and angles and unlike a stage comedy and these had to marry precisely in cutting and editing to ensure pace and successful flow." It was finally agreed to let Kay and Finch improvise during rehearsals, to try and get a good comic flow between them before the imposition of timing and staging was imposed on them. Box later admitted sadly that "We had a sort of armed neutrality for the rest of the film."

Ian Carmichael affirms today that Muriel Box "was not exactly a William Wyler. She was alright on the technical side of it, because she relied on all the technical people around her to point her in the right direction. But I don't think she was terribly inspired." Carmichael also recalls that Kay didn't let that "armed neutrality" toward Box affect her equanimity and good humor toward her other co-workers. "She was great fun, very social, very ebullient, nothing seemed to faze her." Even the dreary, unavoidable delays of filmmaking were taken with patience and good humor. Once, while setting up a shot, delay after delay intruded: the hairdresser called a halt so a lock of Kay's hair could be readjusted. Then, the makeup man had to redo her powder. Next, the lighting crew had to change a light, and the wardrobe woman iron out a crease in Kay's collar. Just as Box was ready to shoot, Kay called out, "Are you sure no one wants to check my oil first?"

This was Muriel Pavlow's third film with Kay, and the two had become social friends through Dirk Bogarde as well. She recalls Kay as being "full of uncertainties, but she was such a natural" on this set, coming out with "ridiculous statements like, 'Oh, I'm so ugly.' One took it in one's stride and was like, 'Oh, come on, dear, pull yourself together.'"

On its release in December, *Simon and Laura* met with agreeable but not overwhelming reception from the public and press. Kay, Ian Carmichael (cute as a button as the twitchy producer), and Thora Hird (as the Fosters' star-struck maid) got the best notices. *The New York Times* was typical: Bosley Crowther admired a few of the performances (and Kay's dazzling appearance in designer Julie Harris's glamorous gowns) but felt that the movie itself was "pretty forced and flat. . . . *Simon and Laura* takes an idea that is pretty pat at the start and makes it even patter." *Simon and Laura*, however, has aged better than most of Kay's films: it survives as a witty, fast-paced period piece. Kay looks stunning—lighted, made-up, and coiffed like the glamour queen she now was; in her chic, high-fashion gowns, her waistline seems to be cinched to the width of her spinal column. There was even a post-modern reference to *Genevieve*, as Laura Foster wails, "I have acted with octogenarians, dipsomaniacs, dope fiends, amnesiacs, and veteran cars . . ."

J. Arthur Rank was disappointed with the film's lukewarm reception—though of course he had no idea that *Simon and Laura* was to turn out to be the last film Kay was to make for his studio; the remainder of her projects would be on loan-out. By the time *Simon and Laura* was wrapped, Kay was preparing herself to say goodbye to Rex Harrison, who was set to leave for New York in the fall of 1955 to star in the Broadway show that would change both of their lives.

Chapter Fourteen

"My career is still important, but it's not that important."

While Kay had been filming *Quentin Durward* and *Simon and Laura*, Harrison was dipping his toes into preparations for *My Fair Lady*. It had all begun back in February 1955, when Dirk Bogarde's friend, playwright Alan Jay Lerner, had begged for a meeting with Rex Harrison. Lerner had been working with his composing partner Frederick Loewe on a project based on *Pygmalion*. Tentatively titled *Lady Liza*, the show would be, Lerner felt, a perfect vehicle for Harrison—though he was hardly first choice for the role, as Harrison later loved to claim. Everyone from David Niven to Noël Coward to George Sanders had either rejected, or been rejected for, the part. Harrison, too, was a very difficult man to pin down. Bogarde and Tony Forwood tipped Kay off to the plan, and she dragged Harrison to Beel House for a February weekend trip. Lerner and his wife Nancy were introduced as "two friends from New York," and everything went swimmingly. Bogarde suggested everyone go for a stroll while he prepared lunch, and Kay feigned a headache. Bogarde recalled, "When they came back they were all great friends and Alan said, coming into the hall . . . 'Have you got a piano in this house of yours?'" He settled for a spinet, and played what had been so far written of the score—both Harrison and Kay were sold. One interesting sidelight added by Bogarde is that "I've Grown Accustomed to Her Face" had not yet been written—according to him, it was later inspired by, and dedicated to, Kay. It must be noted that Harrison biographer Roy Moseley says that "this version of Dirk's is absolute nonsense—Rex and Lerner met in London and went over the show. Dirk could be *such* a liar."

Although Harrison had agreed to play Prof. Henry Higgins, he was far from calm about the prospects. He knew he'd be competing not only against Leslie Howard's film performance in *Pygmalion* but against whatever actress was playing Eliza Doolittle (there was never any serious thought of putting the non-musical Kay into the role). Rex Harrison was no singer, either, and spent many fretful weeks in a rehearsal room trying to work his raspy tenor around the score. After the decision that he should talk his songs in character rather than trying to sing, things went much more smoothly. Producer Herman Levin bought out of the rest of Harrison's *Bell, Book and Candle* contract—Binkie Beaumont got twenty-five thousand pounds and a chunk of the play's grosses—and in December 1955 Harrison flew to New York to begin rehearsals. Kay had every intention of following him, about which prospect Harrison had mixed feelings—he was already terrified at the prospect of this new show, and he wasn't sure if he could handle Kay's dramatics as well. His leave-taking proved to be a very public scene, as he and Kay kissed openly in the airport's departures lounge, to the edification of reporters. After Harrison's plane took off, Kay sat right down in the lounge and cried.

Harrison borrowed actor Tyrone Power's Manhattan apartment and set to work. Playwright (*You Can't Take It With You, The Man Who Came to Dinner*) and director Moss Hart was hired to head the project. Hart had handled such difficult stars as Marilyn Miller and Gertrude Lawrence, but Rex Harrison was prepared to take "difficult" to a whole new level. Hart was recovering from a coronary, was an insomniac, and had just been put on antidepressants when rehearsals began. Also in the cast of *My Fair Lady* were Stanley Holloway as Eliza Doolittle's Cockney dad and Cathleen Nesbitt as Higgins' aristocratic mother. The remarkable, stylized Edwardian costumes were designed by Cecil Beaton—except for Harrison's tweed hat, which was bought in Bond Street and eventually became his trademark (Harrison was quite balding by this time and the hat made it easier to go without his toupee).

Playing the female lead was twenty-year-old Julie Andrews, adding to Harrison's nervousness. Andrews was a veteran of British revues and had made her Broadway debut as the lead in *The Boy Friend* a year earlier. Harrison was afraid that her remarkable singing voice would blow him off the stage, and he was annoyed by her inability to immediately grasp the role. "I got worse, not better," Andrews told Moss Hart's biographer, Steven Bach. "It was obvious to everyone that I was out of my depth, and the awful thing was I knew it." Harrison was on his worst behavior, loudly threatening to quit every few days. Hart managed to coerce Eliza Doolittle out of Julie Andrews, while Harrison worried over every word he spoke and every line he sang.

Through late 1955 and early 1956, *My Fair Lady* rehearsed in New York, tried out in Philadelphia, and previewed in Connecticut, while Kay's transatlantic phone bills mounted. She had turned down all film offers since *Simon and Laura* had wrapped, and by now she was slogging through the end of her tour in *Bell, Book and Candle*: all she wanted was to get her financial and social affairs in order so she could fly to New York and be with Harrison. By this time, sister Kim was married to George F. Baker Jr., of a prominent banking family (the Bakers had an apartment on Park Avenue and a home on Long Island)—so Kay was looking forward to a pleasant family reunion as well. Their mother paid occasional visits to Kim, though, so Kay did have a few reservations about the "pleasant" part.

As 1955 ended, Kay's world had been turned upside-down. She'd had another three films released—two of them well-received; one a big-budget turkey. Offers piled up for her services: Hollywood was begging Rank to loan her out. But Kay no longer cared about anything but Rex Harrison and about herself becoming the next Mrs. Rex Harrison. From now on, her career would take a back seat to her love life. Even bigger success and brighter stardom were still in Kay's future, but they practically had to be shoved down her unwilling throat. "I don't fret," she sighed contentedly. "My career is still important, but it's not *that* important." No longer would Kay "live like a champagne bottle—always about to pop my cork."

My Fair Lady opened at the Mark Hellinger Theater on March 15, 1956, and went on to become the biggest musical hit in Broadway history to date, with a run of six years (not all, of course, with Rex Harrison in the lead). Suddenly Kay found herself romantically attached to the biggest star on Broadway—certainly, Henry Higgins brought Harrison a fame and acceptance he'd never had before (and which he thought he'd forfeited forever with Carole Landis's death). He, Julie Andrews, and Kay's old friend Stanley Holloway coasted on a wave of great press and nightly cheers. There was little competition that year; the only other new musical to make a hit was *The Most Happy Fella*.

Kay was not able to be at the opening night, much to her regret. In April, she asked Rank for "a few weeks' holiday in America, to visit a friend." Her producers were understandably nervous and mistrustful but had no legal right to deny her—even they had no suspicion that it would be some two years before Kay would return to England. She arrived in New York in April and moved right into the new hideaway Harrison had found for them. Now that *My Fair Lady* looked to have a long run, he gave up the

Manhattan apartment and rented polo player Michael Phipps's estate in Old Westbury, Long Island. Kay was delighted with the home, the bucolic setting, and with playing backstage wife. While her lover performed, Kay frequently strolled around the theater district with playwright and screenwriter Harry Kurnitz, who remembered that "there was not a doorman or taxi driver the length and breadth of that sleazy boulevard who didn't greet her with a cheery, 'Hi, Kay,' or to whom she didn't respond with matched enthusiasm and pleasure." Harrison's older son Noel agrees that "Taxi drivers, newspaper sellers, ordinary working people knew her and loved her and she treated them all as equals."

Kay frequently hung around backstage, watching the show over and over again. She would drift from Harrison's dressing room to the wings just in time to hear him sing "I've Grown Accustomed to Her Face"—Harrison gazed at her while he sang and she beamed back. But not even the most devoted of lovers could watch *My Fair Lady* more than a dozen or so times, and Kay soon began to detest both the show itself and the time and energy it took away from her relationship with Harrison. Friends dropped by to keep her occupied: Carol Matthau's former husband William Saroyan met Kay backstage one night. She batted her eyes in pretty confusion when introduced to the famous writer, then said in her most upper-class tones, "Saroyan . . . Oh, yes. Yes. You're a great friend of my wifey's." Kay's brother Terry brought his wife and baby son Neil to New York during the show's run, and Cecil Beaton kindly loaned them his Waldorf-Astoria suite for the night. Terry and Pamela left auntie Kay to babysit Neil: completely flummoxed by her unaccustomed role as nanny, Kay stood over the infant and darkly warned him, "don't you *dare* mess all over Cecil's white satin pillows!"

Kay also attended many parties that were thrown both for the *My Fair Lady* cast and for other Broadway shows. Her friend Peggy Dexter recalled one at which Sammy Davis Jr. performed: "When he walked into the room, she got down on her knees and did the salaam in honor of his talent." Another time-killing friend was actor Jack Merivale, future husband of Kay's *Genevieve* co-star Dinah Sheridan. He was appearing on Broadway with Celia Johnson in *The Reluctant Debutante*, a show that was soon to have an impact on Kay's own career. "Every evening, Jack used to meet Katie or Katie would go to Jack's dressing room after his show was over and then they'd do the town before they went to pick up Rex and go home," recalls Sheridan. "Rex was never jealous, there was nothing in it."

No matter where they went, she laughs, "the barman would always say, 'Hi, Kay!' so obviously she knew every barman in New York."

Playing at the theater next door in *No Time for Sergeants* was Roddy McDowell, who had made a splash as a child star and was now reinventing himself as an adult stage actor. McDowell would step out into the alley between acts for a breath of fresh air, and there was this tall, lovely woman, "so larky and so dear," who eagerly latched onto him. As usual, Kay immediately began complaining to her newfound acquaintance about her nose and how she "wanted to get it done." McDowell objected, "Don't be ridiculous, you have a wonderful nose—like Myrna Loy or somebody. A very original nose," which was what Kay had been angling for all along. McDowell didn't have the slightest idea who she was, and Kay laughed, "I'm a kept woman—why don't you take me for coffee or something?"

Kay and McDowell quickly became good friends—he knew he was "in" when he was bestowed with one of her nicknames ("Sammy the Seal," because he loved to swim). "She just enveloped you—but I don't mean like a praying mantis," McDowell recalled of his budding friendship. "She was just so completely attentive. She really *looked* at you, she really connected. She enjoyed people very much." He was invited for weekends on Long Island and happened to be there the week that Kay had fired all the servants after discovering that they were avidly reading celebrity tabloid stories about their employers. "We're just going to be hand-to-mouth this weekend," she apologized, staring helplessly at the kitchen. "Just hand-to-mouth." As McDowell discovered, the one part of this housewifely life Kay was not prepared to deal with was servants and cooks. "Housekeeping and cooking is something I don't know too much about," she admitted, "but one learns." She tried devotedly to polish and vacuum and come up with tempting dinners, even asking a reporter from *Cue* magazine to write down a lasagna recipe for her to attempt. Harrison went out fishing on his days off, but all he seemed able to hook was flounder, which Kay did her level best to scale and bone and toss into the oven or frying pan. "We eat hardly anything out here but flounder," she sighed. "Baked flounder, fried flounder, grilled flounder, all sorts of flounder."

McDowell eventually came to admire Kay not only as an actress but as one of the last of the old-time stars. "She was a magical creature," he said shortly before his death in 1998. "Everywhere you went, people used to stop and stare because of her carriage and what she radiated. And the way she wore clothes." He was also impressed with the way she brought her particularly scatty characters to life onscreen. Like Carole Lombard, Kay "knew how to make irresponsible, selfish people with no conscience, people with no social acumen at all, make them seem childlike and adorable." But as close as McDowell got to be with Kay—"like brother and sister"—he never warmed up to Rex Harrison. "He was so incendiary, so perverse. It was really very difficult to deal with Rex." Kay kept trying to get McDowell to meet Dirk Bogarde—sadly, her two great friends "Sammy the Seal" and "Diggy" didn't meet until Kay's memorial service.

Another friend Kay made in New York was tiny, blonde Eva Gabor. Still a decade away from her greatest success, on TV's *Green Acres*, Gabor had achieved a certain minor fame in nightclubs, Broadway, and such films as *The Last Time I Saw Paris* and *Artists and Models*. As bubbly and glamorous as Kay, Eva found a soulmate. The two enjoyed lengthy "I hate my looks" gripe-sessions (Eva hated her shortness as much as Kay hated her height). Kay described to reporter Geoffrey Bocca their typical Girls' Nights: Gabor brought over a bottle of vodka, and Kay proudly produced a forty-dollar pot of caviar. "Dinner is ready!" she crowed, and the ladies set to.

Kay treated her sister to a rare experience: lunch at the Waldorf with all three Gabor sisters—Eva, Zsa Zsa, and Magda—along with Dominican playboy and diplomat Porfirio Rubirosa. Zsa Zsa had broken off a scandalous, sometimes violent, four-year romance with Rubirosa in 1955, but she was able to stay on good terms with her many exes. Although Kim found the Gabors blindingly glamorous, "What I couldn't understand was Rubirosa. He looked like a monkey—though I expect he had charms which weren't evident over a lunch table."

Everywhere Kay went in New York, radios and restaurant bands were playing the songs she heard from the audience or backstage every night: "Wouldn't It Be Loverly," "I Could Have Danced All Night," "On the Street Where You Live," and the tune that she liked to think of as hers, "I've Grown Accustomed to Her Face." By now, Kay was used to being a star in her own right, but neither she nor Harrison had ever encountered the sort of fame he was now enjoying. This brought on a few moments of panic when Harrison was being interviewed by *Time* magazine for a July 23 cover story—America in the mid-1950s was not ready for a married actor to be living openly with his girlfriend. Kay had to hide all signs of her residence: clothing, photos, knickknacks all had to be kept from the eagle eyes of *Time*. While she later claimed to have sneaked from room to room one step ahead of the reporter, it is much more likely that she simply spent the day with her sister or with friends in the city.

As she watched Julie Andrews transform from a bawdy Cockney into an Edwardian society belle each night, Kay was herself undergoing something of a metamorphosis, and it was one her family and friends did not wholly approve of. Many noticed a slight change, a skewing in Kay's public persona after she was well established not only as a star in her own right but as the consort of the great Rex Harrison. "She enjoyed the glamour of being an actress," said Dirk Bogarde, adding that Kay was capable of being a huge snob. "She knew exactly who was worth what and where she should go and not go," he added. "She knew exactly how to play her cards and with whom to play them." Her old friend Princess Lilian also noticed that Kay changed a bit after success had overwhelmed her life.

"If there were people around who wanted her autograph, she'd say no, and that wasn't like the Katie I knew," Lilian says. "Maybe it went to her head." Kay's sister was also surprised to see her shrink from fans after a show: Harrison lunged into a cab, snarling, "Come on, hurry up—these terrible people," and Kay fell right into line, huffing, "Oh, it's awful—why do they do this?" Kim took her to task: "This is your bread and butter!" she objected, mocking Kay's attitude of "Fancy them touching the hem of my gown!"

Success had not so much changed Kay as it had given free reign to a part of her personality that she'd not yet been able to fully indulge. Back in her chorus-girl days, she was able to loftily call a barkeep "my good man" and it was thought cute and zany. Now she could—and did—adopt such attitudes for real. Of course, this indicated that Kay was finally enjoying the stardom and riches she'd worked for all her life. She grasped fame with both hands and trilled elegantly to reporter Anne Sharpley about what a bore it could all be: she couldn't order ale in a pub because people "think I'm mad not to be drinking champagne." Though she adored riding high atop double-decker busses, "they stare at you as though you were a . . . er . . . *monkey!*" She loved every minute of it. Putting on her best Lady Bracknell voice, Kay purred, "After all, I have been working since I was eleven. . . . It's not *wrong* to wear a mink coat, is it?"

But still, Kay was not Mrs. Rex Harrison and had her doubts as to whether she ever would be. Harrison was so wrapped up in *My Fair Lady* that the thought of actually divorcing Lilli had retreated somewhere to the back of his head. Carol Matthau recalls Kay showing up at her home in the middle of the night sobbing, "Wifey, I can't. . . . Do you think it will ever work out?" Matthau would reassure her: "He's with you. He loves you. I mean, that's all that counts."

Kay also tried to make a hit with the social elite of New York, with very limited success. Kim was something of a young society matron herself, but Kay had ways of ferreting out the "right people." She didn't need her sister's sponsorship. She met the rising hairstylist Kenneth Battelle, who would soon fashion the famous bouffants of Jackie Kennedy, Marilyn Monroe, and half the society women of New York. He perfected Kay's pouffed do and became a family friend; her sister still patronizes Kenneth when in New York. But the society matrons of Manhattan and Long Island did not take to Kay: "These were dull ladies," recalls Carol Matthau. "They all dressed alike, they looked alike, they spoke alike." Kay, on the other hand, was young, beautiful, could wear clothes like a model, and was alarmingly brash and outspoken. Lilli Palmer also had friends in high places in New York, and they made sure Kay was cut dead at every turn. She tried to be philosophical about it: "It isn't me," she said to friends. "They're being loyal to Lilli." But it still hurt, very much.

The only "society swan" to befriend Kay was Babe Paley, the beautiful blonde wife of CBS founder William Paley. A Boston blue blood and former *Vogue* fashion editor, Babe had enough wit and social pull not to be threatened by Kay. The Paleys knew how it felt to be on the outside: being Jewish, William Paley was pointedly excluded from the Social Register set himself. Kay, in her turn, was bowled over by the glamorous social butterfly: "She's so wonderful," Kay raved to her sister about Babe. "She does her gardening in Mainbocher!" Harrison was more than a little jealous of Kay's new friendship. Once, at El Morocco, he sat and glared as Kay whirled around the dance floor with an obviously smitten William Paley. When she returned to their table, he snapped at her, "Well? How many shares of CBS did you get?" The Paleys often had the Harrisons over to Kiluna Farm, their Long Island estate, and soon John ("Jock") Hay Whitney was part of their social circle, too (he was married to Babe Paley's sister, Betsy). Whitney was not only an internationally ranked polo player, but he dabbled with astonishing success in art collecting, publishing, and producing as well.

Kay managed to keep Harrison's house perking with activity and trauma that summer of 1956. When things got too dull, she would take care of that: once, she left a ransom note from her "kidnappers" and hid behind the curtains. Harrison and their house guests went frantic, of course, and called the police. As their friends tried to comfort the bereft host, Kay jumped out and giggled—Rex lost control and smacked her; she burst into sobs. Their guests melted embarrassed into other rooms as the two tearfully made up. Still, Harrison recalled that summer in his memoirs as "a lovely, mad time," dismissing Kay's sometimes demented pranks as "simply for fun . . . delighted with the fuss she had occasioned."

Whatever frustration Kay may have felt about her long vacation from acting, she sublimated it and seemed blissfully happy to both friends and reporters. She even turned down a terrific role in a nationwide showcase: Noël Coward notes in his diaries that Kay was offered the part of Queenie, the discontented daughter, in a CBS television production of *This Happy Breed*, his saga about a working-class family between the wars. "Then the silly bitch refused, so she can stew for all I care," Coward sniffed. He hired Patricia Cutts instead and noted Kay's plan to "live secretly in sin with Rex" as "madness." Kay didn't care about the loss of the role or the opinions of her friends: she was too happy just living day to day.

Kay Kendall in Britain was tempting enough to Hollywood producers—once she set foot in the U.S., she was deluged with film offers, and J. Arthur Rank was anxious for her to do something—anything—to bring in money. "Oh, that loot!" Kay squealed to a reporter about the offers coming in. "Wouldn't I love to get my hands on that loot!" But still, she resisted all comers. "I hate to give up the chance," she said, but she just did not want to leave Harrison's side.

Producer Sol Siegel was more persistent than most and was determined to cast Kay in an upcoming MGM musical, *Les Girls*, set to begin filming early in 1957. The mid-1950s was a slow time for Hollywood musicals, and the combination of Kay, co-star Gene Kelly, director George Cukor, and music by Cole Porter was bound to be successful. There would be little competition: the only other hit film musicals in 1957 were to be the delightful *Funny Face* and the Elvis Presley vehicle *Jailhouse Rock*; the adaptations of Broadway hits *The Pajama Game* and *Pal Joey* failed to draw big audiences. With so much music on TV, Hollywood was concentrating on drama that year: *The Three Faces of Eve*, *The Bridge On the River Kwai*, *Peyton Place*.

Two things finally convinced Kay to take on the role: "that loot," and the chance to work with Cukor. "It was George Cukor who finally sold me," Kay told gossip columnist Hedda Hopper. "I've always thought he was one of the finest directors in the business. And besides, he assured me on our first meeting in New York that we'd have a barrel of fun making the picture." Still undecided, Kay told Siegel she would only do the film for a $100,000 bonus over her Rank salary, thinking they would turn her down flat. Much to her shock, he agreed, and she found herself backed into a corner. The first thing she did was rush out and spend nearly her entire salary on Christmas gifts for her friends and family (for Harrison, a first edition of Byron and a mink-lined coat). Siegel was delighted: "She could be the top comedienne in the business and one of the all-time box office greats if she'd only settle down and become serious about her career," he told Hopper.

Chapter Fifteen

"I won't be any good at it! She needs a strong person."

In the autumn of 1956, as the new theatrical season started, the producers of *My Fair Lady* suggested that Harrison check into Columbia-Presbyterian Medical Center for a series of routine tests. Kay had been feeling weak, feverish, and headachy for some time, so she accompanied him. Their doctor was Dana W. Atchley, "physician to the stars" (and for whom Columbia-Presbyterian's Atchley Pavilion was named). Atchley could be depended on to keep secrets, which, as it turned out, was a good thing. He told Harrison that he was concerned about Kay's tests and that she needed to have further blood work done—Atchley also got in touch with Carl Goldman, who had been the Kendalls' family physician in London since the 1940s. "I don't know what the fuck they're doing," Kay groused to Carol Matthau when she had to go in for further tests. "It's just for overnight or something."

Meanwhile, Kay was happily planning her first big, "family" Christmas bash, decking the Long Island house out in lights and wreaths, with a huge tree. Harrison put off Dr. Atchley's repeated requests for an emergency consultation to go over Kay's results: he strongly suspected that this was going to be bad news, and he just didn't want to hear it until Christmas was over. Dirk Bogarde and Tony Forwood came to Long Island to spend three weeks. As the holiday season wore on, guests wandered in and out: Forwood's son by Glynis Johns, Gareth; Harrison's co-star Cathleen Nesbitt; Kay's sister Kim and her husband. Harrison had purchased an expensive record player, and Kay played the soundtrack of the new Judy Holliday musical, *Bells Are Ringing*, over and over again until everyone wanted to kill her. Bogarde recalled Kay gazing lovingly at Harrison, singing along with Holliday (and her co-star, Sydney Chaplin), "Just in time, I found you just in time. . . . Before you came my time was running low."

Kay managed to drag Bogarde to a Christmas party in Manhattan at the home of theatrical producer Gilbert Miller and his socialite wife, Kitty. Convincing him was no easy task, as he wanted to spend his holiday lazing about Long Island and not playing the show-biz game. He grumbled and refused, and a furious Kay stormed off to the city, shouting, "You just don't understand—this isn't the kind of party you turn down—people *murder* to get invited to the Millers'!" Chastened, Bogarde dressed and followed her— at the party, he was delighted to meet not only Greta Garbo but Judy Garland, who had Kay perched adoringly at her feet all night. Bogarde and Garland became friends and were to co-star in her last film, *I Could Go On Singing*, in 1962.

It was one of the happiest times in Kay's life: she finally had Harrison all to herself (except for having to share him with Eliza Doolittle every night). She had Hollywood begging for her services and throwing great whacking gobs of cash at her. And now she was playing Lady of the Manor to her best friends, showering them with gifts and hospitality. After one long dinner, Bogarde found Kay huddled up happily in a large armchair, exhausted, smiling and muttering, "Oh, wifey, I'm getting to be an old, old woman. . . . Oh! I am a lucky lady. . . . I've got all my loves about me."

Even Kay's oft-estranged mother, Gladys, came to visit the couple on Long Island. Harrison could only take so much of Gladys and her friend Jean Baird, who had come along with her, so Kay called her sister and begged Kim to invite the ladies out to her own Long Island home. "I took mother and Jean to stay with us, to help Kay out," says Kim. "Then every-thing hit the fan! Kay called me up and said, 'How could you do this? How could you take mother away?' And all this after she'd *asked* me to!" Kay's relationship with Gladys continued to be rocky, and Harrison didn't help matters. As soon as Kay had come into money, she began sending her mother a monthly check, despite their differences. One month she was late and Gladys called to inquire after her stipend. As Kim remembers, "Rex wrote her a *terrible* letter, saying she was the most inhuman mother ever."

The New Year arrived, and Rex Harrison couldn't put it off any longer: on January 2, 1957, he appeared at Dr. Atchley's office. Atchley asked if Kay had any family, and he answered, "not anyone she cares about"—a reply which was to prove quite a shock to her parents and siblings in later years. Seeing as Harrison was the closest person to her, Atchley broke the news—Kay had myelocytic leukemia and could be expected to live only another two years at most. "I sat, my own blood draining, unable to say anything," Harrison wrote in his memoirs. "A whole vista of agony stretched out before me, and yet I felt proud that this doctor had given me the task of looking after her."

Chronic myelocytic leukemia most often strikes people between the ages of twenty-five and forty-five; sufferers may not show any symptoms until the disease has been incubating for a year or two. Kay would have begun to experience the weakness, palpitations, indigestion, weight loss, chills, and fevers (though rarely above 101 degrees) that were common with this illness. The life expectancy of someone diagnosed in the 1950s tended to range from one to five years.

Proud Harrison may have been, but he turned immediately to the sensible strength of Lilli Palmer, who was on a ski trip in Austria with their son, Carey. He wired her to fly straight to New York, which she did. The estranged—but still very married—couple met again in Dr. Atchley's office later that week, and an exchange straight from the most torrid of soap operas took place. Harrison and Palmer agreed in their respective autobiographies about what Atchley had to say: if Kay could not be told of her condition and sent back to her family, then Harrison would have to marry her and nurse her to the end. In the 1950s, it was common for people with mortal illnesses to be kept in the dark; it never seems to have occurred to Harrison, Palmer, or Atchley that Kay might have wanted to know her prognosis. "She must never be told, she must never know" became Harrison's mantra for the next two years. He never stepped back from that.

What happened in private over the next few days between Harrison and Palmer was to become a bone of contention between the two over the next twenty years. Harrison's autobiography was published in 1974 and Palmer's a year later; their stories differ considerably, and the pair gave indignant interviews in the late 1970s insisting that their own version was the pure truth. Harrison, of course, made himself sound as noble and self-sacrificing as possible. "I wanted to accept responsibility for Kay, whom I loved very much," he wrote. "I must take care of her. I must be constantly by her side. I would marry her, because I loved her."

Palmer's tale was a little different: She was the one to chirp brightly to Atchley, "You can rest assured that we will be divorced and that Rex will marry Kay and take care of her." In the taxi afterward, Harrison cried out, "I can't! You know I can't! You know how I feel about—about it." She went on to detail Harrison's terror of death and illness, claiming he moaned, "I won't be any good at it! She needs a strong person. . . . And when it's all

over, what will I be left with? I'll be alone. I'll have to start life all over again
. . . I could do it—if I knew that in the end, you would be there." Palmer
wrote that she promised Harrison to remarry him after Kay's death, that it
was the only way she could get him to agree—although she had no intention
of following through. Palmer was already involved with Carlos Thompson
and saw this as a clean, noble way to obtain a divorce and marry her new
love.

One thing that both Harrison and Palmer agreed on in later years
was her continuing role as moral support. "Every week, where ever I happened to be, at least one letter was waiting for me," she recalled, "which
told the true story of anguish and often of despair. But the worst were the
telephone calls. . . . And then there would be five or even ten minutes of
pent-up frustration." Palmer showed Roy Moseley Harrison's letters, though
she refused to let them be reprinted in his biography. "Rex was in negotiation to remarry Lilli and was very open about it," Moseley says. "Rex wanted
Lilli back, but she had already met Carlos and wanted the divorce."

Harrison was right to be scared in that taxi—he was indeed letting
himself in for a horrible, self-sacrificing job. Palmer's friend Noël Coward,
when apprised of the situation, bellowed, "I would never have allowed
myself to be pushed into this ridiculous situation. What kind of cheap
melodrama is this?" Popular author Jacqueline Susann voiced the opinion
of many of Harrison's acquaintances in her 1969 novel *The Love Machine*.
She loosely based the characters Ike Ryan and Amanda on Harrison's and
Kay's situation: an egotistical film producer with a mysterious suicide in
his background, and his glamorous wife, dying of leukemia. "She can help
my image," Ike coolly tells a friend. "My reputation isn't exactly sympathetic. I can use a little good press. When Amanda goes, people will look at
me in a different light. They'll realize I made the last months of a doomed
girl happy ones—great ones. I'm gonna give her the biggest razzle-dazzle
whirl any girl ever had. And when they close the lid on her pretty puss, at
least she'll have gone out in style." Making allowances for Susann's penny-
dreadful prose, many of Kay's friends felt these were Rex Harrison's thoughts
exactly.

Lilli Palmer signed all the necessary papers and took off for Juarez,
Mexico, to file for divorce. She requested no alimony. And Harrison was
able to send Kay off to Los Angeles to begin filming *Les Girls* with a marriage proposal. Neither of them ever told anyone the circumstances of the
proposal: what Harrison said, or where or when; what Kay's reaction was.

Various friends and relatives felt that Kay had never really wanted to marry Harrison, that he had been pursuing her. Others said that Kay was desperate to become Mrs. Harrison and that he was the reluctant one. Whatever their mixed feelings, Kay said "yes" and went to Los Angeles as an engaged woman.

But getting her to the West Coast was not going to be easy. Kay was terrified of flying, hated to be away from Harrison and their cozy Long Island retreat, was sure she'd be a flop in this film—her last musical, after all, had been *London Town!*—and was also scared of being alone in L.A. Additionally, Dirk Bogarde already suspected, "She was ill and she knew that she was ill." Actress Gladys Cooper kindly loaned Kay her Corgi, June, to accompany her on the trip. Bogarde and Tony Forwood drove Kay to Idlewilde Airport while Harrison played a matinee of *My Fair Lady.* She sobbed hysterically into her mink coat the whole drive, trying to find a way out. June, shoved into a pet carrier, was yelping, too: both Kay and June were fed ineffectual tranquilizers by Bogarde.

The L.A. flight was packed with stars. Along with Kay were a foursome soon to be involved in multiple marital high jinks: Debbie Reynolds and her husband, Eddie Fisher; and Elizabeth Taylor and her husband, Michael Wilding; also aboard were Shelley Winters and her fiancé, Tony Franciosa; and Kay's friend Eva Gabor, also en route to MGM. Kay and Gabor sat together and cheered each other up (Kay already missed Harrison horribly, and Gabor was in the midst of a divorce). The two popped still more sleeping pills—which had no effect whatsoever—and chatted volubly for the entire flight.

Chapter Sixteen

"It is Kay Kendall who shines brightest . . . a constant pleasure and surprise."

Kay arrived in Los Angeles and MGM's press attaché took her to a rented apartment: she got one look at it and became hysterical. "It looked like an Amsterdam tart's parlor," recalled Dirk Bogarde, "swagged and buttoned satin, scatter cushions, an immense lilac nylon Teddy bear." Particularly grisly, under the circumstances, was an undertaker's sign in green neon opposite Kay's bedroom window, repeatedly blinking the message, "It's Later Than You Think." The phone rang at Harrison's Long Island home: it was Kay, alternately laughing and crying. "I can't stay a night here, I'll slit my throat, wifey! Oh, I'se sick, Miss Scarlett!" Harrison got hold of MGM, and Kay was bustled off to the much more suitable Beverly Hills Hotel on Sunset Boulevard.

Les Girls began filming in February of 1957; Kay's medical exam for MGM's insurance company proved to be no problem, which Harrison and her doctor had feared: there was as yet no hint of illness, so a blood test was not administered. The film's other "girls" were sparkly-eyed dancer Mitzi Gaynor (a Chicago native who was to have her biggest hit the following year with the film version of *South Pacific*) and Finnish-born Taina Elg, a successful ballet dancer who had appeared in several minor roles at MGM. The film's star was forty-five-year-old Gene Kelly, whose best days were behind him. After the early-1950s successes of *Singin' in the Rain* and *An American In Paris*, he had suffered setbacks with such box-office failures as *Invitation to the Dance* and *It's Always Fair Weather*. A director and choreographer, Kelly found all creative control taken away from him in *Les Girls*: George Cukor directed, and Jack Cole choreographed. Kelly—who was used to doing his own choreography—was not a happy man. Cukor, who did not want Mitzi Gaynor in her role, was also not happy.

Les Girls was the story of Barry Nichols (Kelly) and his trio of dancing girls, who love and fight their way across Europe. The clever framing device had them all testifying to their own version of events when Angele (Elg) sues Sybil (Kay) for libel over her memoirs; sort of a musical-comedy *Rashomon*. The only real false step was the title, which tended to be mispronounced "Lay Girls" or "Lez Girls," both of which give a highly misleading idea of the goings-on.

After costume fittings with Orry-Kelly, Kay had to get down to work. Her three co-stars were famed for their dancing talents, and Kay was terrified of looking foolish. "I have legs like a kangaroo," she moaned to UPI reporter Aline Mosby. "I have a deal with Mitzi Gaynor. I'm going to hide behind her." Kay added—while the MGM publicist visibly cringed in the background—"I'm the same height as Gene Kelly without heels so I guess he'll have to stand on a box." She was also unhappy about the revealingly sexy showgirl costumes she had to wear. "They'll have to photograph me through some old kitchen curtain," she groused self-consciously. She and Kelly had already gotten off to a rocky start: on her first day on the set, there was no greeting from him in her dressing room. She made sure that on Kelly's first day, his dressing room was pointedly stuffed with flowers from her.

Jack Cole rehearsed Kay mercilessly; he had previously guided such highly insecure non-dancing stars as Marilyn Monroe and Lana Turner through musical films, so Kay was not that big a challenge. "I used to crawl back to the Beverly Hills Hotel at night with my legs literally so tired I could hardy move," she recalled. "Then, too, I'd never sung onscreen before [her *London Town* songs had been dubbed]. That took lots of work. I still look for the audience to start for the doors when they hear me." As it turned out, Kay did quite well by herself in the vocal department. She took part in three numbers: the title song; a comic ensemble piece, "Ladies in Waiting"; and a marvelous knockabout duet with Kelly, "You're Just Too, Too." Jack Cole managed to choreograph around her: all of Kay's dance steps could probably have been executed by her eighty-four-year-old grandmother.

George Cukor tried to keep his a happy set, which was not always easy: Gene Kelly was going through a nasty divorce and was not in a good frame of mind. Additionally, Mitzi Gaynor didn't really bond with Kay and Taina Elg, who recalls that "We used to have lots of fun. Sometimes during lunch hour [Kay] would bring some nice wine and cheese and we would have those. Mitzi was a very organized girl—just like in the film—

and she would have vegetables and healthy things to eat and rest in her room." Kay was also battling fatigue, brought on by her poor health. A doctor would visit the set to give her vitamin B^{12} shots, and Elg—who had just had a baby—lined up and said, "Oh, I'll have some, too!" Kay's strength was beginning to decline, but she was not yet undergoing any treatment for her illness: co-star Leslie Phillips recalled that she sometimes had to be shot around, occasioning some grumbling about special treatment.

Kay found Cukor to be a "darling," whose worst criticism was, "Alright, girls, that's fine—let's shoot it again." Cukor told the press that "With many actresses you spend time lowering their ego so it doesn't get in the way of their performance. With Kay it's just the opposite, you've got to build up her self-confidence as you go along." Despite her nerves, Kay managed to do good deeds for two men in the cast: she asked that her friend Leslie Phillips be cast as her character's fiancé, Sir Gerald Wren, and she helped calm down Patrick MacNee, who was appearing in one of his first film roles, as a barrister. MacNee was, he remembers, "down and out, very broke, very frightened, very insecure." During a break in filming, Kay sauntered over to MacNee, "gave me a light kiss on the temple and murmured, 'Has anyone ever told you, you look just like Laurence Olivier?' I became ten feet tall and completed the day in a besotted trance."

Elg and MacNee recall the shooting fondly, but rumors later flew of Something Unpleasant happening on the set. Kay's agent Laurie Evans ominously clams up when the subject is broached. "There was an incident in [*Les Girls*] which I wouldn't ever discuss," says Evans. When pressed, he admits it involved Kay but repeats firmly, "Just . . . something happened that I'd rather not talk about." Taina Elg professes herself mystified by this: "Goodness, I have no idea!" she says. "I really have no clue." Whatever may or may not have happened, it never reached the gossip columns. The only things that Kay expressed real displeasure over were the cheesecake shots she had to pose for (MGM insisted she break her "no legs" rule) and the comic drunk scenes she had to play. "You can't believe how beastly it is to be known as 'that drunken lady who played the trumpet [in *Genevieve*],'" she moaned. "And then I had to play those boozy scenes in *Les Girls!* That's the only part of the picture I hated. . . . I expect I'm already in danger of going down in history as a dipsomaniac. If anyone ever offers me another drunken part I'll knock him on the head with my umbrella." She added sulkily that "The funny thing is, I don't even get to drink as much as I'd like to. Rex has a firm rule about liquor—no drinks until after the evening performance."

While Harrison tried to cover up his illicit relationship with Kay in New York, she talked openly about it to her Hollywood friends and co-workers. No one cared much; Hollywood was used to such affairs. Kay had no trouble reintroducing herself to old friends in the film capitol and meeting new ones. Hedda Hopper wrote, "Not since the late Carole Lombard laughed her way into the hearts of everyone who knew her has Hollywood known such a madcap personality as Kay." Hopper added acidly that "While I adore Kay, Rex is not one of my favorite people. I still remember the Carole Landis suicide and the part Harrison played in that." Kay was the honored party guest of Elizabeth Taylor, David Niven, Judy Garland, fellow *Caesar and Cleopatra* survivor Jean Simmons, Stewart Granger. Taina Elg had her to dinner, and the next night "the doorbell rang and I went to the door and there was a big basket of flowers that she left; she rang the bell and ran, so as not to be seen. That's the kind of thing she would do—she had these impulses and wit."

Kay's biggest thrill was a developing friendship with her idol, Bing Crosby—she even taught Gladys Cooper's Corgi to roll over in ecstasy at the sound of his name. When Kay met Crosby on the MGM lot, she babbled nervously about an older record of his that she'd been looking to buy but which no longer available in stores. During a recording session, Crosby knocked out a private version of it and had the record delivered to her. In return, Kay sent the singer a roomful of roses, delivered right in the middle of a recording session. During shooting, she somehow found the time and energy to visit Crosby in Palm Springs and to take a sightseeing tour of San Francisco. In fact, the high point of her Hollywood sojourn involved her new friend: "I remember when I was doing a difficult scene," she recalled. "Bing Crosby and Fred Astaire walked on to the set and watched me. Afterward they told me how much they enjoyed my performance. Now, *that* was a big thrill to me and very rewarding."

The press was delighted with Kay, who gave good interview—as long as her love life was not brought up. "Love is a serious and very private business with me," she said. "It's the one corner of my life I'd like to keep to myself." But Kay was more than willing to play the publicity game when it came to other subjects, from fashion to her own personality. "I guess people expect the cold, haughty English lady," she told UPI's Mosby. "Maybe it's because we come from a cold climate—or it's our voices. Frankly, I love the

American voice—much more attractive than ours. Very warm." *The New York Times Magazine* did a lengthy feature on Kay, during which she held forth against the pneumatic figures of current sex symbols Marilyn Monroe and Jayne Mansfield. "I feel so vitriolic about ladies with enormous bosoms," she fumed. "They give anybody who is my height and slightly flat-chested a bad name." For the *Times*, she let down her guard and spoke about Rex Harrison, who was much more important to her than her burgeoning career. "I don't want to do anything but be with Rex," she said. "I've had too many years of rushing around from hotel to hotel and town to town and waking up alone in the morning. I've had too many hundreds of years of being by myself." It was just the kind of romanticism fans wanted to read: But it gave chills to MGM and J. Arthur Rank.

Interviewers had to be wary, though—Kay's mood swings could be hard on them, as Joe Hyams (*The Herald Tribune*) and Charles Rice (*This Week*) discovered. She was in a snappish mood when Hyams arrived in her dressing room for a chat. "If you ask about my private life, I shall strike you," she said. When Hyams protested his innocent intentions, she continued: "I don't believe you're not going to ask me something personal. If you don't then you're the most unique journalist in show business." Hyams told her he merely wanted some background on her, and Kay quickly reeled off, "I'm thirty years old and I was born in Yorkshire and had an Irish father and I didn't play the trumpet in *Genevieve*." She then ushered Hyams to the door. He attempted to continue the interview, which went well enough until he noticed Kay's Corgi sitting in the corner contentedly eating her lipstick. When he innocently asked the dog's name, Kay snarled, "I knew it, you're just like all the rest," and tossed him out. A stagehand explained Hyams' mistake to him: the dog's full name was "June Cooper Harrison."

Charles Rice caught Kay on a much better day and treated her to dinner. "Can we have steak?" she batted her eyes at him. "I know it's frightfully expensive, but I haven't had a bite since teatime. And oysters first? The little ones?" Kay chatted happily about her film, her past, how much she adored Queen Elizabeth, and then asked if Rice wouldn't mind switching steaks with her? And might she have his peas instead of her spinach? While Rice tried to ply her on the subject of Rex Harrison, Kay wondered if she might eat some of his lemon ice. Kay then spun a good tale for Rice: Recalling how she'd dyed her hair gray while on tour in *Blithe Spirit*, she improvised one of her madcap adventures: "Some women go out and buy a hat," Kay said, "but I hate hats, so I go out and change my hair. The other day I had the strangest urge to see what I'd look like when I get old and crumbly, so I had my hair dyed gray." Kay went on about how she proudly came back to the hotel to show off her new look for her fiancé. She asked the bellboy in the lobby if Mr. Harrison was in, and he came back with, "Yes, ma'am, the desk clerk says your son just went up in the elevator." All highly improbable, but it wound up in Rice's story, ironically headlined "The Truth About English Girls."

Being a Hollywood star meant that Kay also had to cheerily hold forth on such subjects as fashions and diets. Kay had been beanpole-thin since her youth, but she still patiently and intelligently held forth to reporter Lydia Lane on her "diet tips," saying that "I have tried many diets, but my favorite keeps me from feeling hungry or thinking about food. . . . My big meal is breakfast. . . . because the food we eat early is usually burned up with the day's activities. If you start out well fed you are not concentrating on food or the next meal." The underweight actress added to the reporter that "I never let my weight get out of control so I do not need to be on this diet for more than a week."

Kay also chatted airily about clothes with the expertise of an established fashion plate: "I am happiest in tweeds or sweaters and skirts," she said, professing herself somewhat shocked by all the blinding glamour she encountered in Hollywood, and "these extremely low-cut dresses you see out here. . . . Englishwomen are shy and are brought up with the idea of not being noticed, of feeling it is a bit on the vulgar side to stand out," Kay huffed, apparently forgetting such British bombshells as Diana Dors and Joan Collins. Sounding more and more like Queen Victoria, she continued, "I wouldn't like to feel the only way I could get a man to notice me was with a plunging neckline. These [Hollywood] girls are so pretty they don't need that."

In mid-February, Rex Harrison took two weeks off from *My Fair Lady* and came out to visit a delighted Kay (he was replaced as Higgins by Edward Mulhare, who, coincidentally, would take Harrison's old role in *The Ghost and Mrs. Muir* when it became a TV series). Hollywood at large was not so delighted, and Harrison promptly got into a fight with another hot-tempered actor, Frank Sinatra. On February 16 (the day before Harrison's divorce from Lilli Palmer became final), the three were guests at the home of Kay's former beau, Charles Feldman, and his former wife, Jean Howard. Harrison found Kay and Sinatra outside on a balcony, en-

joying a tete-a-tete. He jealously grabbed Kay's arm and demanded that
she come home with him, and she lightly told him that she was admiring
Sinatra's shirt. "It's just an old shirt. Off-white," said Sinatra, pointedly
adding, "Sort of yellow." Harrison slapped Sinatra and the room ground to
a still halt. "It's still yellow," Sinatra said through clenched teeth before he
walked away.

The papers groped for an explanation for this bizarre incident: Was
the "yellow" comment a crack about Harrison's behavior all those years ago
with Carole Landis—or even a suggestion that Harrison's background was
of mixed race? No reason was ever given, though everyone remarked how
odd it was for the scrappy Sinatra not to have returned the blow. Bing
Crosby later brought Harrison and Sinatra together in Palm Springs, where
the two made up: "He could have gone on hitting me all night," said Sinatra,
uncharacteristically. "I admire the man so."

After *Les Girls* wrapped, Kay flew gratefully back to New York. The
Hollywood press wrote of her as a coming star and expected she would be
back time and again as roles and studio contracts were offered her. But Kay
was never to return to California. In New York, she and Harrison moved
from the Phipps home into "the Boathouse" on Jock Whitney's Long Island estate. Despite its offhand name, it was actually a large, luxurious,
and airy annex to the Whitney main house. *My Fair Lady* churned on and
on, and Kay went back to her lazy, casual life of socializing and shopping.

By this time, Carol Matthau knew of her friend's illness; Rex Harrison
had taken her to lunch at the Oak Room and filled her in. "I think Lilli
will spread it about," she recalls him telling her, "and you know practically
everyone in New York that we know. If you should hear it, make sure it is
denied by you as Kay's very best friend." Matthau did indeed hear it: she
remembers one "rather famous and fat" woman at a party gossiping about
how Kay Kendall was dying of cancer, that she had it straight from Lilli
Palmer. "I know that is not true," retorted Matthau, hotly. "I know what is
wrong with her—she has an ulcer, and it has been cured." Matthau got on
her high horse and told off the assembly: "What a terrible thing to say," she
snapped witheringly. "They're in the throes of breaking up a marriage and
you're attaching it to a lethal disease. You people!"

Matthau never did find out how the story of Kay's illness had spread
so quickly throughout New York society, but Harrison had let it slip to so
many people that it's not surprising. Only Kay herself, and Kay's family,
were never let in on the secret—though it was inevitable that some of the

rumors would reach Kay. "I've seen those wonderful ladies we both know," she told Matthau during a phone chat in 1957. "They're all horrors and liars."

When *Les Girls* opened later that year, Kay's stardom was assured. The film itself got a lukewarm reception: Porter's music was "unexceptional but cheerful," the script had "many small touches of wit, but also quite a few dull stretches." But everyone agreed that Kay Kendall was, in the words of *The American Weekly*, "a Sheraton highboy in a garden furniture department." *The New York Times* called her "a formidable match for Beatrice Lillie as a light comedienne," and another reviewer raved: "It is Kay Kendall who shines brightest. A lanky beauty of thoroughbred features, she is also a comedienne who can be funny in the mere tilting of an eyebrow, and the movie is at its best when she is on hand. . . . she is a constant pleasure and surprise."

MGM and Rank were also pleasantly surprised: Rank wanted Kay home to begin filming *Wyndham's Way*, to co-star Dirk Bogarde, and MGM offered her the role of Debbie Reynolds's headmistress in a musical called *The Girl Friend* (which, as it turned out, was never made). Kay blithely turned them both down; when she flew back to New York, Rex Harrison was waiting for her with a wedding ring.

Chapter Seventeen

"I just wanted that sense of being at home— my first real home."

On the morning of June 23, Kim got a call from her sister: "Darling, Rex and I have taken out the banns and we're going to get married after the show tonight, but I don't want the press to know. So don't wear anything too good-looking." Kim attended that night's performance of *My Fair Lady* and noticed Harrison nervously flubbing his lines. Shortly before midnight, the wedding party took off for the Upper West Side: Harrison in a suit, Kay in a beige silk shantung dress with pleats, a scarf wrapped around her hair. Besides Kim, they were joined by actress Margaret Leighton; Harrison's dresser, Manson; and his lawyer, Aaron Frosch.

The altar of the Universalist Church of the Divine Paternity came as rather a surprise to the wedding party, being decked out with symbols of every major religion. The man who conducted the service was, in his own way, as remarkable as the bride and groom. Charles Francis Potter had founded New York's first Humanist Society as well as Euthanasia of America, an early right-to-die foundation. He was an expert for the defense of John Scopes, the Tennessee teacher tried for teaching evolution in 1925's infamous "monkey trial." He had become a celebrity two years earlier by debating Fundamentalist Baptist preacher John Roach Straton—by 1957, Potter was as respected in the religious world as Rex Harrison was on Broadway.

The ceremony did not go smoothly: both bride and groom were highly nervous, and Kay veered between giggles and tears to the point where Potter threatened to call the whole wedding off if she did not calm down. With a squeezed hand and a kick in the shins from her intended, Kay managed to stifle herself. The ceremony ended in haste and confusion, as reporter Earl Wilson appeared from nowhere and began shooting photos. With cries of "oh, the horrid press!" the party dashed outside to their cars. At this point, Potter handed Kim the legal papers, which the newlyweds had neglected to sign. "Oh, I'm sorry, they're very emotional," Kim apologized, as she ran out into the night, waving the papers and screaming for Kay and Harrison to come back and make everything legal. The night ended at Orsini's restaurant, Kay sobbing into her spaghetti.

It was not the wedding she had always pictured, but at least she was safely and legally bound to the man she loved. Harrison's own emotions were more complicated: he had made himself a newlywed and a widower in one sweep. Genuinely concerned above all with Kay's happiness, he arranged for the Paleys and Leyland Hayward to throw them a "real" wedding on their adjoining Long Island estates about a week later. "The second time was great fun, and we both enjoyed it enormously," he recalled in later years.

Then, Kay settled happily into the role of the perfect 1950s housewife. She'd been an actress on the run for nearly all of her life and even as a child had had no settled home life. Her parents and her paternal grandparents had divorced, so Kay set all of her considerable energy into becoming the cheerful, supportive Hausfrau. "I was brought up an Englishwoman," she beamed contentedly. "I've married and I expect to go wherever my husband goes. I have no choice—even the *Queen* is an English wife." A reporter asked dubiously what would happen if Harrison were to bellow, "Kay! Where the devil are my slippers?" Kay retorted that "He wouldn't have to. His slippers would already be there." Friends of the couple knew full well that, in such a case, Kay would tell her husband exactly where he could put his slippers.

Kay even let her husband advise her on her clothes: "I never pay too much attention to the new collections," she told reporter Lydia Lane, "but Rex has wonderful taste and seems to know better than I what is right for me. I no longer dread going shopping when he goes with me." This was a bit much for Americans to take, even years before women's liberation took hold. Didn't British wives want equality with their husbands? "Not at all," Kay answered prettily for her countrywomen. "We'd rather have husbands than equality. There's something in Englishwomen's attitudes toward their husbands that might be worth thinking about," she lectured. "Though heaven knows we probably have a thousand small ways of irritating them that American women never thought of."

Kay was more than able to stand up for Harrison when necessary— and was also able to defuse dangerous situations with humor. Noel Harrison remembers a society party outside Paris, hosted by Diana Cooper. An "insufferably self-satisfied jet-set duchess" loomed up to the elder Harrison and said, "I saw you in *My Fair Lady* in New York. It was a matinee. I didn't think you were trying." Harrison was stunned silent for only a second before retorting, "Madam! Have you ever worked in your *life?!*" Kay leaped to her feet and shouted, "Come on, Rex! Come on, Noley! We're just *actors*, we don't belong here! We shouldn't have come through the front door—we'll go out through the kitchen!" which they did, says Noel Harrison, "and laughed all the way back to Paris."

During that leisurely summer of 1957, "I just did nothing for months," Kay later recalled. "I just wanted that sense of being at home—my first real home—in New York and going fishing or walking or just waiting for that final curtain." By this time, she could not bear to sit in the audience, unless a special friend really needed her company. More often, Kay would drop by backstage and socialize with the cast and crew, or with people playing at nearby theaters.

Kay and Harrison managed a belated honeymoon in mid-July. They flew to Jamaica, where they booked a cottage at Round Hill, a chic resort opened in 1954 by John Pringle, a self-described "control freak" ("I wanted to control every flower, every tree"). Round Hill had become the favored getaway of such social lions as Noël Coward, Claudette Colbert, Cole Porter, and William and Babe Paley. It should have been paradise—a relaxing week away from the press and *My Fair Lady*. But the honeymoon was a brief one: Harrison insulted a local with a racial epithet, and Pringle "saw him to the gate immediately." As Kay and Harrison packed and made their sullen way to the airport, Pringle was on the phone with gossip columnist Cholly Knickerbocker, assuring them of as much bad press as he could. The honeymooners arrived back in New York via a Pan American Clipper on July 22—hardly rested or relaxed.

June—Gladys Cooper's Corgi—having been returned to her owner, Kay devoted herself to her new pug dogs, Woolsack and Higgins, presented to her by Dirk Bogarde. Though Kay remained devoted to the dogs, Bogarde felt she treated them rather offhandedly. "The point was she was married to Rex," said Bogarde, "she was draped in mink, she was extremely rich, she was groomed, her life was Gucci and Pucci and . . . what she envisaged were two darling little pugs—they were a fashion accessory, and she had a pair. It took a very long time to get a pair because they were extremely unfashionable in those days and rather hard to find." "Oh, rubbish!" says Laurie Evans, who insists that both Harrisons adored the dogs and were distraught when they had to be quarantined for six months on re-entry to Britain. "Kay didn't need anything to enhance her image," he adds. "She had her own image and she was delighted with it."

In the fall of 1957, Harrison took another break from *My Fair Lady*, and the couple set sail for Europe and Harrison's Portofino house. Already, the press was guessing at Kay's true illness. It was during this getaway that Harrison first had to face head-on the job he'd undertaken. Kay came to him, puzzled, with an Italian magazine describing her battle with leuke-mia. "What rubbish they print," she said, hopefully. Harrison laughed, then blithely crumpled up the magazine and said, "Idiots—they meant 'anemia.' They obviously don't know what they're talking about." Kay also shrugged it off, but this was most likely the first inkling she had that her husband and her doctor were not being straight with her. That feeling would grow and become more pressing and ominous for her over the next few months, until her suspicions became undeniable. Harrison began to turn more and more against the press, telling a friend, "Is it possible to imagine the depravity of a man who will write a magazine article without caring whether or not Kay knew the truth? If anything proves how right I am to give the whole fucking press a wide berth, it's this."

Back in the U.S., Harrison took up the mantle of Henry Higgins again, and Kay finally shook off her newlywed laziness and realized she had to get back to work or go mad from boredom. Actress Polly Bergen hosted a variety show on TV that season, and Kay eagerly signed on as a guest. She made her U.S. TV debut on *The Polly Bergen Show* in October 1957. The episode co-starred comic actor Howard Morris, and among the skits was a version of the "Triplets" number from *The Band Wagon*, the three perform-ers dolled up like babies and dancing about on their knees.

Rex Harrison played his last Broadway performance of *My Fair Lady* on December 2, 1957. Kay was so delighted to see the end of this run that she cooked up a practical joke: She and director Moss Hart arranged to take the places of the performers playing the Queen of Transylvania and her escort in the Embassy Ball scene. Few people recognized the dark, com-pact Hart, but the theater buzzed with excitement and amusement when Kay made what was to be her only Broadway appearance.

Shortly before they returned to Britain, Kay shot an episode of *The Bilko Show*, starring Phil Silvers. Kay appeared as herself on the half-hour sitcom: on a promotional tour through the U.S., Kay lands in Fort Baxter, where the ever-devious Sergeant Bilko cons her into appearing in a production of *Romeo and Juliet*, for which he is secretly charging ten dollars a ticket. When Kay discovers this, she tricks him into returning the money by pretending to show up drunk (a bit of comedy business she was already heartily sick of). The script—co-written by future playwright Neil Simon— was pleasantly amusing and gave Kay the opportunity for some broad, funny exchanges with Silvers, a seasoned comic. The episode was broadcast in January 1958—but, because of the high residuals demanded by Rank, it was never rerun or put into syndication; *Bilko Presents Kay Kendall* has become a real collector's item for Silvers fans.

Chapter Eighteen

"They were just lost, they were so deeply in love with each other."

To celebrate the beginning of 1958—their first new year as husband and wife and, for all Harrison knew, their last—the couple took the Queen Mary from New York to Cherbourg. "We want rest, just rest," Harrison said—but in fact, the two were already deep in negotiations for a film together. Laurie Evans and his wife, Mary, met them in Southampton in the middle of a snowstorm, and Kay was having fits because her pug dogs had to go into quarantine. Kay took her new husband to her hometown to show him off to the family. They took rooms at Withernsea's Queen's Hotel and threw a reception: Kay's aunt Eva met Harrison and said in an aside to Gladys—in her broad Yorkshire accent—"'e's ower oud for *me!*" ["He's too old for *me!*"]

Kay and Harrison traveled to Switzerland to visit Charles and Oona Chaplin, and both narrowly missed being in Charles Chaplin's final two film projects. Harrison turned down the chance to star in *A Countess from Hong Kong*—Marlon Brando finally made it, nearly ten years later. Chaplin had also been considering Kay for the leading lady part in *A King in New York*, a pointed comedy poking fun at American TV and politics. She was delighted, and not a bit put off by Chaplin's problems with the U.S. government (his entry visa had been revoked in 1952). Producer Jerry Epstein, thinking to clinch the deal, ran off a copy of *Genevieve* for Chaplin. "It bored Charlie to tears," Epstein found, to his dismay. The plan backfired, as Chaplin decided against casting Kay: "She's too English," he said. "She has to be American." Epstein dreaded breaking the news, but "sweet Kay made it very easy for me." Kay's friendly attitude seems all the more remarkable, considering the "American" part went to Dawn Addams, who hailed from Felixstowe, Suffolk.

After visiting the Chaplins, Kay and Harrison took out a two-month lease on a chalet in St. Moritz, at one hundred pounds a week. It was small but had magnificent views of the Alps. It became somewhat smaller when playwright Terence Rattigan joined them as houseguest. Jack Buchanan's widow, Suzzie Dillon, recalls a weekend at Rattigan's house near Ascot at about this time, in company with Kay, Harrison, and actresses Vivien Leigh and Margaret Leighton. Kay's wicked sense of humor was in full flight: "Everyone knew that Terry had finished a new play," says Dillon. "The actress guests were trying to find out something about the play; whether or not there was a chance of a splendid leading lady role. Each used a different ploy to pry the details out of Terry, but he successfully avoided all." Non-professional Dillon had great fun watching her friends. "Each actress played her own scene, showing different sides of her personality; showing, in fact, that they could adapt to any role. Terry was bombarded with veiled questions, and such a personality parade of talent shown at lunch had seldom been seen."

Later, Dillon and Kay went out in the garden to have a nap in the sun, and Rattigan came by with Margaret Leighton, showing her the grounds. Leighton made a hugely theatrical entrance, still playing up to her host and sounding him out; this was too much for Kay, who "gave a wicked imitation of Maggie: the way she walked, tilted her head adoringly at her host and her fawning manner," says Dillon. "I don't know if Terry or Maggie heard. I tried to shush Kay, but she continued until Rex came out and told her to behave. She was a talented mimic." In an audible stage whisper, Kay told Dillon, "Oh, she won't get it, she's too *old*—if anyone does, it'll be Viv!"

Rattigan's presence in St. Moritz became a lifesaver to Harrison in early 1958, as Kay quickly fell ill—very ill, indeed. Harrison found a doctor from Zurich, who examined Kay and had her quickly shipped off to a clinic in St. Moritz, where she ran a high temperature and hovered perilously between life and death. Harrison "roamed around the town of St. Moritz, lost." His sons came to offer moral support (it was then that Harrison confided Kay's true condition to Noel), and Rattigan accompanied him to the town's tourist sites. A local professor was experimenting with leukemia medications, and Harrison agreed to try out these new pills (along with blood transfusions) on Kay: within three weeks her blood count was back to normal, and she was able to slowly gain her strength back in the Alpine chalet. A cover story was sent out to the press: "It was a flareup of an old liver condition and she is now out of the hospital," one paper printed on January 3.

There were a number of treatments available for chronic myelocytic leukemia in the mid-1950s, though none could do more than alleviate symptoms for a year or two. One text noted, "treatment, though it may not increase survival time by more than 6 months or a year, can for much of the time make the difference between a state of chronic invalidism and a condition of well-being which may approach normality." This is what Harrison and her doctors hoped to achieve for whatever time Kay had left. Radiation therapy (roentgen ray and radioactive phosphorus) were commonly used—though this was never tried on Kay, probably because there was no way to do this without giving up the charade.

Blood transfusions were recommended only sparingly and conventional wisdom at the time decreed that they "should be reserved for very serious bleeding, since such transfusions lose their effectiveness in time." But, for whatever reason, Kay was given transfusions rather frequently and was told she was being treated for anemia. As far as drugs, Kay's St. Moritz doctor may have been trying out some of the latest therapies on her. Triethylenemelamine was a powerful hematopoietic depressant but could also be quite toxic; chlorambucil was often better tolerated by the patient. For short-term cycles, busulfan in daily doses could also be effective; or demecolcin, if the former drug didn't seem to work. For the next year and a half, Kay's various doctors—first Atchley in the U.S., then Goldman in Britain—would experiment with a combination of these medications and transfusions—never, of course, consulting Kay herself about her course of treatment.

In one of the few interviews about her illnesses, Kay spoke to a reporter shortly after this bout. "It was to be our first real holiday," she said. "We would climb up mountains and things, and it would be wonderful. That was the idea. And then," she recalled, "I fell ill. I had to go to bed almost as soon as we arrived. I became so ill I thought I was going to die. For two whole nights Rex sat by my bed. Whenever I opened my eyes he was there. . . . He got no rest at all." Kay had little to do during her agonizingly slow recovery but think, and she "decided that nothing in work was really worth getting ulcers over and what I wanted most was a home and security and my career could come after that." Perhaps she didn't yet realize intellectually that she was going to die—but Kay was starting to put her affairs in order emotionally.

She soon got well enough to go tobogganing during a visit to the writer Colette in Klosters. "No one and nothing could keep Katie down," said Harrison. "She had the courage of a lion." Unfortunately, she also had the tobogganing skills of a lion: Kay tipped out of her toboggan and found herself in excruciating pain when she tried to climb back to the top of the slope. Back to the clinic in Zurich, where she had so recently cheated death: an X ray revealed a hairline fracture of her pelvis. Not serious; it would soon mend, as long as she lay still and didn't exert herself. The only problem was that Kay was due to start shooting her next film in March, and she still had to go through costume fittings, rehearsals, and lighting tests. Not to mention passing a studio medical exam for insurance purposes.

Ever since they had married, Kay and Harrison had been looking for a project to do together. It finally came in the form of *The Reluctant Debutante*, which had been a modestly successful play on Broadway and in London. MGM's Pandro Berman sent the script to director Vincente Minnelli, who was just finishing post-production on *Gigi*. Berman and Minnelli both saw it as the perfect vehicle for the Harrisons: a daffy upper-class British couple who introduce their teenage daughter into society. Minnelli sent the script off to Harrison in Switzerland; he looked it over and telephoned back: "We'd love to do it, but the script is no good." Rewrites were tried out, but Harrison responded with, "We wouldn't play one word of that lousy script!"

William Douglas Home, the show's original playwright, was called in—and, happily, he turned out to be more than amenable. Home got along famously with Kay and Harrison—and indeed wound up nursing the script through the whole shooting process, sometimes adapting Harrison's "requests" that night for the next day's filming. Home later recalled an incident that typified Kay's joy in shocking the timid: he and Harrison were busy opening a champagne bottle in the Harrisons' Lancaster Hotel suite in Paris when the phone began ringing. Kay—as the only woman present—was expected to answer, despite the fact that she was in the bathtub. "Kay! Get the phone!" Harrison yelled. The next moment, Kay emerged, dripping wet, with a towel wrapped around her head but otherwise stark naked. She blithely picked up the phone and accepted a weekend dinner invitation from the British Ambassador, warning him politely that "Rex and I like to dip our fingernails in the gin bottle on Saturday night, if you know what I mean." Kay waved goodbye to the stunned Home and sashayed back into the bathroom. "The most splendid girl in the world," Home summed up.

MGM coughed up a hundred thousand dollars to the Rank Organisation for Kay's services, and the wheels were set in motion. The happy couple flew to Paris, where the film had to be hurriedly shot in March 1958 so that Harrison could return to London in time for his *My Fair Lady* opening on the West End. The medical examination by MGM's doctors was not the horror that Rex Harrison had been fretting over: it was very cursory and involved no blood tests. Kay was having a good day and passed with flying colors: even her mending pelvis didn't seem to faze the physicians. Indeed, Kay managed to disguise her recuperation as a bit of movie-star glamour: she gave all of her pre-production interviews swathed in chiffon, draped elegantly over a chaise longue. No one (not even director Minnelli) suspected that walking was still problematic for her.

Only costume designer Pierre Balmain knew that Kay was in any pain; he accommodated her by doing as many of her fittings and pinnings horizontally as was possible. It paid off; her clothes in this film are a delight: a series of slim sheath gowns, with voluminous wraps of fur or feathers or chiffon. Kay looked a treat, her hair streaked auburn and gold and feathered into an elegant bouffant.

The Reluctant Debutante was a very British story; few foreigners would know about debutantes being presented to the Queen or care about the end, that year, of this tradition. But the movie had to be filmed (except for some establishing exteriors) in France because of Harrison's tax status. MGM's press attaché recounted some of the difficulties of shooting a British film in Paris: "Moving the London airport to Paris, shooting in the streets without catching a side glimpse of the Eiffel Tower or the Arc de Triomphe, and combing French schools for English teenagers. . . . I'm sure that every Britisher in Paris appeared at least once in the film." Harrison was not made any happier by the casting of very American teen heartthrobs Sandra Dee and John Saxon as the youthful love interests: the film was becoming less and less English by the minute. Sandra Dee was explained away as Harrison's daughter by an American first wife, raised in the U.S. Saxon's status as an Italian duke was tougher to buy. Providing another sharp comic partner for Kay was Angela Lansbury, who played Kay's bitchy social competitor.

Kay's only injunction to Minnelli, he recalled, was "Careful how you photograph my Cyrano nose, darling." The only trouble she caused during filming was on her husband's behalf—and Minnelli suspected that Harrison put her up to it. One night they both came rushing to the director's hotel room, Kay waving the script and shouting, "My husband is the world's greatest actor—I have a part that is so good, and he needs more to do! Look at this scene. I have fifty lines of dialogue and he has only three. You've got to rewrite this." Minnelli assured the two that the scene—wherein Kay and Harrison listen to actor Peter Myers drone on and on about London traffic—would hinge upon Harrison's comic reactions. "And that's exactly what happened," Minnelli later affirmed. Harrison continued to use Kay as his mouthpiece. He would tell her what he wanted changed, what he didn't like, and she would face down Vincente Minnelli. Harrison would stand behind her and bark, "Yes! Yes!"

Kay worked hard on this film, despite occasional bouts of fever and weakness. One day she had particular trouble with her trademark physical comedy, a simple little trip on a staircase. "I told Vincente Minnelli, a dear, sweet man, that I couldn't do it. It was much too difficult. I was almost in tears with frustration and anger trying to get it right. Ten times I did it. *Ten times*."

But still, Kay managed to have fun on the set, recalls John Saxon. Saxon himself was having a good time, flirting with the many female extras—Kay found this adorable and "would greet me each morning in makeup with, 'good morning, old cock,'" he says. One day, while filming her closeups, Kay invited her young co-star out to lunch. "We went to a very nice restaurant," he recalls, "and Kay ordered a full bottle of very good French wine. I'm sure I said something like, 'that was too much wine for me at lunch,' but she insisted." Once back at the set, the closeups did not go as smoothly as they had that morning: "I was behind the camera delivering my lines to her, and each time she was to respond she looked at me and began to giggle. I can't remember how many times this occurred, but it did last some time. And I do remember Minnelli being very annoyed and looking at me, wondering if he could put the blame for this on me."

Kay seemed to have completely recovered from her illness of a month earlier, and no one on the set suspected that she was slowly dying. "It never crossed my mind that Kay was seriously ill," said author Home. "Just the reverse: she seemed in a continuous mood of endearing unpredictability— and would do anything for a joke." Only Harrison and perhaps director Minnelli knew, the latter telling his wife that Kay was "in very delicate health." Lee Minnelli feels that Harrison tipped off the director to make filming easier for Kay: "Vincente was very careful how he handled her, that she didn't get tired or anything."

Dirk Bogarde and Tony Forwood had helped the Harrisons settle in

Paris, smuggling them past the press off the boat at Cherbourg and moving them into the Lancaster, where MGM had booked them. Bogarde paid back some money that Harrison had loaned him, "a big roll of pound notes." Kay snipped the elastic band holding it together and the roll burst open in the bathroom, where she was running the shower and Harrison was trying to shave. "She went 'wheeee!' and sent four hundred pounds worth of notes all over the bathroom," recalled Bogarde. "I was so angry. . . . I was going round the lavatory picking up wet notes and putting them in my pocket." But that month in Paris Bogarde also saw a more romantic side to the pair. After dinner at a West Bank café, the Harrisons said they'd rather walk back to their hotel. Bogarde and Forwood drove off in their Rolls. "I remember looking out of the back of the Rolls and seeing these two figures in a huge embrace in the middle of a traffic island. All there was beyond them was the Place de la Concorde with the fountains going and all the traffic lights going red, yellow and green, and they were just lost, they were so deeply in love with each other," Bogarde remembered.

The only other cast member staying at the Lancaster was Angela Lansbury, who had a tiny penthouse—a far cry from the huge suite shared by the Harrisons. The pair took her under their wing and frequently invited her to dinner at their favorite restaurant, La Paruse. She recalls Rex Harrison—usually "terribly self-involved and self-important and putting people down left, right and center"—as unusually well-behaved and friendly on this shoot. He took over a local bistro and insisted the cast have decent lunches and carefully made sure everything was done to keep Kay as comfortable as possible. Kay would show up the morning "looking absolutely gray and tired, but by the time the boys got through with her makeup and hair and everything, she looked absolutely ravishing," Lansbury says.

Lee Minnelli remembers that Kay and Harrison "were wonderful together. He adored her. You could see when he looked at her, his eyes lit up. They balanced each other perfectly—they played off each other." But she also noticed how quickly Kay tired during filming, though "she did everything to be wonderful and lovely and full of the joy of life. If she came into a room, she had us all laughing in five minutes. Even if you felt a little down, you talked to Kay and by the time you left you were floating, you were up in the air."

The only real unpleasantness during filming came from Harrison, not Kay: his *My Fair Lady* co-star Stanley Holloway gave an interview portraying Harrison as an arrogant boor, heartily disliked by the cast and crew:

"When Rex was leaving the show he gave a small cocktail party for the cast and stage hands," said Holloway. "Not a single stage hand showed up." Holloway's complaints were no doubt spot-on; Harrison was well-known for being difficult. But that sort of public backstabbing was simply not done; certainly not in the midst of a long run. Kay was in a particularly uncomfortable spot, as Holloway was a friend who had appeared in five movies with her. Harrison threatened to sue Holloway, who apologized and claimed to have been misquoted. But it didn't make either of the Harrisons look forward to their London homecoming and the imminent West End opening of *My Fair Lady*.

Kay gave post-production interviews to the press, trying her best to be cooperative. Sounding every inch the gracious movie star, she told reporters, "Most important was the fact that we worked together as husband and wife in the film, a chance that seldom comes in a careertime." Soon, the graciousness dropped and Kay's humor (and her insecurities) showed through: "I was frightened out of my wits," she laughed. "I told Rex that they would no doubt have to photograph me through layers of old kitchen curtains. All of the directors in England have complained about my face." Harrison tried to silence her by breaking in: "Nonsense—look at me. They always claimed that my face was too long to photograph, but I've been around films for twenty years."

Harrison was not only giving Kay acting tips but performing as her personal Henry Higgins as well. "He's always telling me I don't talk properly," she meekly admitted. "The other night we were having a splendid argument and I called him a bloody turncoach. He said, 'You mean bloody turncoat, you silly wench!' And he was right, of course." Depending on her moods, Kay either took this from him with gratitude or chucked a vase at his head. Some of his advice was actually helpful and supportive: "Rex also taught me to be critical and to take criticism without bursting into tears," Kay said in one of her post-*Debutante* interviews. "He also taught me not to worry about the way I look. I was always worried by my appearance— like a greyhound, too long and lean."

Reviewers were lukewarm toward the film but loved the leading couple—especially Kay. *The New York Times* called *The Reluctant Debutante* "thin and boneless" but fell all over itself about the leading lady: "If there are any doubts that Miss Kendall is a super-slick comedienne, her work . . . should dispel them. . . . Small talk becomes a minor art as she voices it." London's *Evening News* enthused, "Is Kay Kendall the most splendid thing in comediennes the screen has found since the end of the war? Yes! Yes!" Critic Fred Majdalany wrote that Kay was "now securely in the chair long left vacant by the death of Gertrude Lawrence." Only William Peper voiced the opinion that the script and Minnelli "have required her to be so unrelievedly scatterbrained that she gets a bit tiresome after awhile."

The Reluctant Debutante holds up fairly well today—but, like *Les Girls*, it runs on far too long and could have done with some judicious trimming. It is a beautiful, lush film with flashes of dry wit, the Harrisons stealing it from the rest of the talented cast. Kay and Harrison played off each other like the expert team they were: Kay dithering madly, Harrison gazing at her baffled through his poached-egg eyes; they were like a British George Burns and Gracie Allen. Their funniest scene came while alternately hiding in the kitchen and making "passion noises" for the other in the parlor to see if they would be able to hear Sandra Dee being molested by John Saxon. Kay was particularly good in a stammering monologue, simultaneously talking on the phone to Angela Lansbury and admonishing Sandra Dee: "Now, write this down and—stop picking your nose—oh, Mabel, darling, don't be silly, I was talking to Jane. You were, too? What a strange coincidence."

But *The Reluctant Debutante* was, at the dawn of the 1960s, part of a dying breed, a throwback to the cocktails-and-moonlight days of Noël Coward and Ivor Novello. In order to compete with darker, modern theater and the immediacy of television, films had also been veering toward realism and kitchen-sink dramas. Ealing comedies were giving way to black-and-white dramas of lorry drivers, and low-budget horror flicks. Sweetie-pie youngsters like Sandra Dee and John Saxon were fast becoming outdated in an age of youth revolt and Angry Young Men. Kay, only thirty-one years old, seemed like a vision from another age next to the velvet-collared Teddy Boys and incipient Mods who were commanding the tabloid headlines (rock 'n' roll had invaded the country by 1958, but Kay remained loyal to Bing Crosby). One jarring scene in *The Reluctant Debutante* came when Kay whirled Harrison frantically around while a band played "Rock Around the Clock." It was like seeing Elvis Presley doing a minuet.

Other film stars, too, were emerging to compete with Kay's old-style glamour and elegance. Tousle-haired waifs such as Brigitte Bardot and Juliette Greco foreshadowed the 1960s, with their bare feet, blue jeans, and casual chic. As much as she liked going about in slacks and no makeup in private, Kay was still an old-fashioned film star: in public she was dressed to the nines, her hair teased and sprayed into perfection and her jewels glittering. Kay even had a new movie-star car to swan about in: she and Harrison bought a six-thousand-pound Rolls-Royce in the spring of 1958 to complete their glittering status. Harrison had also bought Kay a luxurious fur coat, but Woolsack and Higgins chewed it to pieces when she left it unguarded.

Chapter Nineteen

"Diggy, I think I'm dying . . . and they won't tell me."

Kay and Harrison returned to London on April 4 to prepare for the London opening of *My Fair Lady* at the Drury Lane Theatre on April 30. They rented the home of the Earl of Warwick in Swan Walk but soon had a falling-out that resulted in Kay's going house-shopping. "I'm looking for a home," she told reporter David Lewin that spring. "Something for Rex and me—not too big. A study for Rex and a garden for me and the two dogs. We'll be here for a year, and you can't live in an hotel for all that time, can you?" She soon found a nice eighteenth-century house in Chelsea, on Cheyne Row, and the couple settled in for the rest of 1958. "We've never had a home for three years, we've always rented houses," Kay said, hopefully talking about buying a house in London by 1960, although "we most probably . . . will find ourselves working in New York." Renting these lovely old homes was not as glamorous as people might think, she explained. "I'm always sitting in corners sobbing and weeping because I've got to pack up again."

Opening night was an all-star event: Kay (by now able to recite the entire play by heart), Dirk Bogarde, Harrison's sister and brother-in-law, the play's authors and producers (including Moss Hart and his wife, Kitty Carlisle; Alan Jay Lerner; and Frederick Loewe), a smattering of British and Hollywood royalty. To no one's surprise, the play and Harrison were huge hits and could have played for years had the star not insisted on a one-year-only contract. Two weeks into the run, a Gala Performance was given for the Queen and Prince Philip. Kay wore one of her *Reluctant Debutante* gowns with a huge white ostrich-feather boa that she had dyed pink. When she saw the boa being dragged across the floor to the cloakroom after the show, she threw herself at it, screaming, "Oh, beat it, beat it! Kill it with a stick!" much to the press' amusement.

Vivien Leigh's godson and Rex's future biographer Roy Moseley attended an opening-night party Kay hosted at the Drury Lane. "Everyone was there," he recalls, "absolutely *everyone*. Katie was ecstatically happy, the happiest I've ever seen her; dispensing champagne, saying this was much better than the Broadway production. An exquisite hostess, and so proud of Rex." She also won Moseley's affection by standing up to her friend Dirk Bogarde: "I had just come in and Dirk was extremely unpleasant to me, ordered me out. Kay heard that and said, 'That's no way to behave, this young man is very welcome at my party!'"

After the opening, Kay became philosophical, as she settled in to play patient housewife to "Professor Higgins" again. "I'm thirty now, and I have been working—more or less—since I was eleven," she told reporter Lewin. She was happy, she insisted, not to be filming herself: "I'd have to get up at six in the morning, and I'd be back home from the studios at seven in the evening. At seven in the evening Rex would be at the theater, and by the time he was through by eleven I'd have to be in bed to get up again by six the following morning. That is not a satisfactory married life." But Kay was not prepared to give up show business altogether. Despite her increasing weakness and her continuing happiness in marriage, she never for a moment lost her urge to act. "What I'd really like to do is a play," she said. "Then Rex and I would have every day together. I'm reading scripts like mad now—but everything I have been offered is a star part," and that frightened her to no end. "I have never starred in anything in the West End . . . and I don't think I should start off as the main lead."

Whatever help her Swiss doctor's pills were doing was wearing off, and in the spring and summer of 1958, Kay began to fade again. She collapsed and had to be hospitalized while vacationing in St. Moritz. A Dr. P.R. Berry told the press that she was suffering from appendicitis, and after a few days she and Harrison were able to take off for a Cote d'Azur holiday with Kay's friend Lilian and her future husband, Prince Bertil of Sweden.

By the summer of 1958, Kay was finding it more difficult to play innocent about her physical condition. All the hospitalizations, the constant transfusions, the newspaper accounts of her leukemia—blithely dismissed by her husband as anemia—were impossible to laugh off. Kay was not a stupid woman, and no one can be that sick for that long without knowing something is seriously wrong. But the only direct evidence that Kay knew of her dire situation comes from Dirk Bogarde. Kay had fled from London that summer to stay with Bogarde and Forwood at Beel House.

Bogarde missed Kay during a croquet game and found her in the aviary, "shivering and pinched, humped into a corner." Suddenly weak and terrified, she begged Bogarde to finally tell her the truth: "Diggy, I think I'm dying. I've got some terrible disease and they won't tell me. I think I've got cancer."

This put Bogarde into a terrible spot: he had promised Harrison never to tell Kay of her condition, but here was his best friend, obviously panicked and beginning to get rather paranoid. Her doctors, her friends, her husband, were conspiring to keep her in the dark about her health. Kay didn't know who she could trust anymore. Bogarde kept his promise to Harrison and tried to laugh off her fears: "Balls! Of course you haven't, don't be such an idiot. . . . You've probably got the curse or something." Kay shook her head and said, "I've got something . . ." Bogarde was convinced from then on that Kay knew perfectly well what the game was. "She was no fool," he said years later. "You don't sit huddled up in a mink coat on the hottest day of the year, begging for Guinness and port . . ."

Even Dr. Atchley's son William—himself a doctor—admits today that his father knew that Kay wasn't taken in. "She was playing the opposite game," he says. "She didn't want to let on and upset Harrison. It was a matter of spy and counterspy. It was a matter of who was the better actor in this loving deceit."

While Rex continued in *My Fair Lady*, Kay kept herself busy looking about for projects and socializing with friends in London. In August, she appeared at the annual 100 Stars charity show at the London Palladium, doing a costume skit with Margaret Leighton, Joyce Grenfell, and Julie Wilson. That same month, Noël Coward offered Kay a Broadway role in *South Sea Bubble*; Vivien Leigh had appeared in the play's brief West End run in 1957. But Kay refused to leave Rex. Coward sighed that she was "fairly scatty anyhow. It is sad to think how many of our glamorous leading ladies are round the bend. . . . I am getting a little tired of badgering leading ladies to play a wonderful part in a jolly good comedy" (*South Sea Bubble* didn't make it to Broadway, achieving only a brief run in Connecticut). On August 24, Coward wrote in his diary of his "high-powered, tear-diffused, heart-to-heart talks" with Lilli Palmer. Palmer was "still carrying a torch for Rex, although she loves Carlos." As for Kay, "The poor dear may have behaved badly in the first place when she went bald-headed after Rex, but having got her own way she is certainly paying a ghastly price for it."

As time went on, Kay and Harrison became more reclusive and drew further into themselves. No one at the time knew it, but Harrison was terrified of her illness becoming more known than it already was: Kay—and her secret—belonged to him, and he was not disposed to share her even with her family and best friends. By 1958, she was becoming a bit distant, a bit hard to reach. "She was his possession," said her old friend Peggy Dexter. "He isolated Kay and we sort of grew apart." In addition, Dexter added pointedly, the snobbish Harrison "wasn't thrilled with her relationship with me at all—he thought I was just a chorus girl, and beneath her." Harrison also discouraged Kay's friendship with her sister: "He broke a friendship like he broke a family trust with us," says Kim.

In September 1958 Harrison arranged for some time off and he and Kay made for Portofino. Lilli Palmer, who had used the house that summer, politely vacated in time for them to move in. Kay was beginning to get restless: the charity show and turning down *South Sea Bubble* had reminded her that she had not acted onstage in quite some time. As fun as it had been to show up in a Broadway cameo the night of Harrison's closing, it rankled somewhat that he was so far outpacing her careerwise. So Kay began casting about for a show to appear in.

It had been on her mind for some time. In mid-1958, she reiterated to Lowell E. Redelings that she "couldn't possibly do a picture now." She would be at the studio all day and Harrison would be on stage all night: "What kind of marriage would it be?" Scripts were coming in, but she was being very choosy about which role would best showcase her. "To jump into such responsibility would be frightening. What I'd really like is a good supporting role, preferably one in which I'm killed off in the first act, or shortly thereafter!"

The vehicle she finally settled on was by first-time playwright Judy Campbell, an actress who used the pen name J.M. Fulton. Noël Coward, also a friend of Campbell's, had steered the two women toward each other: "Noël would do anything for people he was fond of," says Roy Moseley, "so he helped put this together." *The Bright One* was an eight-character, three-act comedy about studious botanist Agatha Purvis, who, while vacationing in Greece, is possessed by the spirit of an ancient nymph. Zaniness, as it tends to do, ensues: the reborn nymph romances a sporty American and a hearty English farmer; a jealous Zeus materializes as a swan, a bull, and a thundercloud. The mix-up ends up with Agatha married, pregnant, struck by lightning, and finally vacated by her ghostly inhabitant. The whole feeling of the project went against longtime stage professional Rex Harrison's better judgment: not only was the vehicle itself extremely flimsy and overly whimsical, but the strain of rehearsing and performing—on time, every night—might prove to be too much for Kay. But, as he told Bogarde, "If I hadn't made Kate do it, she'd have been immediately suspicious that I'd changed my mood and that I was concerned for her, because if I was concerned for her, then something really *is* wrong with her. I wasn't going to do that."

Hugh McDermott and Michael Gwynn were cast as Kay's romantic leading men, and stage great Gladys Cooper played the British farmer's wry grandmother. Cooper, then sixty years old, had been a World War I pin-up girl and a star since 1922, when she had appeared in Pinero's *The Second Mrs. Tanqueray*. Her career had been one stage and screen success after another since then, and she was a good friend of the Harrisons' (she'd already loaned Kay her Corgi, and later played Henry Higgins's mother in the film version of *My Fair Lady*). Kay sighed happily about being back onstage, airing her feeling that "In the movies, let's face it, you're making faces at a camera. . . . Onstage, there's just the two of you—you and your audience. There's more satisfaction in it."

Kay dumped the logistics of the play into Harrison's lap. He convinced his friend Jack Minster, a producer and former BBC newscaster, to invest heavily. Harrison borrowed the rest of the money from various friends and booked the Winter Garden Theatre on Drury Lane. Then, another problem: Kay insisted—forcefully and with occasional hysterics—that her husband direct the show. He was still starring nightly in *My Fair Lady*, of course, and it may have been jealousy of that play as well as her own insecurities that made Kay demand Harrison direct her during the day while working nights.

A very nervous Kay opened in previews in Brighton on November 24. She missed several performances as the play moved to Liverpool and then to London, where it had its debut on December 10. The show was presold to the tune of one thousand pounds, many fans anxious to see Kay in person. But reviews doused the cast and potential customers with ice water. *The Bright One*, said the *London Observer*'s reviewer, "has all the English whimsy that is the curse of our stage. Everybody is so delightfully 'crazy' and lovably 'goofy' that it made me more depressed than I've felt for a long time." Critic Milton Shulman added that Harrison's directing "is as prosaic as my bank statement, and about as depressing."

Only Kay herself came through relatively unscathed. "Her anarchic brand of inspired fooling is delightful to watch," wrote Shulman, and *Variety* agreed that "Whatever success the production may achieve will be almost exclusively due to Miss Kendall's delicious and supremely witty performance." *Punch* wrote encouragingly that "she does everything she could for it, changing delightfully from the hockey-striding confidence of the schoolmarm to the wide-eyed mischief of the intruder." Only the *London Times* took her to task: "Miss Kay Kendall talks rather as a well brought up young lady would talk if somebody had told her that she was really a pagan nymph."

"Kay Kendall saved the evening," critic Felix Barker optimistically wrote. But nothing could save *The Bright One*: Kay's weakness (she missed several performances) and bad reviews doomed it from opening night. After ten days, co-producer Jack Minster pulled the plug, and closing notices were posted. Kay was furious, and Harrison agreed that "the play has not been given a chance. . . . I thought [it] should have been allowed to carry on over Christmas." Kay burst into tears watching Gladys Cooper and the stage hands packing up after the final curtain: "I was crying because of the people left with no jobs over Christmas and no compensation," she said.

Jack Minster was made the villain of the piece, and the following day a "damned angry" Kay raged to the press: "I never want to speak to the man again!" Blissfully ignorant of the backing arrangements, she added that "Rex and I have lost all our savings—everything. . . . The financial disaster . . . was my fault because it was I who discovered the play and persuaded Rex to put up the money." Within a few days, Harrison had calmly explained to her that they were quite all right financially, that only Minster himself and the many friends from whom Harrison had borrowed money were taking the loss. As UPI dryly noted, "Harrison will still be able to afford his $16,800 Rolls-Royce automobile and most of the other finer things of life." Jack Minster, when contacted, had his secretary issue a statement that he was "maintaining a dignified silence." Playwright Judy Campbell was tracked down, and she snapped that "It was my first play. I have had enough hell over it. I want to forget it all."

In retrospect, it's not surprising that the show failed in 1958; airy-light froth like *The Bright One* was going out of style on the West End. Absurdism (Samuel Beckett's 1955 *Waiting for Godot*) and bleak kitchen-sink dramas (most notably John Osborne's 1956 *Look Back in Anger* and Shelagh Delaney's 1958 *A Taste of Honey*) changed not only theater but TV and movies as well. Imports from France (Jean-Paul Sartre, Jean Genet) and America (Arthur Miller, Lee Strasberg's "method" acting) further pushed the British theater toward a new style. But Kay was still a part of the bright and glittering show business of Noël Coward and Gertie Lawrence—fey flirtations, cocktails, and evening clothes. Though still a young woman, her day was passing, and she had more in common with Oscar Wilde than with Bertold Brecht. Only musicals seemed unaffected: not only was *My Fair Lady* a hit but the 1950s saw successful runs for *The King and I, Guys and Dolls,* and *South Pacific,* among others. But *The Bright One*—which might have enjoyed a respectable run ten years earlier—didn't have a chance.

Kay had grown up quite a bit since the disastrous failure of *London Town* had all but destroyed her. Now, she had other priorities in life and was able to shake off the precipitous closing of *The Bright One*. She had her marriage, her friends, all of London at her feet. Reporters who flocked to her door still saw her as a viable star, and one who provided good copy. As 1959 began, she seemed to be in top form and good humor.

Kay told one reporter that she preferred beautiful women as her female friends: "They are less inclined to be catty, and I like to feel safe from gossip when I leave a room." Early in 1959, she began palling around with two women who certainly fit the bill: Lauren Bacall (who had lost her husband, Humphrey Bogart, two years earlier) and Vivien Leigh (whose tempestuous marriage to Laurence Olivier was in one of its down cycles). The three night-clubbed, dined, and went to the theater all through the early months of 1959, providing newspapers with fodder for their gossip columns and fashion pages alike ("The Gay Trio Who Are the Talk of the Town!"). "Suddenly everyone's talking about Vivien, Betty [Bacall] and me as though we were up to something sinister," Kay laughed. "We all love going to the theater. It's our passion, our homework." Leigh shrugged, "We just like being together and seeing plays and doing jigsaws, anything, in fact."

Bacall was soon off to make a film in India, but Kay stayed close to Leigh. In fact, Kay's only political activities (minor as they were) came through her left-wing, liberal friend. Early in 1959, the two women joined a march demonstrating in favor of integrated schools in London. Kay tried to perk up her husband's enthusiasm for her new-found social conscience, with no luck whatsoever. The couple, while strolling in London at about this time, encountered a group picketing against a South African apartheid ruling that separated white and black universities. A photographer for the *Evening Standard* caught a photo of Kay marching under a banner reading

"Education Has No Colour Bar" and eagerly quizzing participants. A few minutes of this was all Harrison could take, and he ushered his wife into a cab.

Kay and Vivien Leigh also spent their free hours with an informal "Theatre Wives Club for Saturday Lunch," composed of themselves; Ralph Richardson's wife, Muriel; and Jack Buchanan's widow, Suzzie Dillon. "They were very happy times," recalls Dillon. The group would often go to "riotous luncheons at Les Ambassadeurs," or to a film, where "the remarks made by my actress pals were often audible, critical and amusing. The mere presence of such stars in a movie audience would cause considerable attention, and usually the manager would rescue us from the autograph seekers when the film was over."

Dillon also brings up the possibility that Kay might have undergone a hysterectomy at about this time. Kay's sister Kim remembers her making hopeful noises after her marriage about having children, or at least adopting a daughter, since Harrison already had two sons. But soon talk of becoming a mother faded away. Dillon remembers a lunch appointment for which Kay arrived late and "not up to her usual form." She explained to Dillon that she'd been to the doctor, "and he had told her he thought it wise for her to have a procedure to prevent her from becoming pregnant, as she had a blood disorder. He assured her that the operation would be reversible so that she could have a child later on if she so wished." Dillon found this ambiguous, to say the least, but she didn't pry. That night, a call from Vivien Leigh cleared things up: Leigh had heard the truth about Kay's condition from Harrison, who was doing a very poor job at keeping it a putative "secret." By now, it seemed that half of London knew that Kay had leukemia, but everyone kept their hopes up that Kay herself was still in the dark.

Chapter Twenty

"If you think I'm coming here to die, you're wrong!"

An important but increasingly dreary chapter in Kay's life closed on March 30, when Rex Harrison played his final London performance in *My Fair Lady*. Kay finally felt herself free from Professor Higgins. She and Harrison could now start looking about for film, theater, and television projects to do together. While Laurence Olivier and Vivien Leigh were hardly good role models for a working marriage, there was still Lunt and Fontanne to pattern themselves after. Hume Cronyn and Jessica Tandy (married since 1942) and youngsters Paul Newman and Joanne Woodward (married just the previous year) were making a go of it, too—no reason why Kay and Harrison couldn't share the stage.

For the time being, however Kay stayed professionally inactive. Through the early months of 1959, she remained at liberty, just enjoying the luxury of free time with her husband. The closest things to work she did were appearing as a panelist on the TV quiz show *What's My Line?* and making a guest appearance on an episode of *This Is Your Life* devoted to Kenneth More. Kay's former co-star Muriel Pavlow had lost touch with Kay but got together with her at about this time to see Dirk Bogarde in a Brighton show. Pavlow had heard no rumors of Kay's illness but noticed that she was "painfully thin. I remember thinking, 'Oh, she's a naughty girl to diet the way she does.' I can be very obtuse," Pavlow laughs ruefully.

Kay must have felt her strength failing, but she gave no outward indication to friends. Still, by the spring of 1959, she was seeing her doctors more often, and for more alarming treatments. "Sometimes I would come back to the house in Cheyne Walk to find her having a blood transfusion in the bedroom," Harrison wrote in his memoirs. It was getting harder and harder for her to play the game, but she kept it up nonetheless. "I don't think Kay really was deceived," says Noel Harrison. "She wasn't stupid and must have known how ill she was. . . . They carried out the charade for one another." Noel Harrison visited Kay in these last waning months and found her "pale and very sick, but her humour was still irrepressible."

Ike Ryan, the Rex Harrison character in Jacqueline Susann's *The Love Machine*, voiced what Harrison himself told his friends about Kay and his life with her at this time: "I can see when she's tired and pretends not to be. I can also see something like the beginning of fear in her eyes. She knows it's not natural to be this tired. I kid her and pretend I'm tired too. . . . I catch her reading all the medical columns in the newspapers. Deep down, she knows something's dead wrong, but she doesn't want to believe it. And she's always smiling, always worrying about me. . . . She's got more gallantry than anyone I've ever met."

Soon afterward, Kay bid goodbye to Dirk Bogarde for the last time, toward the end of Harrison's run in *My Fair Lady*. By this time, Bogarde said, they both knew it would be their last meeting. He was off to make a film in the U.S. and was giving a farewell party at the Dorchester. Kay picked her husband up at the Drury Lane Theatre, and the two headed over to Bogarde's party. To the end of his life, he remembered exactly what she was wearing and how she looked that night: "A white chiffon dress, a Balmain, with autumn leaves and orange and beige on it. Very, very simple with beautiful shoes and that great mane of hair."

"We all knew that Kate knew she was dying," said Bogarde. "There was no way that she didn't know when she kissed me goodbye in the lift at the Dorchester and turned back with tears pouring down her face." "I don't think I'll ever see you again," Kay told him—Bogarde tried to laugh it off, as usual, so Kay gamely parried with, "You're going to Hollywood and you'll probably love it and never come back." But Bogarde later said, "She knew perfectly well that by the time I came back, which would be in another five months, that she would probably have gone."

Kay had not filmed for a year, and the disaster of *The Bright One* had left her anxious both for a return to the safety of film comedy and the security of a paycheck. Early in 1959, she got an offer too good to dismiss: Stanley Donen requested her for the female lead in *Once More With Feeling!*, a Columbia-produced comedy with Yul Brynner. Donen, a former dancer and choreographer, had worked with Gene Kelly on several films, including *On the Town* and *Singin' in the Rain*, and had directed such hits as *Seven Brides for Seven Brothers*, *Funny Face*, and *Damn Yankees*. Columbia agreed to have this new film shot in Paris—Harrison had won Kay over to his avoidance of British shooting and the subsequent British taxes. On

January 9, 1959, Kay flew to France to meet with Donen while Harrison prepared to wrap up his reign as Henry Higgins.

The real mystery of *Once More With Feeling!* is not that Kay was feeling up to filming or that Harrison encouraged her to do so—it's how she managed to pass the insurance examination that Columbia Pictures required for all the leading performers. The film had a three-million-dollar budget, and a leading lady in the later stages of leukemia would never have knowingly been cast. Stanley Donen—both producer and director of the film—pointedly refuses to discuss this matter. In any event, Kay was given the go-ahead and was soon being fitted for her costumes, designed by Hubert de Givenchy, who was contemporaneously creating Audrey Hepburn's chic and pared-down look.

Kay's co-star was forty-four-year-old Yul Brynner, whose shaved head and Russian accent had made him the most exotic of male sex symbols. Brynner was fresh off the successes of *The Brothers Karamazov* and *Solomon and Sheba* and was scheduled to begin filming *The Magnificent Seven* after his project with Kay wrapped. Also in the cast was Gregory Ratoff, who'd last worked with Kay in the disastrous *Abdullah the Great*. Brynner played an egomaniacal orchestra conductor; Kay his harpist wife. The plot turns on his career falling apart when she leaves him and their agent trying to reconcile them for his career's sake. (The roles had been played by Arlene Francis and Joseph Cotten when *Once More With Feeling!* had been on Broadway).

Harry Kurnitz, who had written the Broadway play, was hired to adapt the script. He'd been a fan of Kay's for years, ever since catching one of her films during a bad crossing on the Queen Elizabeth: "I had fallen hopelessly and quite irretrievably in love," he later wrote. While Kay was still a rising starlet, he'd met her at the Connaught Hotel. He had timidly approached her as a fan. "Move on, or I shall call the manager," she snapped haughtily, adding, "Unless, of course, you *are* the manager." By 1959, Kay and Kurnitz had become close friends, so he looked forward to adapting his play for her. He later recalled a story conference held in a noisy, crowded Left Bank restaurant. Strolling musicians, shouting waiters, and loudly conversing customers all blared and crashed as Kay tried to talk to Harrison from a wall phone. "Where *are* you?" he asked. "I'm being a very good girl, darling," Kurnitz heard Kay shout over the din. "I'm in the Christian Science Reading Room with Harry."

Filming began in late May. The role was an exhausting one; it would have prostrated even a healthy actress. As Dolly Fabian, Kay had numerous temper tantrums, flailing about in fury, shouting, smashing furniture. She also faked harp-playing as expertly as she'd faked the piano in *Simon and Laura* and the trumpet in *Genevieve*. It's among her best moments in the film—strumming away serenely, alternating intense concentration with Harpo Marx faces and arched eyebrows. Though obviously underweight, Kay looked a treat: her stylish Givenchy gowns and suits presaged the Jackie Kennedy look of the early 1960s, her hair teased and pouffed into an auburn chrysanthemum.

That wardrobe—designed solely in blacks and whites—provided Kay with one of the brightest spots of filming, and she delighted in it. Actress Arlene Dahl interviewed Kay in her dressing room for a syndicated column, and she happily flourished her gowns and suits for inspection. "I was a little frightened of the black and white at first, because I love colors," Kay told Dahl. "I rotate orange, yellow and navy blue throughout the seasons, but this is such fun for a change." Never too ill or tired for some girl talk, Kay added that she no longer wore the frilly clothes of earlier days, "which looked terrible on me." She explained that Humphrey Bogart had once seen her wearing a simple sweater, skirt and flat shoes, and had told her how flattering it was. "That's my style now, and I stick to it." As Rex Harrison arrived to take Woolsack and Higgins out for a walk, Kay dithered on about her beauty routine ("I do all the things I shouldn't do, like washing my face too often and not using enough hand lotion").

But these normal, gossipy moments were to be few and far between during this shoot, which was an even worse ordeal than Harrison and Dr. Goldman had feared—Kay was losing strength day by day. "Kay could be infuriating at times," admitted Donen to one of Harrison's biographers, Alexander Walker. "Overstrung by her illness, I guess." She perspired heavily under the hot lights; her makeup needed constant touch-ups and her bouffant hair re-teasing and spraying. This was an unavoidably physical role, and Kay's reserves of strength were at low ebb. "She was very brave," said Donen, "but it was poignant to watch her. Everything was now an effort. You could see her fragility getting more and more pronounced as we screened each day's set of rushes." Despite her weakness, Kay's professionalism and natural talent triumphed. Harry Kurnitz later recalled that many of her funniest moments were not because of his script or Donen's direction; rather, "the best things she did were instinctive, and they were 100 percent infallible." Donen agreed, telling *Life* magazine that "she was completely unpredictable. . . . No one has had it since Carole Lombard—and Kay was a better actress."

Two weeks into shooting, Kay felt herself losing the battle. She said to Donen, "Can we shoot all we can today, for I simply don't know if I'll be here tomorrow." By late May, it looked like *Once More With Feeling!* might go uncompleted: on May 31, Kay collapsed with a high fever and was carted off to the American Hospital in Paris. Dr. Goldman was flown over from London, the insurance company alerted, and production shut down while Columbia debated replacing her. Goldman insisted Kay be removed to the London Clinic, where a blood specialist, Dr. R. Bodley Scott, was called in. The film was only two-thirds completed, and if the set was closed down for the estimated ten days, the company would lose $250,000. Since Donen was producing as well as directing the film, he was able to convince Columbia to keep Kay on. Word got out to the newspapers that she had either pneumonia or bronchitis, and "a serious blood disorder" was also darkly hinted at. Harrison was cornered: "The only reason a blood specialist has been called in is that she has anemia," he told the press, and that blood disorder was responsible for complicating her present lung infection. He added that "She is feeling enormously better and she is quite happy."

That first week of June was made even more unendurable when J. Arthur Rank—unaware of her illness—sued Kay for breach of contract. She had been turning down script after script he had offered her, only accepting the higher-quality loan-out projects being produced by foreign studios. Kay had not made an actual Rank-produced film since *Simon and Laura* in the summer of 1955. The suit was due to go to the High Court—but, of course, was never resolved.

Roy Moseley came by to visit when he heard the Harrisons were back in London and arrived at their hotel just in time to see a cab pull up: "Rex got out and lifted Kay out of the cab. She had a mink coat 'round her shoulders, and he lifted her and carried her into the hotel." In their suite, Moseley chatted with Kay about her new film and found her very depressed about it. "She hated that film, she knew it was dreadful," he says. "Kay was forced into that project to keep her active and working, and Rex and Donen were friends. But she mentioned to me that she felt Donen couldn't handle Brynner and was taking it out on her. 'What a comedown, after working with Cukor and Minnelli!' she told me."

Scenes were shot with Yul Brynner and Gregory Ratoff while Kay languished in London, and additional sets were constructed (though not very good ones—to indicate a London background to the story, a badly painted studio backdrop was tacked up for "exterior" scenes). To everyone's amazement, Kay once again bounced back from the brink of death and was able to take the ferry back to France by June 8 to finish up the last week of filming. She even had a makeup artist and hairdresser stop by the London Clinic to fix her up for public viewing: on her first day out, she looked thin and shaky but stunning in her black Givenchy dress and Cartier brooch. Stanley Donen, Columbia, and the insurance company breathed respective sighs of relief: the remainder of their three million dollar investment was safe (minus the $250,000 she had just cost them).

Mary and Laurie Evans recall the polite lengths Harrison and his secretary, Edith Jackson, went to keep Kay's illness a secret, even from them. The foursome was about to go out to dinner when Jackson came out to explain, "She isn't well. Her foot is hurting very badly and she wants us all to have dinner upstairs, have room service." The next day, Laurie Evans and Harrison went for a walk and he asked point-blank, "Rex, these awful rumors all over the place about Kay, are they true?" "No," snapped Harrison. Evans recalls that "from that time on it was never discussed. I never thought of ringing up and saying, 'How's Kay today?' He would have said, 'Oh, she's fine.'" As Kay's agent, Evans was in a terrible position: "It is one's obligation to the management to say, 'this is the situation,' but I never did and she never, fortunately, let us down."

During filming, Kay was visited by her half-brother Cavan, now seventeen years old. His main memory of that trip was how harassed Kay was by reporters and photographers—many of whom knew full well by now that she was dying. "I used to watch Kay walk down the streets and the reporters just constantly pestered her all the time," he remembered. At one point they even shinnied up the drainpipe of their hotel, breaking into Cavan's room by mistake: "They weren't interested in me but I was absolutely terrified. I couldn't think what was going on." Kay's relationship with the press had always veered wildly from friendly to hostile, but now she was utterly fed up with them. She found herself surrounded by reporters one day on her way home from grocery shopping. "She turned a loaf of French bread into a machine gun," recalled Cavan, "and just machine gunned them all down, in the Champs de Elysees." By this time, Cavan was getting some acting work on TV, and Dirk Bogarde remembered Kay proudly watching her young brother perform, saying, "He'll be alright if he holds himself together."

Her friend Lilian visited her in Paris after Kay had resumed filming. Lilian noticed that Kay was shivering and wearing woolly red socks under her white chiffon nightgown. "I've just come out of the hospital," Kay told her. "I don't know what's the matter." "She looked so glamorous and beautiful," says Lilian, "but if you touched her she would bruise, if you touched her leg or arm." Lilian met Kay's co-star Yul Brynner, who told her his opinion that Harrison "wasn't very nice to her." Indeed, Harrison was keeping up—even intensifying—his usual overprotective and snappish behavior toward Kay to throw off any suspicion that he might be babying her. During one fight, Harrison tossed Kay's clothes out into the hotel's hallway, then locked her out when she ran to retrieve them. To anyone not in on the deception, he merely looked like an unthinkingly brutish husband. "That's why they'd have shouting matches and all that," says Mary Evans. "It was nothing to do with hostility."

Somehow, Kay managed to finish that last week of filming—those in the know were amazed she even survived; but once again, she actually returned to what appeared to be almost normal health. Still, Kay told the *Daily Express* in one of her last interviews that *Once More With Feeling!* had put her off comedy for good. "I am sick, sick, sick and tired of those frothy comedies," she groused. "It is tremendously hard work and no one outside the acting profession appreciates it. The public thinks you're having a joyous time. . . . Oh, I know there is a lot to be said for a performance which completely fools the public. And of course there is a lot of personal satisfaction to be had from it all." She realized what a chance she'd be taking by leaving the kind of role and film that had brought her fame and success: "If I give up comedy and am unsuccessful, that is hard cheese for me. But if I didn't take the risk I wouldn't be worth much, I mean as a human being. And that's what really counts—being a successful human being. I suppose I sound pompous and idiotic talking like this, but I do feel rather strongly about it." Shaking off her momentary philosophical mood, she added, "At least I've always got comedy to fall back on if I am a dismal failure at anything else."

Even now, at the end of her life, Kay had not come to grips with her self-image. She sighed ruefully to *Life* magazine that summer, "My feet are too big, my bosom is too small. I have huge hips and an enormous bottom. I can hardly breathe through this frightful nose. My hair looks like Danny Kaye in a wig. Altogether, I look like a female impersonator—or a rather angular horse." These comments can not be dismissed as simply harmless jokes to a reporter, as Kay's friends remember her saying the same things in private. Of course, her "angular horse" look might have made her a fortune as a fashion model had she not gone into acting (two of the top models of the era, Dovima and Lisa Fonssagrives-Penn, were dead ringers for Kay). But although she was able to talk intelligently about her acting talent and her marriage, Kay never forgot that Rank executive who had supposedly told her, "you're too ugly and you photograph badly" back in 1946.

With *Once More With Feeling!* completed and all the necessary post-production interviews done, Kay and Harrison took off for his Portofino retreat—where they found Lilli Palmer in residence. Palmer took one look at her former rival and recognized that the end was fast approaching. She quickly and quietly packed her suitcases and vacated the house; a frightened and weary Harrison saw her leave with mixed emotions. The summer of 1959 was unusually hot, with temperatures topping 100 degrees even on the coastline. The Harrisons decamped briefly for St. Moritz but found reporters and photographers lying in wait for them at every hotel, restaurant, and train station. By now, most papers were speaking openly of Kay's illness. Harrison's blithe explanations of "pneumonia" and "anemia" were given, but headlines read "Actress' Illness Feared Grave," and reporters wrote of "unhappy rumors that [Kay] is dying of cancer." Harrison decided that the solitude of Portofino was preferable to St. Moritz, even with the heat.

Kay's sister Kim was in Monte Carlo that August with her husband, where she was awaiting the birth of her daughter, Lavinia. The sisters spoke on the phone, and Kay offered to hire a car and chauffeur so they could drive to Monte Carlo—but neither felt the other was physically strong enough to make such a long trip. A road trip from France to Italy "would have taken ages," says Kim. "August every year was the time all the factory workers were bumper-to-bumper on the road." "I'm not feeling any too great myself," Kay admitted, "but I know you're having the baby, so why don't you leave it, and when I'm in New York in the fall we'll get together." It was the last time the sisters ever spoke.

She saw Carol Matthau for the last time in a Portofino bar—"Right where we started," Kay laughed, and the two reminisced about their deranged 1954 pursuit of Rex Harrison. Harrison himself had called Matthau and suggested the two friends get together, that Kay needed some cheering up after her recent illnesses. Although he didn't make it explicitly clear, he knew that this would be their only chance to say goodbye. Matthau is one of Kay's few friends who has nothing but kind words for Rex Harrison:

while (to this day) many of them recall him as pompous, self-involved, and tyrannical, Carol Matthau insists warmly that "He was very sweet. A nice man. There had been so many things written about Rex Harrison that were so vile, and I thought, nobody realizes that a real heart beats in him." Princess Lilian disagrees strongly. "I could never understand that she married him—Katie was so generous and fun and interesting and he was the opposite," she says. "He was very mean to her. He wasn't very generous." Dirk Bogarde, though he never warmed up to Harrison, shrugged, "He was never difficult with me. He was rude, but he was always very rude to everybody."

However, some of Rex Harrison's friends and family had equal reservations about Kay's qualifications to be his wife and partner. "Kay was a sweet and lovable girl, but totally incapable of looking after Rex's needs," said his sister, Sylvia. "I don't think Rex's marriage to Kay would have lasted if Kay hadn't had a fatal illness. Neither of them was temperamentally suited to settling down with the other in the long run." Witnessing their violently theatrical rows and reconciliations, she reasoned that "They really couldn't have gone on at that pitch forever."

Kay's former lover Sydney Chaplin turned out to be an unexpected helpmate at this time. After the shock of their dramatic breakup eased, he and Kay remained close friends, and Harrison was also drawn into his circle. Harrison wrote that during the filming of *Once More With Feeling!*, he "tried to while away the time by playing golf at St. Cloud . . . in the company of Sydney Chaplin. . . . My golf was atrocious, but Sydney never complained." Some of Kay's friends felt that Sydney, and not Harrison, had been the love of Kay's life, and it cannot have been easy for her husband when Kay asked to see him. Harrison invited Chaplin over to their Portofino house and wandered around town by himself while Chaplin and Kay said their last goodbyes.

Kay ran a fever and began losing strength at the end of August and was rushed to a hospital in Rapallo, where she was treated with transfusions by the resident physician, Dr. Gallupo. Dr. Goldman was summoned and decided that Kay had to be rushed back to London quickly. She had pulled through seemingly fatal declines before, but Goldman didn't want to take any chances. Arrangements were quickly made, and Harrison, Goldman, and Kay took a train back to London on the night of August 29. Laurie Evans recalls that "she had a terrible journey. When she got off the train she was in a wheelchair and by then she looked terrible. She put on a big hat with a very wide brim so that the photographers couldn't really see what she looked like."

The Evanses met them at Victoria Station, at about 8:00 on the morning of August 30. Word had somehow leaked out, and the press had gathered. Harrison helped Kay to stand from her wheelchair and ushered her gently into a waiting limousine: "Kate was smiling," Evans recalls. "She wasn't unconscious or anything, but she was obviously very ill, deathly ill." The car took them straight to the London Clinic, where a crowd of reporters and photographers followed them. Kay looked skeletal but was impeccably turned out in a suit, sweater, spike-heeled pumps, and ladylike white gloves. She had thought to put on some lipstick, but her hair was sadly deflated and her suit hung off her as she turned to reporters, shook her finger, and angrily snapped, "If you think I'm coming here to die, you're wrong. I'm not sick and I'm not dying."

Kay was given a private room on the fourth floor; Harrison took an adjoining room and spent every possible moment by her side. Kay, still surprisingly chipper and alert, sent Carol Matthau a telegram: "Wifey, darling, back in the clinic. Good God, I don't know what I'm doing here. Was hoping to get out." Between transfusions and drug treatments, she sat up in bed, planning a variety show she was hoping to do on American television. Harrison obligingly went over the proposed script with her, making helpful suggestions. "There's nothing to flap about," he told reporters. "She'll be coming to New York with me in seven days' time."

As Kay was sinking, her sister, now on a fishing trip off Nantucket, was trying to get through to the London Clinic on the phone. Although Kim had inklings that Kay was quite ill, Harrison had kept the truth from her—and still did, even at the end. "Oh, I'm so sorry, but she's not taking calls," a nurse told her. "Mr. Harrison will be here at six." On September 5, Kim finally reached Harrison. "Oh, she's alright," he assured her. "She hasn't been well, but she's alright." Had she known her sister was dying, Kim would have rushed to her bedside, but she was never given a chance to say goodbye. More than forty years later, Kim sums up her feelings about her former brother-in-law thus: "He was the bastard of all times."

It's quite possible that, on an emotional level, Kay *hadn't* come there to die. She had been dying by inches for three years, so this last, drastic setback might not have seemed like the final one to her. The sixteenth-century French essayist Montaigne spoke for all who sank slowly with lingering illnesses when he wrote that "being so often led to the port, confident that you are still within the accustomed limits, some morning you and your confidence will have crossed the water unawares."

On September 5, Kay sat up in bed discussing her proposed TV project. The script lay in her lap and an unnamed friend told reporters that "she talked happily with Rex about what she would do when she came out of the clinic. . . . But we knew it was hopeless." That night, Kay looked at Harrison and asked, "Mousey, you would tell me if I was dying?" "Don't be stupid—of course I would," he replied, "you're not dying." Shortly after, she sank into a coma. At noon on Sunday, a release was issued to the BBC admitting for the first time that Kay was indeed seriously ill. The press account of her last moments was highly romantic, with Kay sighing to Harrison, "I love you very much, darling" with her last breath. She died at 12:30 the afternoon of Sunday, September 6.

Chapter Twenty-One

"No one was ever born into the world with such a bright genius for living."

Though many of the Harrisons' friends had known Kay was dying, to her family it came as a complete and sudden shock. Her grandmother, Marie Kendall, was told by her daughter Moya. Gladys was staying in New York and was reached by transatlantic telephone. Kim was sailing with her husband off Nantucket for Labor Day weekend and had been trying to reach Kay through the local party line, with no success. The next day, her step-daughter Pauline heard of Kay's death on the radio and broke the news to Kim. It was perhaps hardest of all on Kay's father, Terry, as his wife, Doric, was herself a week away from death in another hospital. "I was so sure that Kay was going to come through it," a shattered Terry told the press. "Rex has been a wonderful husband to her and she absolutely worshipped him."

Kay was buried on September 9 in London's picturesque Hampstead Cemetery, opened in 1876 and featuring many beautiful monuments. Among her neighbors today are several theater people: Sir Herbert Beerbohm Tree, Anton Walbrook, Marie Lloyd, and Kay's friend Gladys Cooper. Also in Hampstead are the graves of artists Kate Greenaway and John Constable, author Gerald Du Maurier, and medical pioneer Joseph Lister. Noel Harrison remembers sitting in a car outside the graveyard with his father and half-brother, Carey, before the service. "We had a bottle of something comforting," he says, "and had the hardest time getting the cork out. It broke, finally, and we had to push the last bit in. We were all convinced Katie's spirit was responsible for the problem, and there was a treasured moment when we shared the echo of that divine impishness."

Kay's classically shaped, pale green slate tombstone reads "Kay Kendall Harrison" in an elegant script and, below, "Kate, Deeply loved wife of Rex." Supported by his sons, Harrison placed a spray of crimson roses on her grave. Noël Coward wrote in his diary that "I went to the funeral with

Vivien [Leigh], quite small and quiet and nicely done. There were no mobs and shaming demonstrations, only a few scruffy newspaper photographers clambering about on the cemetery railings and snapping the coffin being lowered into the ground."

On September 15, memorials were held for Kay in New York and Los Angeles. Irene Mayer Selznick presided over the one in New York, at the famed "Little Church Around the Corner," known for its theatrical patronage; Rex Harrison asked Dirk Bogarde to read at the one in Los Angeles. "We were all doing it together at the same time, and finally I couldn't do it, I just broke. So Gladys Cooper, who adored Kate, did it very bravely, with tears pouring down her face," said Bogarde. "Rex had made a rule that there were to be no wreaths of any sort. The first one we saw was this bloody great wreath from David Niven. So we hid that behind a door, and then went in to check the church, and on the altar there were hundreds of red roses." They were wired together, so Bogarde had to rip apart the displays with bleeding hands. The U.S. services were packed with celebrities: Moss and Kitty Carlisle Hart, Lauren Bacall, Ingrid Bergman, John Gielgud, Phil Silvers, Margaret Leighton. Bogarde said that "Four major studios closed that morning for Kate. Even the man who sold hot dogs outside the studio came along—he closed his stall. The church was jammed—you couldn't move with people. She'd only made one film in Hollywood."

Kay's British memorial service was held on September 22 at St. Martin-in-the-Fields and was a star-packed affair. Among the thousand participants were Alec Guinness, Terence Rattigan, Julie Andrews, Cecil Beaton, Douglas Fairbanks Jr., and Muriel Pavlow (of her immediate family, only Kay's father and his mother, Marie Kendall, were able to attend). Kim, eight months pregnant and in the U.S., was not able to come to the service ("though I was not invited anyway," she notes). Ralph Richardson read from the Bible, then Vivien Leigh got up to speak: "No one was ever born into the world with such a bright genius for living. . . . It was almost as if she had a premonition that the gift of life would not be hers for very long—with such intensity and gaiety did she take every minute of her stay on earth."

Kay's family received nothing in the way of mementos when her estate was disposed of by Harrison and his lawyers. He handed a lot over to Mary Evans—furs, jewelry—and said, "I want you to sell all this and give the money to cancer research." Princess Lilian was sent a gold coin on a chain. "I always keep it on. She always wore it." Whatever few keepsakes Kim was able to acquire were given to her by Kay's sympathetic friends. Kay left her father, mother, and stepbrother two thousand pounds; she knew her sister was well-provided for through marriage.

Once More With Feeling! finally opened in March of 1960, to luke-warm reviews. Like so many posthumous films, its main attraction was its morbid curiosity value, not any intrinsic merit. Columbia was at a loss as to how to promote it: handouts to theater managers cheerfully stressed the "happy comedy" and "exuberance and pleasure," carefully avoiding any mention of attendant tragedy. Yul Brynner was hailed in press releases; Stanley Donen and Givenchy were also profiled. Kay's rather brief press bios called her "an international star" and mentioned her previous "spec-tacular comedy appearances." But anyone who'd been out of touch would have no idea she was dead. Noël Coward went to see the film, "which was frankly bad. Kay was marvelous and it was heart-breaking to see her being so funny and alluring and realize that she was in that gloomy little grave in Hampstead." Seen today, *Once More With Feeling!* evokes similar emotions; Kay looks beautiful and chic, but it is painful to see her barreling around doing her physical madcap comedy and realizing how ill and weak she was. The film itself was pallid and forgettable, hardly worth the energy it took out of her.

Harrison seemed to be in shock, on his own, after Kay's death. He went right into three terrible, emotionally exhausting movies (*Midnight Lace, The Happy Thieves,* and *Cleopatra*) and several stage shows (including *Platanov,* during which he met his next wife). He didn't hit his stride again until 1964 and the film version of *My Fair Lady,* which won him a shelf full of awards (including an Oscar and a BFA award). The remainder of his film career was downhill from there; only *The Agony and the Ecstasy* (1965) really stood out. But Harrison continued to triumph onstage in such ve-hicles as *Henry IV, Caesar and Cleopatra, Heartbreak House,* and several revivals of *My Fair Lady* (the last in 1981).

Harrison's most bizarre and controversial project was the 1974 Broad-way play *In Praise of Love,* by his old friend Terence Rattigan. It had begun as two short plays, one of which (*After Lydia*) concerned Sebastian and Lydia Crutwell, a writer and his dying wife. Rattigan's biographer said that the play was not only about Kay's illness and Harrison's attempts to cope with it but was also Rattigan's "own obituary; his apologia for his own life" (ironically, Rattigan would also die of leukemia, in 1977). "It is about the inability of the English to express emotion," Rattigan told a reporter. He did not have the nerve to approach Harrison to appear in the London run; it starred Donald Sinden and Joan Greenwood. But when *After Lydia* was lengthened to *In Praise of Love* for a Broadway run, Rattigan did sweet-talk Harrison into playing a theatricalized version of himself (he fudged a bit, insisting that Sebastian was partially based on his friend Cuthbert Worsley).

Harrison proved a terror during rehearsals, rewriting and redirecting the show, shaving down the lines of his leading lady (Julie Harris). Certainly, much of the dialogue cut close to the bone. Lydia tells a friend, "A long, slow, terminal illness is the worst visitation we can inflict on anyone, let alone our nearest and dearest. And Sebastian isn't the best person in the world at being bored. . . . Then, when I came to die I wouldn't have enjoyed looking up into Sebastian's face—and seeing relief." More to the point, Sebastian later admits to the same friend, "Being one of Nature's shits does have its advantages when one's dealing with a dying wife." *In Praise of Love* opened on December 10, 1974, received mixed reviews and closed after 131 performances.

Harrison went on to marry another three times. In 1962 he picked a successor to Kay who was as different from her as was possible, shocking many of her friends. Welsh-born actress Rachel Roberts was brilliantly talented but emotionally unstable and increasingly alcoholic. Roberts's friend Nancy Holmes told her biographer that she "appeared to me like a little girl lost amidst all that sophistication. In Rex's world, she was a Welsh waif. But when it came to looking after her man, she was in her element. She comforted and cosseted Rex, and cooked those solid English dishes he loved, like roasts and Yorkshire pudding and sausage-and-mash and shepherd's pie." The fiery marriage lasted till 1971 (Roberts committed suicide in 1980).

Immediately after his divorce from Roberts, Harrison married Elizabeth Harris. Harris should have known what she was in for, having recently divorced another difficult actor, Richard Harris. This, Harrison's fifth marriage, lasted four years. The sixth and final Mrs. Rex Harrison was Mercia Tinker; she was fortyish when she and the seventy-year-old actor married in 1978. This union lasted an impressive twelve years and ended only with Harrison's death on June 2, 1990. The year before his death, he had been knighted Sir Rex Harrison, which would have delighted Kay no end. He was not buried next to her at St. John's in Hampstead—rather, he requested that his ashes be scattered into the Riviera off Portofino. His sons carried out his wishes. For the rest of his life, Harrison had worn a ring Kay had given him, inscribed with her signature; Carey Harrison treasures it as a memento of both his father and "one of my sequence of beautiful stepmothers." Lilli Palmer (who had stayed married to Carlos Thompson) died in 1986, at the age of seventy-one.

Had she lived, Kay might have enjoyed the careers and played the roles later taken by her near-contemporaries Maggie Smith, Judi Dench, even Anne Bancroft and Rachel Gurney (think how marvelous a Mrs. Robinson she would have been, or Lady Marjorie in *Upstairs Downstairs*). But Kay's family and friends are divided on her possible fate, some insisting that she might have killed herself upon losing her youthful beauty. "It is good that she died when she did, really," says Princess Lilian. "I don't think she would have ever liked to have grown old." Kim agrees that "If she had found gray hair, or bags under her eyes, or started losing her waistline, I don't think she could have stood it." Only Dirk Bogarde said, "I don't think she would have minded. Would she have aged gracefully? Enormously."

Kay has, of course, lived on in her films: *Genevieve* and her lesser vehicles show up regularly on British television. On U.S. TV, only *The Reluctant Debutante*, *Les Girls*, and the unfortunate *Quentin Durward* carry on her legacy. But still, Kay Kendall is adored as a combination of Lucille Ball and Carole Lombard. She starred in only a handful of films after she came to prominence—and it would be foolish not to admit that many of these films had only Kay herself to recommend them, a fact that makes it all the more remarkable that she is so fondly and vividly remembered more than forty years after her death.

Kay also lives on in a more concrete way: since 1989, the lighthouse built by her grandfather has served as a memorial for her. The Withernsea Lighthouse—which stood next to the house in which Kay and her siblings were born—had been decommissioned and closed in 1976. Eleven years later, it was purchased by Kim Kendall and her husband, Rolla D. Campbell Jr., M.D. (Campbell, now retired, had been associate clinical professor of surgery and orthopedics at Cornell University Medical School and co-director of Combined Fracture Service.) Gladys Kendall, then in her eighties, had returned to Withernsea to retire to an assisted living home, where Kim visited her regularly. Seeing her hometown gave Kim the idea of buying the lighthouse and its attached cottage to set up a memorial to Kay as well as a museum to the Royal National Lightboat Institution and its local heroes.

Three students from the Humberside College of Higher Education, overseen by local architect Chris Wardle, were contracted to revamp the lighthouse's cottage into the Kay Kendall Memorial Museum. Kim and her husband worked hard in the late 1980s to find money and artifacts for the museum, for the refurbishing of the lighthouse, and for a tearoom. She was unable to reach Rex Harrison, telling the press, "I know Rex is ill, but I feel sure if he knew all about our project he would love to contribute something of Kay's." That got him on the phone post-haste: "How dare you tell people I'm ill?" he snapped. "I've never felt better." What's more, he thought the memorial museum was "ridiculous—Katie would have hated it." He and Kim never spoke again.

The lighthouse opened to the public in the summer of 1989. A twenty–minute biographical video about Kay (filmed and narrated by her half-brother Cavan) is on display. There are posters from Kay's films and family photos, her modest wedding dress, and a copy of a Pierre Balmain ball gown from *The Reluctant Debutante*, worn by a wax figure of Kay (commissioned in London for eleven thousand pounds). The lighthouse museum contains ships' bells, models, and photos recording the story of the Withernsea lifeboats and crews as well as other local history.

Additional publicity was generated for the Kay Kendall Leukaemia Fund, which had been founded by James Sainsbury on his death in 1984. The Fund's main purpose is to disperse endowments "in the field of medical research into and the treatment of leukaemia . . . and on related haematological malignancies." It also supports patient care programs and supplies equipment for research laboratories. Among the recent beneficiaries have been the Institute of Cancer Research, the acquisition of a haemoto-oncology unit at Addenbrooke's Hospital in Cambridge, and a fellowship at the University of Leeds to study the role of DNA repair in precisely the form of leukemia that killed Kay.

Kay's fame may someday bring in enough money to cure the disease that claimed her—an ultimately important legacy given to only a few celebrities, such as Lou Gehrig (amyotrophic lateral sclerosis), Rita Hayworth (Alzheimer's disease), and Rock Hudson (AIDS). In the long run, Kay's death may turn out to have been even more important to more people than was her brief, madcap life and career.

Filmography

Fiddlers Three (Ealing Studios, 1944)

Director: Harry Watt. Producer: Michael Balcon. Screenplay: Angus MacPhail, Diana Morgan, Harry Watt. Music: Mischa Spoliasky, Harry Jacobson, Geoffrey Wright, Diana Morgan, Robert Hamer, Roland Blackburn, Spike Hughes. Cinematography: Wilkie Cooper. Editing: Eily Boland. Art Direction: Duncan Sutherland. Musical Arranger: Benjamin Frankel. Makeup: Tom Shenton. Costumes: Elizabeth Fanshawe, Marion Horn.

CAST: Tommy Trinder (Tommy), Sonnie Hale (Professor), Diana Decker (Lydia), Frances Day (Poppaea), Francis L. Sullivan (Nero), Elisabeth Welch (Nora), Mary Clare (Volumnia), Ernest Milton (Titus), Frederick Piper (auctioneer), Robert Wyndham (lion keeper), Russell Thorndike (high priest), Danny Green (lictor), James Robertson Justice (centurion). With Alec Mango, Frank Tickle.

Sailors and Wren transported back to ancient Rome.

Dreaming (Ealing Studios, 1944)

Director, Producer: John Baxter. Assoc. Producer: Baynham Honri. Screenplay: Bud Flanagan, Reginald Purdell. Cinematography: Stanley Pavey. Music: Kennedy Russell, Desmond O'Connor, Bud Flanagan. Art Direction: Duncan Sutherland. Editing: E.M. Inman Hunter. Makeup: Tom Shenton, Ernest Taylor. Costumes: Marianne Horn.

CAST: Chesney Allen (Ches), Bud Flanagan (Bud), Hazel Court (Miss Grey), Philip Wade (Dr. Goebbels), Roy Russell (trainer), Dick Francis (Sir Charles Paddock), Ian Maclean (general), Robert Adams (prince), Peter Bernard (soldier), Gerry Wilmot (general). With Sam Baker, Teddy Brown, Alfredo Campoli, Noel Dainton, Raymond Glendenning, Bob Jones, Gordon Richards, George Street, Morris Sweden.

Fantasy dreams of a head-bonked soldier.

Champagne Charlie (Ealing Studios, 1944)

Director: Alberto Cavalcanti. Producer: Michael Balcon. Production Supervisor: Hal Mason. Screenplay: Austin Melford, Angus Macphail, John Dighton. Cinematography: Wilkie Cooper. Art Direction: Michael Relph. Makeup: Tom Shenton. Costumes: Ernest Stern, Marion Horn. Editing: Charles Hasse. Original Music: Una Bart, Lord Berners, T.E.B. Clarke, Frank Eyton, Noel Gay, Billy Mayerl, Ernest Irving.

CAST: Tommy Trinder (George Leybourne), Stanley Holloway (The Great Vance), Betty Warren (Bessie Bellwood), Jean Kent (Dolly Bellwood), Robert Wyndham (Duckworth), Harry Fowler ('orace), Drusilla Wills (Bessie's dresser), Joan Carol (Coral), Billy Shine (stage manager), Guy Middleton (tipsy swell), Frederick Piper (Leoroyd), Andrea Maladrinos (Gatti), Paul Bonifas (Targetino), Austin Trevor (duke), Peter De Greeff (Lord Petersfield), Norman Pierce (Elephant & Castle landlord), Eddie Phillips (Tom Sayers), Leslie Clarke (Fred Sunders), Eric Boon (Clinker).

Feud between two Victorian music-hall stars.

Caesar and Cleopatra (A Gabriel Pascal Production, 1945)

Director, Producer: Gabriel Pascal. Scenario and Dialogue: George Bernard Shaw. Decor and Costumes: Oliver Messel. Art Director: John Bryan. Music: Georges Avric. Editing: Frederick Wilson.

CAST: Claude Rains (Caesar), Vivien Leigh (Cleopatra), Stewart Granger (Apollodorus), Flora Robson (Ftatateeta), Francis L. Sullivan (Pothinus), Basil Sydney (Rufio), Cecil Parker (Britannus), Raymond Lovell (Lucius Septimius), Anthony Eustrel (Achillas), Ernest Thesiger (Theodotus), Anthony Harvey (Ptolemy), Robert Adams (Nubian slave), Olga Edwardes, Harda Swanhilde (Cleopatra's attendants), Michael Rennie, James McKechnie (centurions), Esme Percy (major domo), Stanley Holloway (Belzanor), Leo Genn (Bel Aftris), Felix Aylmer (nobleman).

Julius Caesar teaches the young Queen of Egypt how to rule over her occupied lands.

Waltz Time (British National, 1945)

Director: Paul L. Stein. Producer: Louis H. Jackson. Screenplay: Montgomery Tully, Henry C. James. Music: Hans May. Lyrics: Alan Stranks.

CAST: Carol Raye (Empress Maria), Peter Graves (Count Franz von Hofer), Patricia Medina (Cenci Prohaska), Webster Booth, Anne Ziegler (singers), Albert Sandler (orchestra leader), George Robey (Vogel), Harry Welchman (Count Rodzanko), Thorley Walters (Stefan Ravenne), John Ruddock (Count Prohaska), Brefni O'Rourke (Emperor), Wylie Watson (Josef), Hay Petrie (Minister of War), Ivan Sampson (Captain of Gendarmes), Marie Ault (Cenci's maid), Hugh Dempster (Ferdinand Hohenlohe), Joyce Linden, Ruthene LeClarc, Eileen Moore, Dawn Bingham, Kay Kendall (ladies in waiting), Richard Tauber (singing shepherd).

Romance between a young Empress and a captain of the Guards in old Vienna.

London Town (J. Arthur Rank Organisation, 1946)

Director, Producer: Wesley Ruggles. Screenplay: Siegfried Herzig, Elliot Paul, Wesley Ruggles. Music: Jimmy Van Heusen. Lyrics: Johnny Burke. Cinematography: Erwin Hiller. Editing: Sidney Stone. Art Direction: Ernst Fegte. Costumes: Orry-Kelly. Makeup: Guy Pearce. Hairstylist: Patricia Pearce. U.S. title: *My Heart Goes Crazy*.

CAST: Sid Field (Jerry Sanford), Greta Gynt (Mrs. Barry), Tessie O'Shea (herself), Claude Hulbert (Belgrave), Sonnie Hale (Charlie), Mary Clare (Mrs. Gates), Kay Kendall (Patsy), Petula Clark (Peggy), Beryl Davis (Paula), Jerry Desmonde (George), Scotty McHarg (Bill), W.G. Fay (Mike), Reginald Purdell (stage manager), Alfie Dean (heckler), Charles Paton (novelty shopkeeper), Pamela Carroll, Marion Saunders (street singers), Lucas Hovinga (dancer), Jack Parnell. London Town Dozen & One [*sic*] Girls: Sheila Bligh, Dorothy Cuff, Pat Hughes, Sheila Huntington, Freda Lansley, Mary Midwinter, Giselle Morlais, Louise Newton, Enid Smeeden, Paulie Tyler, Jackie Watson.

Small-time comic comes to London with his daughter seeking success.

Dance Hall (Ealing Studios, 1950)

Director: Charles Crichton. Producer: E.V.H. Emmett. Screenplay: E.V.H. Emmett, Alexander Mackendrick, Diana Morgan. Music: Geraldo. Cinematography: Douglas Slocombe. Editing: Seth Holt. Art Direction: Norman G. Arnold.

CAST: Natasha Parry (Eve), Jane Hylton (Mary), Petula Clark (Georgie), Diana Dors (Carole), Donald Houston (Phil), Bonar Colleano (Alec), Gladys Henson (Mrs. Wilson), Sidney Tafler (manager), Douglas Barr (Peter), Fred Johnson (Mr. Wilson), James Carney (Mike), Kay Kendall (Doreen), Eunice Gayson (Mona), Dandy Nichols (Mrs. Crabtree). With Grace Arnold, Harry Fowler, Wally Fryer, Harold Goodwin, Doris Hare, Hy Hazell, Ted Heath, Michael Trubshawe.

Nights on the town of factory girls and their boyfriends.

Happy Go Lovely (Associated British Picture Corp. Ltd., 1951)

Director: H. Bruce Humberstone. Producer: Marcel Hellman. Screenplay: Val Guest. Music: Mischa Spoliansky. Cinematography: Erwin Hillier. Editing: Bert Bates. Art Direction: John Howell. Choreographer: Jack Billings. Costumes: Anna Duse. Hairstylist: Jean Bear. Makeup: Nell Taylor.

CAST: David Niven (B.G. Bruno), Vera-Ellen (Janet Jones), Cesar Romero (John Frost), Bobby Howes (Charlie), Diane Hart (Mae), Gordon Jackson (Paul Tracy), Barbara Couper (Madame Amanda), Henry Hewitt (Dodds), Gladys Henson (Mrs. Uquhart), Hugh Dempster (Bates), Sandra Dorne, (Betty), Joyce Carey (Bruno's secretary), John Laurie (Jonskill), Wylie Watson (stage door keeper), Joan Heal (Phyllis Gardiner), Hector Ross (Harold), Ambrosine Phillpotts (Lady Martin), Molly Urquhart (Madame Amanda's assistant), Kay Kendall (Frost's secretary).

Chorus girl is mistaken for millionaire's mistress.

Lady Godiva Rides Again (British Lion Film Co., 1951)

Director: Frank Launder. Screenplay: Frank Launder, Val Valentine.

CAST: Pauline Stroud (Marjorie Clark), John McCallum (Larry Burns), Gladys Henson (Mrs. Clark), George Cole (Johnny), Bernadette O'Farrell (Janie), Eddie Byrne (Eddie Mooney), Renee Houston (Beattie), Kay Kendall (Sylvie), Sidney James (Lew Beeson), Diana Dors (Dolores August), Clive Baxter, Paul Connell, Arthur Howard (soap publicity men), Fred Berger (Mr. Green), Arthur Brander, Felix Felton, Sidney Vivian (councillors), Shirley Burniston (student), Cyril Chamberlain (Harry), Dora Dryan (publicity woman), Tommy Duggan (compere), Lyn Evans (Vic Kennedy), Edward Forsyth (singer), Tom Gill (receptionist), Patricia Goddard (Susan), Rowena Gregory (waitress), John Harvey (Buller), Stanley Holloway (Mr. Clark), Walford Hyden (conductor), Lisa

Lee (singer), Eddy Leslie (comic), Henry B. Longhurst (soap director), Peter Martyn (photographer), Charlotte Mitchell (Lucille), Dennis Price (Simon Abott), Michael Ripper (stage manager), Toke Townley (Lucille's husband), Richard Wattis (casting director), Dana Wynter (Myrtle Shaw), Joan Collins (beauty contestant). With cameos by Trevor Howard, Alastair Sim, Googie Withers.

Girl wins local beauty contest and seeks big-time fame.

Curtain Up (J. Arthur Rank Organisation, 1952)

Director: Ralph Smart. Producers: Robert Garrett, George Pitcher. Screenplay: Jack Davies, Michael Pertwee, from Philip King's play "On Monday Next." Music: Malcolm Arnold. Cinematography: Stanley Pavey. Editing: Douglas Robertson. Art Direction: Geoffrey Drake. Costumes: Joan Ellacott. Hair: Gladys Atkinson. Makeup: Bob Lawrance.

CAST: Robert Morley (W.H. Derwent Blacker), Margaret Rutherford (Catherine Beckwith), Kay Kendall (Sandra Beverley), Michael Medwin (Jerry Winterton), Olive Sloane (Maud Baron), Liam Gaffney (Norwood Beverley), Lloyd Lamble (Jackson), Charlotte Mitchell (Daphne Ray), Charles Lamb (George), Constance Lorne (Sarah Stebbins), Margaret Avery (Mary), Stringer Davis (vicar), Joan Hickson (landlady), John Cazabon (Mr. Stebbins), Diana Calderwood (set painter), Joan Rice (Avis), Sam Kydd (ambulance man).

Trials of a small-town repertory company.

Wings of Danger (Exclusive Films, 1952)

Director: Terence Fisher. Producer: Anthony Hinds. Screenplay: John Gilling, Packham Webb (from his novel *Dead On Course*). Cinematography: Walter J. Harvey. Editing: James Needs. Art Direction: Andrew Mazzei. Music: Malcolm Arnold. Costumes: Ellen Trusller. Makeup: Philip Leakey. Hairstylist: Bill Griffiths.

CAST: Zachary Scott (Richard Van Ness), Robert Beatty (Nick Talbot), Kay Kendall (Alexia LaRoche), Naomi Chance (Avril Talbot), Arthur A. Lane (Boyd Spencer), Colin Tapley (Inspector Maxwell), Diane Cilento (Jeannette), Harold Lang (Snell), Jack Allen (Triscott), Sheila Raynor (nurse), Courtney Hope (Mrs. Clarence), June Ashley, Natasha Sokolova, June Mitchell (sportscar blondes), James Steele, Russ Allen (flying officers), Darcy Conyers (signals officer), Laurie Taylor (O'Gorman), Ian Fleming (Mr. Talbot), Anthony Miles (desk clerk), Douglas Muir (Dr. Wilner).

Pilots, blackmailers, gold smugglers.

It Started In Paradise (J. Arthur Rank Organisation, 1952)

Director: Compton Bennett. Producers: Sergei Nolbandov, Leslie Parkyn. Screenplay: Margharita Laski. Cinematography: Jack Cardiff. Music: Malcolm Arnold. Editing: Alan Osbiston. Costumes: Sheila Grahame. Makeup: Billy Partleton. Hairstylists: Biddy Chrystal, Pearl Gardner.

CAST: Jane Hylton (Martha Watkins), Ian Hunter (Arthur Turner), Terence Morgan (Edouard), Muriel Pavlow (Alison Greville), Brian Worth (Michael Carter), Martita Hunt (Madame Alice), Ronald Squire ("Mary Jane"), Kay Kendall (Lady Caroline

Frencham), Joyce Barbour (Lady Burridge), Diana Decker (Crystal Leroy), Jack Allen (Lord Chandos), Harold Lang (Louis), Mara Lane (popsie), Naomi Chance (model). With Margaret Withers, Lucianne Hill, Dana Wynter.

Ambitious fashion designer finds herself ill-equipped to deal with success.

Mantrap (1953)

Director: Terence Fisher. Producers: Michael Carreras, Alexander Paul. Screenplay: Terence Fisher, Paul Tabori, Adam Hall (from his novel *Queen in Danger*). Cinematography: Reginald H. Wyer. Art Direction: J. Elder Wills. Music: Doreen Carwithen. Editing: James Needs. Makeup: D. Bonnor Maris.

CAST: Paul Henreid (Hugo Bishop), Lois Maxwell (Thelma Speight), Keiron Moore (Speight), Hugh Sinclair (Maurice Jerrard), Lloyd Lamble (Inspector Frisnay), Anthony Forwood (Rex), Bill Travers (Victor Tasman), Mary Laura Wood (Susie), Kay Kendall (Vera), John Penrose (Du Vancet), Liam Gaffney (Douval), Conrad Phillips (Barker), John Stuart (doctor), Anna Turner (Marjorie), Arnold Diamond (Alphonse), Geoffrey Murphy (plain-clothesman), Terry Carney (detective), Sally Newland (receptionist). With Barbara Shelley, Christina Forrest, Jane Welsh.

Detective goes undercover to hunt down elusive killer.

Street of Shadows (Merton Park, 1953)

Director/Screenwriter: Richard Vernon. Producer: William H. Williams. Cinematography: Phil Grindrod. Music: Eric Spear. Editing: Geoffrey Muller. Makeup: Jack Craig. Hairstylist: Betty Sherriff. Wardrobe: Elsie Curtis. From Laurence Meynell's novel *The Creaking Chair*. U.S. title: *The Shadow Man.*

CAST: Cesar Romero (Luigi), Kay Kendall (Barbara Gale), Edward Underdown (Inspector Johnstone), Victor Maddern (Limpy), Simone Silva (Angele Abbe), Robert Cawdron (Sergeant Hadley), Liam Gaffney (Fred Roberts), Molly Hamley-Clifford (Starry Darrell), Paul Hardtmuth (Poppa), John Penrose (Capt. Gerald Gale), Bill Travers (Nigel Langley), Eileen Way (Mrs. Toms).

Pinball manager, his assistant, and an unhappily married woman all suspected of murder.

Genevieve (J. Arthur Rank Organisation, 1953)

Director, Producer: Henry Cornelius. Screenplay: William Rose. Music: Larry Adler. Cinematography: Christopher Challis. Editing: Clive Donner. Costumes: Marjory Cornelius. Makeup: Paul Rabiger. Hairstylist: Helen Penfold.

CAST: Dinah Sheridan (Wendy McKim), John Gregson (Alan McKim), Kay Kendall (Rosalind Peters), Kenneth More (Ambrose Claverhouse), Geoffrey Keen (policeman), Joyce Grenfell (hotel proprietress), Reginald Beckwith (motorist), Arthur Wantner (old gentleman), Edie Martin (guest), Leslie Mitchell (himself), Michael Medwin (husband), Harold Siddons (policeman), Michael Balfour (conductor).

Two couples compete in a London-to-Brighton antique car rally.

The Square Ring (J. Arthur Rank Organisation, 1953)

Director: Basil Dearden. Producers: Michael Relph, Michael Balcon. Screenplay: Robert Westerby (from the play by Ralph W. Peterson). Cinematography: Otto Heller. Editing: Peter Bezencenet. Music: Dock Mathieson. Costumes: Anthony Mendleson. Makeup: Harry Frampton. Hairstylist: Daphne Martin.

CAST: Jack Warner (Danny Felton), Robert Beatty (Kid Curtis), Bill Owen (Happy Burns), Maxwell Reed (Rick Martell), George Rose (Whitey Johnson), Bill Travers (Rowdie Rawlings), Alfie Bass (Frank Forbes), Ronald Lewis (Eddie Lloyd), Sidney James (Adams), Joan Collins (Frankie), Kay Kendall (Eve Lewis), Bernadette O'Farrell (Peg Curtis), Eddie Byrne (Lou Lewis), Vic Wise (Joe), Michael Golden (Warren), Joan Sims (Bunty), Vernon Kelso (Reynolds), Alexander Gauge, Sidney Tafler (wiseacres), Michael Ingrams (doctor), Ivan Staff (Mr. Coleman), Madoline Thomas (Mrs. Lloyd), Ben Williams (Mr. Lloyd), Alf Himes (Deakon), Harry Herbert (DeGrazos), Joe Bloom, Kid Berg (referees), C.H. Nichols (timekeeper).

Melodrama of boxers, their managers, and their women.

Meet Mr. Lucifer (J. Arthur Rank Organisation, 1953)

Director: Anthony Pelissier. Producers: Michael Balcon, Monja Danischewsky. Screenplay: Monja Danischewsky, Alec Grahame, Peter Myers, Arnold Ridley (from his play *Beggar My Neighbour*). Cinematography: Desmond Dickinson. Art Direction: Wilfred Shingleton. Music: Eric Rogers. Editing: Jack Harris. Costumes: Anthony Mendleson. Makeup: Harry Frampton, H. Wilton. Hairstylist: Barbara Barnard.

CAST: Stanley Holloway (Sam Hollingsworth/Mr. Lucifer), Peggy Cummins (Kitty Norton), Jack Watling (Jim Norton), Barbara Murray (Patricia Pedelty), Joseph Tomelty (Mr. Pedelty), Kay Kendall (Lonely Hearts singer), Gordon Jackson (Hector McPhee), Charles Victor (Mr. Elder), Humphrey Lestocq (Arthur), Jean Cadell (Mrs. MacDonald), Raymond Huntley (Mr. Patterson), Ernest Thesiger (Mr. MacDonald), Frank Pettingell (Mr. Roberts), Olive Sloane (Mrs. Stannard), Gilbert Harding (himself), Philip Harben (himself), MacDonald Hobley (himself), David Miller (himself), Olga Gwynne (principal boy), Joan Sims (fairy queen), Ian Carmichael (Man Friday), Irene Handl (lady with dog), Gladys Henson (lady in bus), Roddy Hughes (Billings), Eliot Makeham (Edwards), Bill Fraser (bandleader), Dandy Nichols (Mrs. Clarke), Molly Hamley-Clifford (Mrs. Ensor), Toke Townley (trumpet player), Fred Griffiths (removal man), Herbert C. Walton (pub customer). With Diane Cilento, Eddie Leslie, Edie Martin, and Geoffrey Keene as Mr. Lucifer's voice.

Fantasy about the devil using television for his own nefarious purposes.

Fast and Loose (J. Arthur Rank Organisation, 1953)

Director: Gordon Parry. Producer: Teddy Baird. Screenplay: Ben Travers, A.R. Rawlinson. Cinematography: Jack Asher. Editing: Frederick Wilson. Music: Philip Green. Costumes: Joan Ellacott. Makeup: Edgar Wedd. Hairstylist: Helen Penfold.

CAST: Stanley Holloway (Mr. Crabb), Brian Reece (Peter), Kay Kendall (Carol), Fabia Bryan (Mrs. Crabb), Reginald Beckwith (Tripp-Johnson), Dora Bryan (Rawlings),

Vida Hope (Gladys), Aubrey Mather (Noony), June Thorburn (Barbara), Toke Townley (Alfred), Charles Victor (Lumper), Joan Young (Mrs. Gullett). With Eliot Makeham, John Warren.

Young husband caught in an inn with his former girlfriend.

Doctor in the House (J. Arthur Rank Organisation, 1954)

Director: Ralph Thomas. Producer: Betty Box. Screenplay: Nicholas Phipps, Richard Gordon (from his novel). Cinematography: Ernest Steward. Music: Bruce Montgomery. Editing: Gerald Thomas. Art Direction: Carmen Dillon. Costumes: Yvonne Caffin. Makeup: W.T. Partleton.

CAST: Dirk Bogarde (Simon Sparrow), Muriel Pavlow (Joy), Kenneth More (Richard Grimsdyke), Donald Sinden (Beskin), Kay Kendall (Isobel), James Robertson Justice (Lancelot Spratt), Donald Houston (Taffy), Suzanne Cloutier (Stella), George Coulouris (Briggs), Jean Taylor Smith (Sister Virtue), Nicholas Phipps (magistrate), Geoffrey Keen (dean), Martin Boddey, George Benson, Geoffrey Sumner (lecturers), Joan Sims ("Rigor Mortis"), Ann Gudrun (May), Harry Locke (Jessup), Cyril Chamberlain (policeman), Ernest Clark (Mr. Parrish), Maureen Pryor (Mrs. Cooper), Shirley Eaton (Milly Croaker), Joan Hickson (Mrs. Croaker), Brian Outlon (salesman), Mona Washbourne (midwifery sister). With Eliot Makeham, Shirley Burniston, Mark Dignam, Felix Felton, Lisa Gastoni, Wyndham Goldie, Douglas Ives, Anthony Marlowe, Noel Purcell, Amy Veness, Richard Wattis.

The adventures of four medical students.

Abdullah the Great (MISR Universal Film, 1955)

Director, Producer: Gregory Ratoff. Screenplay: Boris Ingster, George St. George, Ismet Regeila (from his novel *My Kingdom for a Woman*). Cinematography: Lee Garmes. Music: Georges Auric. Editing: Maurice Rootes.

CAST: Gregory Ratoff (Abdullah), Sydney Chaplin (Ahmed), Kay Kendall (Ronnie), Marina Berti (Aziza), Alexander D'Arcy (Marco), Marti Stevens.

Egomaniacal monarch pursues unwilling fashion model as his kingdom topples.

The Constant Husband (British Lion Film Co., 1955)

Director: Sidney Gilliat. Producers: Sidney Gilliat, Frank Launder. Screenplay: Sidney Gilliat, Val Valentine. Cinematography: Edward Scaife. Music: Malcolm Arnold. Editing: Gerald Turney-Smith. Costumes: Anna Duse.

CAST: Rex Harrison (Charles Hathaway), Cecil Parker (Llewellyn), Sally Lahee (nurse), Kay Kendall (Monica Hathaway), Nicole Maurey (Lola), Valerie French (Bridget), Ursula Howells (Miss Pargiter), Jill Adams (Miss Brent), Roma Dunville (sixth wife), Robert Coote (Jack Carter), Raymond Huntley (J.F. Hassett), Noel Hood (Gladys), Eric Pohlmann (Papa Sopranelli), Marie Burke (Mama Sopranelli), George Cole (Luigo Sopranelli), Derek Sydney (Giorgio Sopranelli), Guy Deghy (Stromboli), Margaret Leighton (Miss Chesterman), Eric Berry (prosecuting counsel), Michael Hordern (judge), Charles Lloyd Pack (solicitor), Arthur Howard (clerk), Alfred Burke (porter), Joe Clark (Old Bailey warder), Paul Connell (Cardiff barman), Arthur Cortez (Luigi's driver), Doreen Dawn, Pat Kenyon (models), Arnold Diamond (car loan manager), Peter Edwards, Evie Lloyd (fishermen), Nora Gordon (housekeeper), Olive Kirby (car loan assistant), Sam Kydd (Adelphi barman), Geoffrey Lovat (commissionaire), Enid McCall (Welsh chambermaid), Jill Melford (Monica's golf partner), Myrette Morven (Miss Prosser), Janette Richer (typist), Michael Ripper (luggage attendant), John Robinson (secretary), Stuart Saunders (policeman), Monica Stevenson (Olwen), Graham Stuart (government messenger), Robert Sydney, David Yates (detectives), Nicholas Tannar (usher), George Thorne (Horrocks), Stephen Vercoe (Dr. Thompson), Frank Webster (Old Bailey Warden), Leslie Weston (jailor), George Woodbridge (warder), Muriel Young (Clara).

Amnesiac discovers he is a serial bigamist.

Simon and Laura (J. Arthur Rank Organisation, 1955)

Director: Muriel Box. Producer: Teddy Baird. Screenplay: Peter Blackmore, from the play by Alan Melville. Cinematography: Ernest Steward. Music: Benjamin Frankel. Art Direction: Carmen Dillon. Editing: Jean Barker. Costumes: Julie Harris. Makeup: Bob Lawrence. Hairstylist: Biddy Chrystal.

CAST: Peter Finch (Simon Foster), Kay Kendall (Laura Foster), Muriel Pavlow (Janet Honeyman), Hubert Gregg (Bertie Burton), Maurice Denham (Wilson), Ian Carmichael (David Prentice), Richard Wattis (Controller of Television Drama), Thora Hird (Jessie), Clive Parritt (Timothy), Alan Wheatley (Adrian Lee), Charles Hawtrey (railway porter), Marianne Stone (Elsie), Brian Wilde (Peter Harbuttle).

Feuding husband and wife star in treacly domestic TV show.

The Adventures of Quentin Durward (MGM, 1955)

Director: Richard Thorpe. Producer: Pandro S. Berman. Screenplay: Robert Ardrey, from the novel by Sir Walter Scott. Cinematography: Christopher Challis. Music: Bronislau Kaper. Editing: Ernest Walter. Art Direction: Alfred Junge. Costumes: Elizabeth Haffenden. Makeup: William Lodge. Hairstylist: Joan Johnstone.

CAST: Robert Taylor (Quentin Durward), Kay Kendall (Isabelle, Countess of de Croy), Robert Morley (King Louis XI), George Cole (Hayraddin), Alec Clunes (Charles, Duke of Burgundy), Duncan Lamont (Count William de la Marek), Laya Raki (Gypsy dancer), Marius Goring (Count Philip de Creville), Wilfred Hyde-White (Master Oliver), Eric Pohlmann (Gluckmeister), Harcourt Williams (Bishop of Liege), Michael Goodliffe (Count de Dunois), John Carson (Duke of Orleans), Nicholas Hannen (Cardinal Balus), Moultrie Kelsall (Lord Malcolm), Frank Tickle (Petit-Andre), Bill Shine (Trois-Eschelles), Ernest Thesiger (Lord Crawford).

Scotsman woos French noblewoman on behalf of his wealthy patron.

Les Girls (MGM, 1957)

Director: George Cukor. Producers: Sol C. Siegel, Saul Chaplin. Screenplay: Vera Caspary, John Patrick. Music and Lyrics: Cole Porter. Cinematography: Robert Surtees. Choreographer: Jack Cole. Costumes: Orry-Kelly. Editing: Ferris Webster. Makeup: William Tuttle. Hairstylist: Sydney Guilaroff.

CAST: Gene Kelly (Barry Nicols), Mitzi Gaynor (Joy Henderson), Kay Kendall (Lady Sybil Wren), Taina Elg (Angele Ducros), Jacques Bergerac (Pierre Ducros), Leslie Phillips (Sir Gerald Wren), Henry Daniell (judge), Patrick MacNee (Sir Percy), Stephen Vercoe (Mr. Outward), Philip Tonge (associate judge), Richard Alexander (stagehand), Barrie Chase, Lilyan Chauvin (dancers), Adrienne D'Ambricourt (wardrobe woman), George Davis (sleepy Frenchman), Marcel De la Brosse (headwaiter), Cyril Delevanti (fanatic), Maurice Marsac (house manager), Owen McGiveney (court usher), George Navarro (waiter), Nestor Paiva (Spanish peasant), Genevieve Pasques (shopkeeper), Francis Ravel (French stage manager), Gilchrist Stuart (English photographer), Louisa Triana (Flamenco dancer), Maya Van Horn (Frenchwoman).

Romantic adventures of three women in a traveling dance troupe.

The Reluctant Debutante (MGM, 1958)

Director: Vincente Minnelli. Producer: Pandro S. Berman. Screenplay: William Douglas Home, from his play. Cinematography: Joseph Ruttenberg. Art Direction: A.J. d'Aubonne. Costumes: Pierre Balmain, Helen Rose. Music: Eddie Warner. Editing: Adrienne Fazan. Makeup: Jean-Paul Ulysse.

CAST: Rex Harrison (Jimmy Broadbent), Kay Kendall (Sheila Broadbent), John Saxon (David Parkson), Sandra Dee (Jane Broadbent), Angela Lansbury (Mabel Claremont), Peter Myers (David Fenner), Diane Clare (Clarissa Claremont), Charles Cullum (English Colonel). With Charles Herbert, Ambrosine Phillpotts, Sheila Raynor.

Social-climbing Englishwoman treats her unwilling American stepdaughter to a debut.

Once More With Feeling! (Columbia Pictures Corporation, 1960)

Director, Producer: Stanley Donen. Assoc. Producer: Paul B. Radin. Screenplay: Harry Kurnitz, from his play. Cinematography: George Perinal. Editing: Jack Harris. Makeup: Eric Allwright, Jean-Paul Ulysse. Costumes: Givenchy. Jewelry: Cartier.

CAST: Yul Brynner (Victor Fabian), Kay Kendall (Dolly Fabian), Gregory Ratoff (Maxwell Archer), Geoffrey Toone (Dr. Hilliard), Maxwell Shaw (Jasha Gendel), Mervyn Johns (Mr. Wilbur, Jr.), Martin Benson (Bardini), Harry Lockart (Chester), Shirley Ann Field (Angela Harper), Grace Newcombe (Mrs. Wilbur), C.S. Stuart (Manning), Colin Drake (doctor), Andrew Faulds (interviewer), C.E. Joy (Sir Austin Flapp), Barbara Hall (secretary).

Ex-wife of mercurial orchestra conductor is begged by manager to save his career.

Notes

Abbreviations

KKC   Kim Kendall Campbell
EG   Eve Golden
MW   Maraday Wahlborg

Prologue

1-3 Harrison/Kendall wedding: KKC to MW, Nov. 1994
  2 "Kay has the happy": *L.A. Herald,* Dec. 31, 1957
  2 "I've had too many years": *N.Y. Times Magazine,* Sept. 15, 1957.
  3 "Professor 'iggins Weds": *N.Y. Post,* June 24, 1957

Chapter One

  6 "Don't you think": KKC to EG, Oct. 2000
  6 "The waves were mountain high": Kendall, "My Roots Are in Heaven"
  6 "When the wheat had grown": ibid
  7 "With four pretty teenaged daughters": ibid
  7 "It was one of the": ibid
  7 Marie Kendall background: *Music Hall* magazine, June 1980
  7 "Terribly funny": Cavan Kendall to MW, April 27, 1995
  8 McCarthy family background: KKC to EG, Nov. 2000
  8 "I fell hook": Kendall, "My Roots Are in Heaven"
  9 "She told us how the Queen": KKC to EG, June 2001
  9 "A big, handsome man:" ibid
  9 "One policeman said": Kendall, "My Roots Are in Heaven"
  9 "No! Please don't die!": ibid
10 "Isn't the mink lining": KKC to MW, Nov. 1994
10 "She used to pull my leg": James Drewery to MW, May 4, 1995
10 "My dear father": KKC to EG, April 2001
11 "I'm going to kill you kids": KKC to MW, Nov. 1994
11 "Doric is wonderful": Kendall, "My Roots Are in Heaven"
11 "I remember mother": KKC to MW, Nov. 1994
12 "My love lasted": Kendall, "My Roots Are in Heaven"
12 "If she said 'white'": KKC to EG, Nov. 2000
12 "To say I was devastated": Kendall, "My Roots Are in Heaven"
12 "She was perfectly willing": Molly Simpson to MW, spring 1995
12 "Please don't say anything": KKC to MW, Nov. 1994

Chapter Two

14 "That woman": KKC to EG, Nov. 2000
14 Evening of Ballet details from program, July 20, 1939
15 "We will, I think": Simpson to MW, spring 1995
15 "kept us all sane": Shirley Ann Hall to MW, May 10, 1995
15 "There was a little magic": Simpson to MW, spring 1995
16 "It shows how utterly stupid": ibid
16 "Do you have any questions?": KKC to MW, Nov. 1994
16 "Oh, I'll come and help": Hall to MW, May 10, 1995
17 "Of course, there was nobody in London": KKC to EG, April 2001
17 "For somebody of that age": Seabrook to MW, April 28, 1995
17 "Let's go wake mother up:" KKC to MW, Nov. 1994

Chapter Three

18 "Kay would walk in": Joy Drewery to MW, May 4, 1995
18 "A wonderful, great big": KKC to EG, Nov. 2000
18 "Who's that beautiful girl": KKC to MW, Nov. 1994
19 "She'd make up something": Hall to MW, May 10, 1995
19 "I've had to stay with": KKC to EG, Dec. 2000
19 "From the time I was six": *Cue,* Nov. 2, 1957
19 "Oh, just tell them": KKC to EG, Nov. 2000
20 "My man, we would like": Jean Walker to MW, May, 9, 1995
20 "A girl who was sleeping": KKC to MW, Nov. 1994
20 "We worked together": Beryl Turner to MW, Feb. 23, 1995
21 "There never seemed to be": Kendall, "My Roots Are in Heaven"
21 "If the siren went off": Nancy Winter to EG, July 26, 2001
22 "She was a very": Hall to MW, May 10, 1995
22 "Because there's always another": Roddy McDowell to MW, March 14, 1995
22 "Saw London as a city": Hillary, "The Last Enemy"
22 "There was a huge increase": *Daily Mail,* Aug. 19, 1999
22 "She was mad as a hatter": Princess Lilian to MW, May 2, 1995
23 "There you are, darling": Turner to MW, Feb. 23, 1995
23 "She knew all the words": Lilian to MW, May 2, 1995
23 "We want the best table": Walter Andrews to KKC, fall 2001
23 "If you care nothing for money": ibid
24 "Both girls were under age": Kendall, "My Roots Are in Heaven"
24 "Two left feet": Peggy Dexter to MW, Jan. 1995
24 "Kay was sent vials": KKC to MW, Nov. 1994
24 "Let's go to Granny's!": Kendall, "My Roots Are in Heaven"
25 "The food was awful": KKC to EG, Nov. 2000
25 "These two lovely tall girls": Muriel Pavlow to MW, May 11, 1995
26 "Huddled in shelters": Hopkins, "The New Look"
26 "I'm sure we looked beautiful": KKC to MW, Nov. 1994
26 "There weren't too many": ibid

27 "Spoiled the life": ibid
27 "Nobody seemed to want me": *Cue,* Nov. 2, 1957
27 "She was asleep and woke up": McDowell to MW, March 41, 1995

Chapter Four

28 "He gave us each five pounds": KKC to EG, June 2001
29 "Put your leg up": *Preview* magazine (undated)
29 "One of the most hideous": McFarlane, "An Autobiography of British Cinema"
29 "Miss Gynt, do you think": ibid
30 "All the virgins stand up": KKC to MW, Nov. 1994
30 "Everytime we were": ibid
31 "Everybody keeps putting me": McFarlane, "An Autobiography of British Cinema"
31 "I think you've got something": *N.Y. Times Magazine,* Sept. 15, 1957
32 "This is my break": Jean Walker to MW, May, 9, 1995
32 "Only do it for love": KKC to MW, Nov. 1994
33 "It was a very sad kiss": *Preview* magazine (undated)
33 "in agony": Beryl Turner to MW, Feb. 23, 1995
33 "sweet, warm and funny": ibid
33 "When I saw that camera": 1946 newspaper clipping
34 "Audience reaction was lukewarm": Derek Leask to EG, Oct. 17, 1999
34 "Nobody had ever heard of me": Newspaper interview with Morgan Hudgins, 1953

Chapter Five

35 "a triumph in its own class": *London Times,* Sept. 1, 1946
35 "misfire": *Variety,* July 24, 1946
35 "a sad error of judgment": *The Observer,* Sept. 1, 1946
36 "I think I'm just going": Moya Collins to MW, March 29, 1995
36 "picking up little girls": *N.Y. Times Magazine,* Sept. 15, 1957
36 "You are a very ugly girl": *American Weekly,* Jan. 5, 1958
37 "If I weren't a real pro": unident. 1953 newspaper article, "Kendall Kindles Glamour"
37 "I've had it": KKC to MW, Nov. 1994
37 "I had ulcers with worry": Newspaper interview with David Lewin, 1958
37 "Really, darling": *N.Y. Times Magazine,* Sept. 15, 1957
37 "grab this babe": unident. 1954 newspaper article, "Kay Goes Wild"
37 "After the war": Nancy Winter to EG, July 4, 2001
38 "The streets were still drab": Hopkins, "The New Look"
38 "If there were piles": ibid
39 "I haven't heard from Kay": Jean Walker to MW, May, 9, 1995
39 "They were a lovely family": Beryl Turner to EG, June 2001
40 "Kay was not in that show": Nikolas Dana to EG, Sept. 2001
40 "We'd all exercise together": KKC to EG, June 2001
40 "Not bad for a Cockney chorus girl!": Princess Lilian to MW, May 2, 1995
40 "The British Olympic Association": Richard Cox Cowell to MW, Jan. 19, 1995

Chapter Six

43 "Kay hated her nose": as affirmed by nearly all of her friends
43 "People say I'm glamorous": *Cue*, Nov. 2, 1957
43 "She did nothing but grumble": Dinah Sheridan to MW, April 27, 1995
43 "I know what I look like": Carol Saroyan Matthau to MW, March 17, 1995
44 "Look—no cartilage!": KKC to MW, Nov. 1994
44 "Can you imagine anyone": Pictorial Review, Jan. 1930
44 "She said she'd gone through": Dirk Bogarde to MW, April 25, 1995
44 "What rubbish!": KKC to MW, Nov. 1994
44 "I got it from my mother": *Life* magazine, 1959
44 McIndoe to Gustavson: Sander L. Gilman, "Making the Body Beautiful"
44 "I can smell your cigar!": Bogarde to MW, April 25, 1995
44 "Oh, poor me": ibid
44 "I used to have the same problem": KKC to EG, June 2001
45 "Everything, the litter baskets": Hopkins, "The New Look"
45 "After that long, grey winter": ibid
45 "bliss, lovely to work with": McFarlane, "An Autobiography of British Cinema"
45 "a snug nursery": ibid
46 "the studio with the family feeling": ibid
46 "everyone back to my place": KKC to EG, June 2001
46 "All her flats were scattered": ibid
46 "James Sainsbury was a lovely man": James Hanson to EG, May 1999
46 "Lilian, darling, tell her": Princess Lilian to MW, May 2, 1995
46 "James, I think I know": ibid
47 "He was totally love-struck!": Seabrook to MW, April 28, 1995
47 "She would talk of no one else": Sheridan to MW, April 27, 1995
47 "I'm very much in love": Princess Lilian to MW, May 2, 1995
47 "Oh, shit!": Cowell to MW, Jan. 19, 1995
47 "She's just gone to post": Princess Lilian to MW, May 2, 1995
47 "So many of my girlfriends": Suzzie Dillon to EG, Aug. 2001

Chapter Seven

48 "I was a Cockney tart": *Preview* magazine (undated)
50 "Oh, look, it's Mr. Bogarde": Bogarde to MW, April 25, 1995
50 "She's very funny": ibid
50 "She just enveloped you": McDowell to MW, March 14, 1995
50 "When she talked to you": Lee Minnelli to MW, March 15, 1995
51 "What a sweet little housey": Dirk Bogarde, "Snakes and Ladders"
51 "wretched blood capsules": Bogarde to MW, April 25, 1995
51 "There had never been a happier": Bogarde, "Snakes and Ladders"
51 "knitting with her glasses on": Bogarde to MW, April 25, 1995
51 "I just sit for hours": *Preview* magazine (undated)
51 "great intellect, that girl!": ibid

52 "Right, mates, goodnight": Bogarde to MW, April 25, 1995
52 "We laughed": ibid
52 "Oh, me poor little butcher boy": ibid

Chapter Eight

53 "I remember sitting": Pavlow to MW, May 11, 1995
53 "I was their girl": *N.Y. Times Magazine,* Sept. 15, 1957
54 "She had half the men": Princess Lilian to MW, May 2, 1995
54 "What were you doing": KKC to EG, Nov. 2000
54 "You work in the daytime": unident. 1953 newspaper article, "Kendall Kindles Glamour"
55 "the most chinless": Theo Aronson, Princess Margaret, A Biography
55 "He has a title": *Daily Mirror,* June 7, 1954
55 "It's the blood": ibid
55 "We're planning to run away": KKC to EG, Nov. 2000
55 "Marie Kendll's granddaughter": unident. 1953 newspaper article, "Kendall Kindles Glamour"
56 "People think I'm the gayest thing": ibid
56 "Cooch Behar?": *The Evening News,* Feb. 26, 1955
56 "He was mad about her": KKC to MW, Nov. 1994
57 "Poor Tony": KKC to EG, June 2000
57 "Oh, he looks like an earwig": KKC to MW, Nov. 1994
57 "They all loved her": ibid
58 "I see you're sitting": Sheridan to MW, April 27, 1995
58 "We've got to be careful": ibid

Chapter Nine

59 "We were all fighting flu": *The Evening News,* Feb. 26, 1955
60 "I don't mind if you're cold": Sheridan to MW, April 27, 1995
60 "Are we south of Scotland?": ibid
60 "Behind every bush in Bucks": ibid
60 "And began to beat Corny": Kenneth More, "More or Less"
60 "He never got over her": Princess Lilian to MW, May 2, 1995
61 "Oh, God, oh God": Sheridan to MW, April 27, 1995
61 "She really was in a bad way": ibid
61 "nothing but the most appalling noises": ibid
61 "come on, smile!": ibid
62 "very beautiful and very delicate": ibid
62 "I don't want to go home alone": ibid
62 "Why don't you marry him?": ibid
62 "Love those money-makers!": Princess Lilian to MW, May 2, 1995
62 "Why is it, James": ibid
62 "Oh, that is sweet of you": Sheridan to MW, April 27, 1995
63 "It completely bowled me over": *Preview* magazine (undated)
63 "From start to finish": *The Evening News,* Feb. 26, 1955

63 "They sacked me once": unident. 1953 newspaper article, "Kendall Kindles Glamour"
63 "kept us in fits": Sheridan to MW, April 27, 1995
63 "There was a wonderful moment": Pavlow to MW, May 11, 1995
64 "one of the three best": *Daily Mail,* undated review
64 "sparkles with the authentic effervescence": *News of the World,* undated review
64 "altogether more endearing": unident., undated review
64 "unsavory . . .": *The Catholic Times,* undated review
64 "Kay Kendall is a lovely girl": *Daily Express,* undated review
64 "gives a good deal": *Sunday Times,* undated review
64 "places a delicate tongue": unident., undated review
64 "It really is desperately difficult": *Daily Express,* Jan. 16, 1959
65 "I wish people would stop": *Cue,* Nov. 2, 1957
65 "I am not a star": *The Evening News,* Feb. 26, 1955
65 "Such fun": unident. article, 1953

Chapter Ten

66 "Ladies and gentlemen": unident. 1957 newspaper article, "The Nine Lives of Katie Kendall"
66 "Never show me legs": *Daily Mirror,* June 7, 1954
67 "that indefinable quality": unident. 1957 newspaper article, "The Nine Lives of Katie Kendall"
68 "It was great fun to make": *Daily Mirror,* June 7, 1954
68 "It's love": ibid
68 "That's one of the reasons": ibid
69 "Thought it would make a good film": McFarlane, "An Autobiography of British Cinema"
69 "We all loved the script": Pavlow to MW, May 11, 1995
69 "For instance, I had to say": ibid
69 "It was a ragbag of all": McFarlane, "An Autobiography of British Cinema"
69 "We didn't want to use actors": ibid
70 "He had a very short attention span": Margaret Beebe Chaplin to EG, Dec. 3, 2000
70 "She was adorable": Matthau to MW, March 17, 1995
70 "I'll take the second bath": ibid
70 "I don't know why I love Sydney so": ibid
70 "Sydney, you finally found a real girl": ibid
71 "enough Chinese food for six people": ibid
71 "Tell him you are in a terrible state": ibid
71 "What looks best when you're dead?": ibid
71 "I hope you are having a good time": ibid
71 "I am not and never was": *Daily Mirror,* June 7, 1954
71 "He always said that": Chaplin to EG, Dec. 3, 2000

Chapter Eleven

75 "She was very easy": Rex Harrison "Rex, An Autobiography"

75 "I felt instinctively": ibid

75 "You know, darling": KKC to MW, Nov. 1994

76 "Tired?": ibid

76 "not at all difficult": *Weekend* magazine, May 6, 2000

76 "flighty and photgenic farce": *New York Times,* undated review

76 "moment of completely off-guard surprise": Alexander Walker, "Fatal Charm: The Life of Rex Harrison"

77 "What do you think": Roy Moseley to EG, Oct. 8-9, 2001

77 "This was very frustrating": Rex Harrison, "Rex, An Autobiography"

77 "She was a true Cockney": ibid

77 "Kay was exhuberant": Noel Harrison to EG, Aug. 2001

77 "always went to extremes": Rex Harrison, "Rex, An Autobiography"

77 "She was perfectly capable of saying": KKC to MW, Nov. 1994

78 "great battles, fisticuffs": Rex Harrison, "Rex, An Autobiography"

78 "Lilli was very tolerant": Daily Mail, Jan 4, 2001

79 "I will never forget that train ride": Matthau to MW, March 17, 1995

79 "You really don't understand lire": ibid

79 "He told me he never even wanted": ibid

Chapter Twelve

80 "She had arranged it all": Rex Harrison, "Rex, An Autobiography"

80 "I'm going to see that fucking wife": Bogarde to MW, April 25, 1995

80 "He wants to marry me": Matthau to MW, March 17, 1995

81 "We did it in the woods!": ibid

81 "All at once, there it was": Lilli Palmer, "Change Lobsters and Dance"

81 "Kay and I were too obviously": Rex Harrison, "Rex, An Autobiography"

81 "Why are you doing this": Carol Matthau Saroyan, "Among the Porcupines"

81 "Kay, don't tell that to Lilli": ibid

82 "The evening ended icily": Rex Harrison, "Rex, An Autobiography"

82 "Wifey! Wifey!": Carol Matthau Saroyan, "Among the Porcupines"

82 "You are a fucking fool": ibid

83 "It was bad taste": Roy Moseley, "Rex Harrison: A Biography"

83 "It's about the worst case I know": Lilli Palmer, "Change Lobsters and Dance"

83 "How was I going to get through": ibid

83 "horrible for my mother": Carey Harrison to EG, Aug. 2001

83 "Wan't an unduly predatory male": ibid

83 "Indeed, when he was starting": Dillon to EG, Aug. 2001

83 "attractive and intelligent": ibid

84 "She was great fun": ibid

84 "Oh, for God's sake": Alexander Walker, "Fatal Charm: The Life of Rex Harrison"

84 "Kate went mooning": Bogarde to MW, April 25, 1995

84 "Oh, for Christ's sake": ibid

84 "It was dreadful for Lilli": ibid

84 "Isn't it funny, darling": ibid

85 "There were no hard feelings": Carey Harrison to EG, Aug. 2001
85 "I grew up with my mother": Noel Harrison to EG, Aug. 2001
85 "divinely, deliciously naughty": ibid
85 "I told Binkie": Alexander Walker, "Fatal Charm: The Life of Rex Harrison"
85 "The play was a success": ibid

Chapter Thirteen

86 "Oh Rex was never": KKC to MW, Nov. 1994
86 "She was terribly funny": Laurie Evans to MW, May 1995
86 "great humor and tremendous style": Roy Moseley, "Rex Harrison: A Biography"
86 "Kay suddenly showed the stress": Matthau to MW, March 17, 1995
87 "We were always laughing": Princess Lilian to MW, May 2, 1995
87 "Sexy Rexy!": ibid
87 "I didn't know what it was": Cavan Kendall to MW, April 27, 1995
87 "sitting on the settee": ibid
88 "Rex Harrison has fallen": Graham Payn & Sheridan Morley, "The Noel Coward Diaries"
88 "Kay Kendall is a good girl": ibid
88 "Irene Handl": ibid
88 "She was not as good as": Roy Moseley to EG, Oct. 8-9, 2001
88 "She's so vital": N.Y. *Times Magazine,* Sept. 15, 1957
88 "'Common' doesn't mean": ibid
89 "She's been offered": *Daily Herald,* Dec. 1954
89 "She's a clever actress": *The Evening News,* Feb. 26, 1955
89 "She is not a temperamental star": *Daily Herald,* Dec. 1954
89 "Nobody can blame Rank": *Johannesberg Daily News,* Dec. 1954
90 "Nothing I had done": *Los Angeles Times,* May 22, 1955
91 "This is all just gossip": ibid
91 "They shaved my eyebrows": *N.Y. Times Magazine,* Sept. 15, 1957
91 "You go and ask Mr. Rank": unident. 1957 newspaper article, "The Nine Lives of Katie Kendall"
92 "Normally the casting": McFarlane, "An Autobiography of British Cinema"
92 "I feel all these camera angles": Trader Faulkner, Peter Finch
92 "a steadier and more stable man": ibid
92 "Nothing I said": McFarlane, "An Autobiography of British Cinema"
93 "I can't understand why": ibid
93 "which had to be visualized": ibid
93 "we had a sort of armed neutrality": ibid
93 "was not exactly a William Wyler": Ian Carmichael to MW, April 25, 1995
93 "she was great fun": Carmichael to EG, Sept. 11, 2000
93 "Are you sure no one wants": ibid
94 "full of uncertainties": Pavlow to MW, May 11, 1995
94 "pretty forced and flat": *New York Times,* July 3, 1956

Chapter Fourteen

102 "She's so wonderful": KKC to MW, Nov. 1994

102 "How many shares": ibid

103 "a lovely, mad time": Rex Harrison, "Rex, An Autobiography"

103 "Then the silly bitch": Graham Payn & Sheridan Morley, "The Noel Coward Diaries"

103 "Oh, that loot!": *This Week,* Nov. 17, 1957

103 "I hate to give up": ibid

103 "It was George Cukor": Hedda Hopper's Hollywood, June 16, 1957

103 "I've always thought": ibid

104 "She coud be the top": *Chicago Sunday Tribune Magazine,* 1957

Chapter Fifteen

105 "I don't know what the fuck": Matthau to MW, March 17, 1995

106 "You just don't understand": Bogarde to MW, April 25, 1995

106 "Oh, wifey": Dirk Bogarde, Snakes and Ladders

106 "I took mother and Jean": KKC to EG, Nov. 2000

106 "Rex wrote her a terrible letter": ibid

106 "Not anyone she cares about": Lilli Palmer, "Change Lobsters and Dance"

106 "I sat, my own blood draining": Rex Harrison, "Rex, An Autobiography"

107 "A whole vista of agony": ibid

107 "I wanted to accept responsibility": ibid

107 "You can rest assured": Lilli Palmer, "Change Lobsters and Dance"

107 "I can't!": ibid

108 "Every week, wherever": ibid

108 "Rex was in negotiation": Moseley to EG, Oct. 8-9, 2001

108 "I would never have allowed": Lilli Palmer, "Change Lobsters and Dance"

108 "She can help my image": Jacqueline Susann, "The Love Machine"

109 "She was ill": Bogarde to MW, April 25, 1995

Chapter Sixteen

110 "It looked like an Amsterdam": Dirk Bogarde, "Snakes and Ladders"

110 "I can't stay a night here:" ibid

111 "I have legs like a kangaroo": *Citizen-News,* Feb. 2, 1957

111 "I'm the same height as Gene Kelly": ibid

111 "They'll have to photograph me": unident. newspaper article, "Life with Rex"

111 "I used to crawl back": *Hedda Hopper's Hollywood,* June 16, 1957

111 "Then, too": ibid

111 "We used to have lots of fun": Taina Elg to EG, May 7, 1999

112 "Oh, I'll have some, too!": ibid

112 "a darling": *Cue,* Nov. 2, 1957

112 "Alright, girls": ibid

112 "down and out": Patrick MacNee to MW, April 14, 1995
112 "gave me a light kiss": ibid
112 "There was an incident": Laurie Evans to MW, May 1995
112 "Goodness, I have no idea!": Taina Elg to EG, May 7, 1999
112 "You can't believe how beastly": *This Week,* Nov. 17, 1957
112 "The funny thing is": ibid
113 "Not since the late Carole Lombard": *Hedda Hopper's Hollywood,* June 16, 1957
113 "While I dore Kay": ibid
113 "the doorbell rang": Elg to EG, May 7, 1999
113 "I remember when I was doing": *Daily Express,* Jan. 16, 1959
113 "Love is a serious": *Chicago Sunday Tribune Magazine,* 1957
113 "I guess people expect": *Citizen-News,* Feb. 2, 1957
114 "I feel so vitriolic": *N.Y. Times Magazine,* Sept. 15, 1957
114 "I don't want to do anything": ibid
114 "If you ask about my private life": *Herald Tribune,* Jan. 14, 1957
114 "I'm thirty years old": ibid
114 "I knew it": ibid
114 "Can we have steak?": *This Week,* Nov. 17, 1957
114 "Some women go out": ibid
115 "Yes, ma'am": ibid
115 "I have tried many diets": *L.A. Times,* Jan 12, 1958
115 "I never let my weight": ibid
115 "I am happiest in tweeds": ibid
115 "I wouldn't like to feel": ibid
116 "It's just an old shirt": unident. artice, Feb. 17, 1957
116 "He could have gone on": ibid
116 "I think Lilli will spread it about": Matthau to MW, March 17, 1995
116 "rather famous and fat": ibid
116 "I know that is not true": ibid
117 "I've seen those wonderful ladies": ibid
117 "unexceptional but cheerful": unident. review, 1957
117 "a Sheraton highboy": *American Weekly,* Jan. 5, 1958
117 "a formidable match": *N.Y. Times,* undated review

Chapter Seventeen

118 "Darling, Rex and I": KKC to MW, Nov. 1994
118 "oh, the horrid press": ibid
119 "Oh, I'm sorry": ibid
119 "The second time was great fun": Rex Harrison, "A Damned Serious Business"
119 "I was brought up an Englishwoman": *This Week,* Nov. 17, 1957
119 "I never pay too much attention": *L.A. Times,* Jan 12, 1958
119 "Not at all": *This Week,* Nov. 17, 1957
120 "insufferably self-satisfied": Noel Harrison to EG, Aug. 2001
120 "I just did nothing for months": unident. 1958 article, "Life with Rex"

120 "I wanted to control every flower": *Vogue,* Dec. 2000

120 "saw him to the gate": ibid

120 "The point was": Bogarde to MW, April 25, 1995

120 "Oh, rubbish!": Laurie Evans to MW, May 1995

121 "What rubbish they print": Alexander Walker, "Fatal Charm: The Life of Rex Harrison"

121 "Idiots—they meant 'anemia'": ibid

121 "Is it possible to imagine": ibid

Chapter Eighteen

123 "We want rest": unident. article, Jan. 1958

123 "'e's ower oud for me!'": KKC to EG, Nov. 2000

123 "It bored Charlie to tears": Jerry Epstein, "Remembering Charlie"

124 "Everyone knew that Terry": Dillon to EG, Aug. 2001

124 "gave a wicked imitation": ibid

124 "roamed around the town": Rex Harrison, "Rex, An Autobiography"

124 "It was a flareup": unident. newspaper article, Jan. 3, 1958

125 "Treatment, though it may not increase": Raymond D. Adams, et al, "Principes of Internal Medicine"

125 "should be reserved" ibid

125 "It was to be our first": unident. 1958 article, "Life with Rex"

125 "decided that nothing in work": ibid

125 "No one and nothing": Rex Harrison, "Rex, An Autobiography"

126 "We'd love to do it": Vincente Minnelli, "I Remember It Well"

126 "Kay! Get the phone!": Roy Moseley, "Rex Harrison: A Biography"

126 "Rex and I like to dip": ibid

127 "Moving the London airport": "Reluctant Debutante" press release

127 "Careful how you photograph:" Vincente Minnelli, "I Remember It Well"

127 "My husband is the world's": ibid

128 "And that's exactly what happened": ibid

128 "I told Vincente Minnelli": *Daily Express,* Jan. 16, 1959

128 "would greet me each morning": John Saxon to EG, July 17, 2000

128 "It never crossed my mind": Roy Moseley, "Rex Harrison: A Biography"

128 "in very delicate health": Lee Minnelli to MW, March 15, 1995

128 "Vincente was very careful": ibid

129 "a big roll of pound notes": Bogarde to MW, April 25, 1995

129 "I remember looking out": ibid

129 "terribly self-involved": Angela Lansbury to MW, May 10, 1995

129 "Kay would show up": ibid

129 "were wonderful together": Lee Minnelli to MW, March 15, 1995

129 "did everything to be wonderful": ibid

130 "When Rex was leaving the show": Roy Moseley, "Rex Harrison: A Biography"

130 "Most important was the fact": "Reluctant Debutante" press release

130 "I was frightened out of my wits": unident. newspaper article, "Life with Rex"

130 "He's always telling me": *This Week,* Nov. 17, 1957
130 "He also taught me": unident. 1958 article, "Life with Rex"
130 "thin and boneless": *N.Y. Times,* undated undated
130 "Is Kay Kendall": *Evening News,* undated review
131 "Now securely in the chair": undated, unident. review
131 "have required her to be": undated, unident. review

Chapter Nineteen

133 "We've never had a home": unident. 1958 article, "Life with Rex"
133 "We've never had a home": unident. 1958 article, "Now Let's Take a Look at the Real Kay Kendall"
133 "I'm always sitting in corners": ibid
133 "Oh, beat it, beat it!": Bogarde to MW, April 25, 1995
134 "Everyone was there": Moseley to EG, Oct. 8-9, 2001
134 "I'm thirty now": unident. 1958 article, "Now Let's Take a Look at the Real Kay Kendall"
134 "What I'd really like to do": ibid
135 "shivering and pinched": Dirk Bogarde, "Snakes and Ladders"
135 "Diggy, I think I'm dying": ibid
135 "Balls! Of course you haven't:" ibid
135 "She was no fool": Bogarde to MW, April 25, 1995
135 "She was playing the opposite game": William Atchley to EG, Sept. 15, 2000
135 "fairly scatty anyhow": Graham Payn & Sheridan Morley, "The Noel Coward Diaries"
135 "high-powered, tear-diffused": ibid
135 "the poor dear may have behaved": ibid
136 "She was his possession": Dexter to MW, Jan. 1995
136 "He broke a friendship": KKC to MW, Nov. 1994
136 "couldn't possibly do a picture": *Hollywood Citizen-News,* Aug. 18, 1958
136 "To jump into responsibility": ibid
136 "Noel would do anything": Moseley to EG, Oct. 8-9, 2001
137 "If I hadn't made Kate do it": Bogarde to MW, April 25, 1995
137 "In the movies, let's face it": *Cue,* Nov. 2, 1957
137 "has all the English whimsy": *London Observer,* Dec. 14, 1958
137 "is as prosaic": unident. review, Dec. 11, 1958
138 "Her anarchic brand of inspired fooling": ibid
138 "Whatever success the production may achieve": *Variety,* Dec. 17, 1958
138 "she does everything she could": *Punch,* Dec. 17, 1958
138 "Miss Kay Kendall talks": *London Times,* Dec. 11, 1958
138 "Kay Kendall saved the evening": *Evening News,* Dec. 11, 1958
138 "The play has not been given a chance": *Daily Telegram,* Dec. 22, 1958
138 "I was crying because of the people": *Daily Mail,* Dec. 22, 1958
138 "I never want to speak to the main": ibid
138 "Harrison will be able to afford": UPI release, Dec. 24, 1958

138 "maintaining a dignified silence": *Daily Mail,* Dec. 22, 1958
138 "It was my first play": ibid
139 "They are less inclined to be catty": *Hollywood Citizen-News,* June 16, 1959
139 "Suddenly everyone's talking about": unident. 1959 article, "Now Let's Take a Real Look at Kay Kendall"
140 "They were very happy times": Dillon to EG, Aug. 2001
140 "not up to her usual form": ibid

Chapter Twenty

141 "Oh, she's a naughty girl": Pavlow to MW, May 11, 1995
141 "Sometimes I would come back": Rex Harrison, "Rex, An Autobiography"
141 "I don't think Kay": *Daily Mail,* Jan. 4, 2001
142 "pale and very sick": ibid
142 "I can see when she's tired": Jacqueline Susann, "The Love Machine"
142 "A white chiffon dress": Bogarde to MW, April 25, 1995
142 "We all knew that Kate": ibid
143 "I had fallen hopelessly": unident. 1959 article
143 "Where are you?" ibid
144 "I was a little frightened": *Hollywood Citizen-News,* June 16, 1959
144 "Kay could be infuriating": Alexander Walker, "Fatal Charm: The Life of Rex Harrison"
144 "She was very brave": ibid
144 "the best things she did": *Life* magazine, 1959
144 "she was completely unpredictable": ibid
145 "Can we shoot all we can today": Alexander Walker, "Fatal Charm: The Life of Rex Harrison"
145 "serious blood disorder": *L.A. Herald,* June 2, 1959
145 "The only reason a blood specialist": ibid
145 "She is feeling enormously better": *World Telegram,* June 1, 1959
145 "Rex got out": Moseley to EG, Oct. 8-9, 2001
145 "She hated that film": ibid
146 "She isn't well": Laurie Evans to MW, May 1995
146 "I used to watch Kay": Cavan Kendall to MW, April 27, 1995
146 "They weren't interested in me": ibid
146 "She turned a load of French bread": ibid
146 "He'll be alright": Bogarde to MW, April 25, 1995
147 "I've just come out of the hospital": Princess Lilian to MW, May 2, 1995
147 "wasn't very nice to her": Jhan Robbins, "Yul Brynner, The Inscrutable King"
147 "That's why they'd have shouting matches": Mary Evans to MW, May 1995
147 "I am sick, sick, sick": *Daily Express,* Jan. 16, 1959
147 "If I give up comedy": ibid
147 "At least I've always got comedy": ibid
147 "My feet are too big": *Life* magazine, 1959
148 "unhappy rumors": unident. article, July 2, 1959

148 "would have taken ages": KKC to EG, Oct. 2000

148 "Right where we started": Matthau to MW, March 17, 1995

149 "He was very sweet": ibid

149 "I could never understand": Princess Lilian to MW, May 2, 1995

149 "He was never difficult to me": Bogarde to MW, April 25, 1995

149 "Kay was a sweet and lovable girl": Alexander Walker, "Fatal Charm: The Life of Rex Harrison"

149 "Tried to while away the time": Rex Harrison, "Rex, An Autobiography"

149 "She had a terrible journey": Laurie Evans to MW, May 1995

150 "Kate was smiling": ibid

150 "If you think I'm coming here to die": unident. article, Sept. 1959

150 "Wifey, darling": Matthau to MW, March 17, 1995

150 "There's nothing to flap about": unident. article, July 2, 1959

150 "Oh, I'm sorry": KKC to MW, Nov. 1994

150 "He was the bastard of all times": ibid

151 "She talked happily with Rex": *Daily Herald,* Sept. 7, 195

151 "Mousey, you would tell me": KKC to MW, Nov. 1994

151 "I love you very much": *Daily Mirror,* Sept. 7, 1959

Chapter Twenty-one

152 "I was so sure that Kay": *Daily Herald,* Sept. 7, 1959

152 "We had a bottle of something": Noel Harrison to EG, Aug. 2001

152 "I went to the funeral": Graham Payn & Sheridan Morley, "The Noel Coward Diaries"

153 "We were all doing it": Bogarde to MW, April 25, 1995

153 "Four major studios": ibid

153 "though I was not invited": KKC to MW, Nov. 1994

153 "No one was ever born": *Daily Mail,* Sept. 23, 1959

153 "I want you to sell all this": Mary Evans to MW, May 1995

154 "I always keep it on": Princess Lilian to MW, May 2, 1995

154 "happy comedy . . . exuberance and pleasure": Columbia press release

154 "Which was frankly bad": Graham Payn & Sheridan Morley, "The Noel Coward Diaries"

154 "own obituary": Geoffrey Wansell, "Terence Rattigan: A Biography"

155 "appeared to me like a little girl": Alexander Walker, "No Bells on Sunday: The Rachel Roberts Journals"

156 "one of my sequence of": Carey Harrison to EG, Aug. 2001

156 "It is good that she died when": Princess Lilian to MW, May 2, 1995

156 "If she had found gray hair": KKC to MW, Nov. 1994

156 "I don't think she would have minded": Bogarde to MW, April 25, 1995

157 "I know Rex is ill": *The Independent,* Aug, 5, 1987

157 "How dare you tell people": KKC to MW, Nov. 1994

157 "in the field of medical research": Kay Kendall Leukaemia Fund 2000 annual report

Bibliography

Adams, Raymond D., Ivan L. Bennett Jr., T.R. Harrison, William H. Resnik Jr., George W. Thorn, M.M. Wintrobe. *Principles of Internal Medicine.* New York: McGraw-Hill Book Company, 1966.

Aronson, Theo. *Princess Margaret, A Biography.* Washington, D.C.: Regnery Publishing, Inc., 1997.

Bach, Steven. *Dazzler: The Life and Times of Moss Hart.* New York: Alfred A. Knopf, 2001.

Barr, Charles. *All Our Yesterdays: Ninety Years of British Cinema.* London: British Film Institute, 1986.

Bogarde, Dirk. *Snakes and Ladders.* New York: Holt, Rinehart and Winston, 1978.

Epstein, Jerry. *Remembering Charlie.* New York: Doubleday, 1989.

Faulkner, Trader. *Peter Finch.* New York: Taplinger Publishing Company, 1979.

Fisher, John. *What a Performance: The Life of Sid Field.* London: Seeley, Service & Company, 1975.

Gifford, Denis. *The Illustrated Who's Who in British Films.* London: B.T. Batsford Ltd., 1978.

Gilman, Sander L. *Making the Body Beautiful.* Princeton, N.J.: Princeton University Press, 1999.

Harrison, Rex. *Rex: An Autobiography.* London: Macmillan, 1974.

Harrison, Rex. *A Damned Serious Business.* New York: Bantam Books, 1991.

Hillary, Richard. *The Last Enemy.* London: Macmillan, 1943.

Hopkins, Harry. *The New Look: A Social History of the Forties and Fifties in Britain.* London: Secker & Warburg, 1964.

Katz, Ephraim. *The Film Encyclopedia.* New York: HarperCollins Publishers, Inc., 1994.

Kendall, Gladys. *My Roots Are In Heaven.* Glen Head, New York: Glen Harbour Printers, 1978.

Keylin, Arleen, ed. *Hollywood Album 2.* New York: Arno Press, 1979.

Matthau, Carol. *Among the Porcupines.* New York: Turtle Bay Books, 1992.

McFarlane, Brian. *An Autobiography of British Cinema.* London: Random House, 1997.

Minnelli, Vincente. *I Remember It Well.* Garden City, NY: Doubleday, 1974.

More, Kenneth. *More or Less.* London: Hodder and Stoughton, 1978.

Moseley, Roy. *Rex Harrison: A Biography.* New York: St. Martin's Press, 1987.

Palmer, Lilli. *Change Lobsters and Dance.* New York: Macmillan Publishing Co., Inc., 1975.

Palmer, Scott. *A Who's Who of British Film Actors.* Metuchen, New Jersey: The Scarecrow Press, Inc., 1981.

Payn, Graham, and Sheridan Morley, eds. *The Noël Coward Diaries.* Boston: Little, Brown and Company, 1982.

Raffles, Mark. *Magic All the Way: Diamond Jubilee Memoirs.* Ayr, Scotland: John Moore, 1997.

Rattigan, Terence. *In Praise of Love*. London: Hamish Hamilton Ltd., 1973

Robbins, Jhan. *Yul Brynner, The Inscrutable King*. New York: Dodd, Mead and Company, 1987.

Shellard, Dominic, ed. *British Theatre in the 1950s*. Sheffield, England: Sheffield Academic Press, 2000.

Shipman, David. *The Great Movie Stars: The Golden Years*. New York: Bonanza Books, 1970.

Shipman, David. *The Great Movie Stars: The International Years*. New York: St. Martin's Press, Inc., 1973.

Susann, Jacqueline. *The Love Machine*. New York: Simon and Schuster, 1969.

Trager, James. *The People's Chronology*. New York: Henry Holt & Company, 1992.

Vickers, Hugo. *Vivien Leigh*. Boston: Little, Brown and Company, 1988.

Walker, Alexander. *Fatal Charm: The Life of Rex Harrison*. New York: St. Martin's Press, 1992.

———, ed. *No Bells on Sunday: The Rachel Roberts Journals*. New York: Harper and Row, 1984.

Wansell, Geoffrey. *Terence Rattigan: A Biography*. New York: St. Martin's Press, 1997.

Warren, Patricia. *British Film Studios*. London: B.T. Batsford Ltd., 1995.

Williams, Bridget. *The Best Butter in the World: A History of Sainsbury's*. London: Ebury Press, 1994.

Wood, Alan. *Mr. Rank: A Study of J. Arthur Rank and British Films*. London: Hodder and Stoughton, 1952.

Acknowledgements

Of course, this book would not exist without Kim Kendall Campbell, who set the wheels in motion and opened communications with Kay's many relatives, friends, and coworkers who cooperated in granting interviews. Thanks, too, to Maraday Wahlborg, who diligently completed so many of those interviews and ferreted out so many newspaper articles and reviews in 1994–95.

The following people were also invaluable in providing interviews and/or documentary materials for this book: Andy Aliffe, Dr. William Atchley, Gerry Atkins, Jean Baird, Letitia Baldrige, the late Dirk Bogarde, Barbara Seabrook Boyle, Kevin Brownlow, Ronald Bruce, Ian Carmichael, Geraldine Chaplin, Saul Chaplin, Sydney and Margaret Beebe Chaplin, Petula Clark, Moya Collins, Eric Concklin, David Conway, Richard Cox Cowell, Nikolas Dana, the late Peggy Dexter, Susan Dillon, Kenneth Dootson, James and Joy Drewery, Peter Drewery, Robert Edwards, Taina Elg, Laurie and Mary Evans, Steve Evereitt, Lord James Hanson, Carey Harrison, Noel Harrison, Shirley Hall Harnett, Gordon Irving, Dinah Sheridan Ison, Alex Jennings, Kath and Cyril Jones, the late Cavan Kendall, Jane Klain (Museum of Television and Radio, New York), Fiona and Stephen Kendall Lane, Angela Lansbury, Derek Leask, the late Jack Lemmon, Howard Lee Levine, Princess Lilian of Sweden, Moira Lister, Patrick MacNee, Carol Saroyan Matthau, the late Roddy McDowell, Lady Connie McIndoe, Lee Minnelli, John Moore, Roy Moseley, Stephen O'Brien, Muriel Pavlow, Max Pierce, Leslie Phillips, Michael Powazinik, John Saxon, Molly Simpson, Erik Stogo, Elizabeth Storer (The Kay Kendall Leukaemia Fund), Beryl Turner, Jean Walker, Bridget Williams (J Sainsbury plc), Nancy Winter, David Wyatt.

A special thank you to Veronica Hitchcock (who tracked down videos of even Kay's most obscure films), and Julie Snelling of the BBC (who uncovered details of all of Kay's radio and television appearances). Thanks also to Barbara Candee.

The following Web sites were useful for locating people, books, and other information—though anything found online must, of course, be double-checked for factual accuracy: bookfinder.com, britishpictures.com, britmovie.com, imdb.com, queenvic.demon.co.uk, rylibweb.man.ac.uk, and southbucks.gov.uk. Thanks, too, to The Straight Dope Message Board's helpful and enthusiastic "Teeming Millions."

The Withernsea Lighthouse Museum can be reached at Hull Road, Withernsea, East Yorkshire, HU19 2DY, England.

Index